14-5-98

TURKE

Gue

12·

Patrick Kneuang.

THE BALLAD OF
THE THIN MAN

THE BALLAD OF THE THIN MAN

THE AUTHORISED BIOGRAPHY OF
PHIL LYNOTT & THIN LIZZY
STUART BAILIE

BOXTREE

B[*]XTREE

First published 1996 by Boxtree
an imprint of Macmillan Publishers Ltd
25 Eccleston Place, London SW1W 9NF
and Basingstoke

Associated companies throughout the world

ISBN: 0 7522 0395 9

9 8 7 6 5 4 3 2 1

A CIP catalogue record for this book is available from the
British Library

Photography: Denis O'Regan; Decca Records Co. Ltd; Chalkie
Davies; John Paul. The Licensor has made every effort to trace
copyright holders. Any errors and omissions are entirely
unintentional.
Design by Graphyk
Typeset by SX Composing DTP, Rayleigh, Essex
Printed and bound at The Bath Press, Bath

Thanks to the following, who have made this book possible: Julian Anderson, Roger Armstrong, Paul Ashford, Eric Bell, Tony Brainsby, Paul Brannigan, Smiley Bolger, Tim Booth, Robbie Brennan, Eamon Carr, Roy Carr, Ted Carroll, Philip Chevron, Gail Claydon, Adam Clayton, Carol Clerk, Francis Coates, Chalkie Davies, Fred Dellar, Brian Downey, Mike Edgar, BP Fallon, Peter Fallon, Brendon Fitzgerald, Jim Fitzpatrick, Bob Geldof, Scott Gorham, Annie Goulding, Nigel Grainge, Paul Hardcastle, Jackie Hayden, Shay Healy, Terri Hooley, Nick Kent, Philip King, Paul McGuinness, Paul Mauger, Régine Moylett, Frank Murray, Chris O'Donnell, Michael O'Flanagan, Terry O'Neill, Pat Quigley, Fran Riley, Brian Robertson, Frank Rodgers, Chris Salewicz, Charles Shaar Murray, Brush Shiels, Matt Smith, Joe Staunton, Steve Sutherland, Darren Wharton and Eric Wrixon. Thanks also to Jake Lingwood at Boxtree.

A special salute to the late Bill Graham of *Hot Press*.

This book is dedicated to Collette, Lily, Jim and Margaret Bailie.

1

Phil Lynott had rehearsed this scene for many years. He always figured that he'd be king of the town some day – that his looks, talent and famous energy levels would result in a legendary homecoming. And on this fine August weekend in 1977 nobody, not even George Best, his footballing pal, was a greater star on the island. Phil was nervous, sure, but he knew that Dublin was ready to welcome his band – to take part in a glorious musical event, to be wowed utterly by Thin Lizzy's charm and thunder.

Phil and the boys could excite any town they visited. Their music was timelessly cool. They'd won international success while they were still young enough to enjoy the outcome. It was a total lifestyle; even when they'd finished their regular shows, they'd take off to a tiny club, plug in their gear and start playing all over again, purely for the buzz of it. They'd never merely settle for a gig when they could throw an event; the show, the party, the jam session, another party, maybe even a fight – until the community either rolled with the celebrations or got severely twisted in opposition to the idea. Being around Thin Lizzy in those days was nearly all pleasure.

Many other bands used the power of rock and roll to create an image of escape – of cutting loose, trashing the past, starting all over again. But Phil liked to sing about coming home from his adventures; battle-scarred, wiser and better. For him, the hero's return was his myth and his personal thrill. Dublin had welcomed him in as a half-caste kid back in the 1950s, after the unbearable bigotry and squalor he'd suffered with his mother in England. So Phil regularly came back to his adoptive heartland. He loved the old town and always wanted the approval of his friends and relations there.

This upcoming musical event – a day's worth of top acts at the

1

football stadium of Dalymount Park – was a perfect way to mark the occasion. By now Lizzy had become too big to play in the normal venues anyway, so the size of the audience was lifting them to this spectacular level of success. However, organising Dalymount had been tricky. Save for the recent Rory Gallagher show at Macroom, near Cork, they'd never witnessed anything on this scale before in Ireland. But Phil's people had spent an awful lot of time on this project, so hopefully it would work. Lizzy, Graham Parker And The Rumour, The Boomtown Rats, The Radiators From Space, Fairport Convention, The Undertones – it was the makings of an epochal show.

While he was home, Phil was going to enjoy all of the other possibilities on offer. A family reunion. A magnificent birthday party. The company of stimulating friends and beautiful women. Choice refreshments. Some press coverage to catch him at his best. And of course, a little recreational time in the pubs on the lively strip around Grafton Street and Duke Street. Those same boozers that were already jammed with fans, freeloaders, touts, friends and gatecrashers, spreading the word around, mad to see Philo back in town.

As the plane buzzed westwards from London over the Irish Sea, Phil considered his fortunes. Only six years before, he'd posed with some music biz friends by the glass passageway of Grafton Arcade in Dublin. Phil had worn his best funky gear and had carried a guitar case. He'd been staging a photo session for Ireland's *New Spotlight* magazine, pretending that he'd landed at Heathrow airport after a mega Irish tour. In those days, Phil had no money, and he actually travelled by boat. But hey, Lynott argued, why not tell a few lies, the old poetic licence? Sure, if you give the punters the flavour of the big time, maybe you'll achieve those expectations after a while.

And of course, Lizzy had flourished through the 1970s. They'd released masses of strong records – powering the band through chaos and physical disasters, numerous sackings and near bankruptcy. In the summer of 1976 they'd released 'The Boys Are Back In Town', a song that captured the heat of that restless season and scored high in the US and British charts. Now they were joshing around in a plane rammed full of rock and roll, the greatest.

Phil looked around the cabin. The Lizzy members were all

present. Brian Downey was a long-time buddy and neighbour from the Crumlin estate. He was a class drummer, technically brilliant and able to second-guess Phil's intentions after twelve years of working together. Brian was a calming influence, a tolerant personality within a gang of crazies. He was also a critical judge of character. If Downey hated somebody, then he must definitely be an asshole.

Scott Gorham, the guitarist, was Phil's closest mate. Raised in Glendale, near Los Angeles, Scott was cheerful and cool, with the cheekbones, the good teeth and the long hair that you'd never equal east of California. This made him a rival when it came to charming the girls, especially in Ireland, where an American accent was a premium. Scott was sometimes insecure about his playing, though, and he'd often allow other guitarists to dominate the show. But on the just-finished Lizzy album *Bad Reputation*, he'd prevailed on his own much of the time, and everybody said he'd done a supreme job. And now he felt happy and invigorated.

Completing the band was guitarist Brian Robertson, just out of his teens, a Glaswegian fireball who kept the music and the management edgy with his dangerous ways. There were traces of a bitemark on his forehead, where an enraged girl in the inappropriately named town of Normal, Illinois, had taken a lump out of him in 1975. His hands were hacked and cross-hatched by scars where he'd encountered bottles, heads and steel – carving up skin, tendon and arteries, testimony to an untamed youth. He'd left the band at the end of 1976 in bloody circumstances, but now he claimed to be a reformed character.

But Robbo was only two weeks back on tour and already he'd been party to infernal scenes in Finland – taking on the local Vikings and only quitting when he'd been physically unable to throw a marble table across the hotel reception. He'd been struggling with the unexpected weight of this furniture when the Finns had pummelled him into submission. Such a guy. Such a classic line-up.

There were many other friends, journalists, roadies and attention-grabbers on the jet. Thin Lizzy had adopted a band of punk chancers from Dublin, The Boomtown Rats. Their lead singer was Bob Geldof, whose chin and ambitions were, like Phil's, uncommonly large. For now, the two singers enjoyed the

3

respectful status of mentor and cub – but that would soon change as the Rats were forever pulling stunts and trying to upstage their rivals and headliners. During a recent tour with Tom Petty And The Heartbreakers, they'd unveiled a cheap banner that read: BOOMTOWN RATS EAT HEARTBREAKERS FOR BREAKFAST. Geldolf had even hired a publicist and vibes-minister called BP Fallon, an exotic Dubliner who'd previously travelled with the likes of Led Zeppelin and Marc Bolan. Soon, BP was party to many of these strokes, and the band became famous for their shenanigans: packaging dead lab rats in plastic bags filled with formaldehyde before chucking them at punters, even creating a new dance called The Rat – all stupid, remarkable stuff.

Geldof was selfish, single-minded, and proud of it. His band's début single was called 'Looking After Number One' – a dismissal of the kind of camaraderie that Phil had built into the Lizzy regime. The Rats' record had just been awarded Single Of The Week in Geldof's old workplace, *New Musical Express*. As a former journalist, Geldof understood the value of extravagant statements, and he knew that this weekend was an ideal time to further his reputation. This seemed to be the deal when the party arrived at Dublin airport, and people sensed a scam. The Lizzy crowd realised that someone had hired a bus for the day, and had packed it full of roughneck kids from the city centre. They'd been driven to the airport and loaded up with Boomtown Rats gear – posters, record sleeves and placards – and told to cause a scene to impress the visiting music writers and make it look as if Ratmania was the new Irish epidemic. However, the kids hadn't been told that Phil and his posse would be on the same plane too.

The two bands left customs together, the wannabees and the stars. The Rats favoured scruffy bomber jackets and skinny ties, pyjama trousers, baseball boots and soaped-up, razored hair. BP Fallon wore a soft-brimmed hat set off with a rakish green plume. His jacket was made from a quilted bedsheet that he'd liberated from the Sheraton – cut and sewn so that the hotel's insignia featured large on the back panel. BP, like many others, was mourning the recent death of Elvis Presley. He'd sat there with his friend Marc Bolan, reading the papers, sadly aware that Maria Callas had also passed away on 16 August, and was hardly noticed. 'Well, I'm glad that I didn't die today,' Marc had said. Yet he too would be gone a month later.

4

Lizzy walked out in Cuban heels, waistcoats and belts inset with silver conches. They wore appliqué satin and crushed-velvet gear from London's Kensington Market – an old-school, gypsy élite look, but Lizzy wore it well. And besides, this time Phil was also duded up in his black biker jacket and his drainpipe jeans – looking sleek and definitive, his standing undamaged by the arrival of so many punk contenders who'd dismissed Rod Stewart, Led Zeppelin, The Who, and even The Rolling Stones as being outmoded and out of touch. But with Phil, the new breed recognised a kindred soul – totally into adrenalised times, fierce parties and wild music.

The kids at the airport saw another aspect of Phil's personality. They knew he was a character, a true son of this city – a Dub. He was just like the writer Brendan Behan and the singer Luke Kelly from The Dubliners in that respect. His accent was untouched by his travels abroad. He still lived out his life in the centre of town when he was home – rarely hiding away or posing as the untouchable star. Phil had the Dub humour, salty and unreconstituted. Ancient biddies could stop him in the street and tell him a joke. The old fellas, pushing their bicycles down the main drag, would wave and wink. Young musicians would ask for advice, and he'd always be obliging and useful. And so the fans knew Phil would have some time for them, too.

Therefore they gathered around him in the airport concourse, pushing bits of paper at him, asking him to autograph whatever came to hand – even one of those Boomtown Rats sleeves if necessary. He obliged with good grace, aware of the fact that Geldof stood virtually alone. Bob was never going to compete with this. Their stunt had failed. It was Phil's moment and nobody here was going to steal it away.

Lizzy's homecoming may have felt like the greatest ritual ever, but it also required another section of townsfolk to play a different role. The Irish police wanted to be recognised as doing their duty. They had to be seen to contain these decadent long-hairs and their flaunting, sinful ways. Why, there'd even been ructions at the door of The Gresham Hotel on the very first night of their arrival, when one of those yahoo rock and rollers tried to bring female company back to his room. Not just one young girl, for pity's sake – but didn't he have a *couple* of them with him at once! And then he says, well, can I bring just the *one* in? Merciful God!

The special police directive for the summer was to clamp down on drugs. This initiative had started earlier in August, when they'd tracked a supply of cannabis headed for Ireland. They seized 12 lbs of the stuff, and promptly fed the news of this capture to the local press, who ran up hysterical reports of a Dublin drug ring and the appalling consequences of this trend. Pleased with the results of this bust, the police decided to make a symbolic raid into the heart of the Lizzy camp.

19 August: the police let their targets alone on the Friday night, as Lynott, inevitably dressed to kill, moseyed down to Moran's Hotel in Gardiner Street to see The Boomtown Rats play. The crowd was delighted when Phil got up on stage with Geldof, and these two super-egos battled and riffed together, Phil blamming on a borrowed Rickenbacker bass and Bob throwing shapes just like Mick Jagger. Some guy with scary, home-made tattoos leapt on to the stage and got Phil in a headlock and people freaked, but he was only being friendly, and Phil just laughed it off.

The police also left Thin Lizzy alone during the day, when Phil visited his favourite bars, and took his journalist mates up to the top end of Grafton Street and proudly showed them Saint Stephen's Green, the place where he'd spent some defining times as a young man. In the lovely Victorian landscapes of the park, Phil used to drink cheap wine and enjoy the ambience of Dublin coming to terms with the 1960s. This was the closest Ireland would get to Golden Gate Park in San Francisco, so the hippies and the heads would congregate there, smoking and playing music. Eric Bell, the former Lizzy guitarist, had adored it. He'd be tripping like mad, and waving to somebody at the far side of the green, and they'd smile and return the salute. And Eric would be so blissed out that it seemed like there were jewels and rays of light splashing from the hands of those other friends.

He thought that his life was going to be like that for ever. That was one of the reasons why the photo session for Lizzy's second album, *Shades Of A Blue Orphanage*, was shot there. It was their touchstone, a special place. Whenever Phil got into a smokers' conversation and people asked him what his favourite kind of hash was – Lebanese or Moroccan, red, gold or black – the singer would smile and tell them that he was a sucker for Stephen's Green.

Phil also used to hang around there on the chance of meeting some tourist girls. He'd strike up a conversation with the prettiest back-packers and let slip that he knew all of the great spots around Dublin, places they really should see.

'I'd love to show you around,' Phil would say in his saddest, sweetest tones, 'but I've got no money.'

And of course they'd soften up right away, and offer to feed him and let him be their guide for the day. Easy.

Phil snapped out of his reverie, back to 1977 and his polished Valentino persona.

'So that was it. You were in! I wasn't a gigolo . . . but it was pretty close.'

Back down the road at The Bailey pub, Phil established his court with a mixture of old pals and newcomers. He'd shake hands with those he knew and immediately enquire, 'How's yer mother?' Phil knew the names of everyone's ma, their wife and their kids. It was part of his considerate nature and also a method for putting his less famous mates at ease. He was the smoothest. His voice was deep and lilting – his sentences often tailing off into handsome flourishes – a style that he also sustained in his handwriting. An English girl wanted to know how he pronounced his surname and he gave her a much-practised line.

'You call me Lie-Not. I tell no lies.'

There was a significance in the way that people addressed the singer. Those who had known him in the 1960s – when he'd frequented the folk clubs, had his ego mashed by hallucinogens and came across as a sensitive, shy soul – they chose to call him Philip. It was a personal thing, like you knew him really well. Sometimes Philip would reveal himself to an old musician friend, privately laughing at how he'd come this far, the extent to which this musical trip had taken him. Just for a few seconds he'd roll his eyes and guffaw. None of this stardom was taken for granted, even if his public personality made it seem like the easiest thing ever.

But of course, he'd been toughing it for years. Phil had worked to a phenomenal degree – involving himself in interviews, promotions, styling, songwriting, singing, artwork, bass playing, tour programmes, merchandising, stage sets, tour economics, press photos, lighting rigs and the supporters' club. Phil was hands-on to an extent that it sometimes made him a pain in the ass to work for. He would never settle for work casually executed – you were off the firm if you weren't fired up, working your best.

And yet Phil still found time to party. In order to squeeze in his time somewhere, the Lynott metabolism allowed him to survive with minimal sleep – even after wild nights, he was up before the rest. And he could see business chances everywhere. He could even justify his love life in terms of Lizzy's fortunes – he said that another conquest was another record unit sold. Knowarrimean?

If his full name Philip represented the poet and the private man, then Phil was his rock and roll tag, the goodfella that everybody felt they could buddy up to. The Dubs had a variation on this, calling him Bold Philo. He sometimes referred to these aspects of his life as 'me act', and it became a difficult front to maintain in the later years, when he sometimes felt sad and alone. But in 1977, Phil was still on the rise; playing fast, winning fans, taking care of everything.

Saturday, 20 August was Phil's twenty-eighth birthday. The party was held west of Dublin, at Castletown House in County Kildare, a grand Georgian establishment built in 1722. The neighbouring village of Celbridge was settled on the banks of the River Liffey, and Phil was excitedly taking his guests across the grass to see this famous waterway. It ran all the way down to Dublin Bay, some of it passing into the Guinness brewery at St James' Gate en route, to make the creamy drink that was also flowing so plentifully on this midsummer night.

Tony Boland, a senior producer for the Irish TV station RTE and the tenant of Castletown, was worried about the possible damage that might befall the house. A previous New Year's Eve party had resulted in a fire that ruined one of the great rooms, so Phil's hooley was held on the west wing, away from the more fragile parts of the building. This was a sensible move, because in addition to Phil's 200 guests, there were as many gatecrashers on the site, partying hard, celebrating this new social phenomenon in Ireland, the rock and roll ascendancy.

Phil had been worried earlier in the night that there might not be any female guests. He was a famous ladies' man, hence the title given to him by the road crew: Phil Line 'Em Up. But he was happily reassured at Castletown. He was talking to a few girls in the hayloft late into the night when Drugs Squad detectives and uniformed Gardai from Naas station arrived. This in itself was no shock, since Phil had been given a tip-off several hours before, and many people had thrown their bags of grass on to the fire, creating a powerful, unmistakable perfume.

The singer was deeply angry at this intrusion, a tiresome piece of point-scoring, but he greeted the cops and they returned the compliment. They seemed to be good-natured about their business, and Phil offered to let them search him. He even put his hands in the air and stood by the stable wall. They went through his pockets and found nothing. So the Gardai moved on, taking a little hash off a couple of unofficial guests and thus saving their own reputation.

When the cops had left the stable area, Phil produced a small wrap of paper that he'd been hiding in his hand all the time that he was sweet-talking the police. Inside was a gram of fine white powder – cocaine, the old Devil's dandruff. BP Fallon thought this was hilarious. Just at that moment, Robbo made his entrance, rattling up the driveway in a tractor belonging to ML Trucking, the sound company belonging to The Who, there to cover Dalymount. Robertson had been sulking earlier in the night – some spat with Phil already forgotten. So he'd bummed a lift out to Kildare on this unconventional machine. Just as some other guests were wilting, here came the hellish reinforcements. The party could resume.

Thin Lizzy's drug situation was still at a relatively harmless stage in 1977. The band worked incredibly hard, and occasionally took some stimulants that made their job seem easier to endure. Since Thin Lizzy wasn't incredibly rich yet, and cocaine was a reward rather than a necessity. Phil once blew a huge wad of his earnings on some pure Peruvian, but he didn't talk about this in a boastful way; it was just as if he'd treated himself to a bottle of expensive wine, a pleasurable indulgence. The drugs had yet to bring a feeling of dread into the camp. That would start two years later, when frustrations and boredom would cause him to binge to an escalating degree on heroin and alcohol. That's when the singer became Phil Why-Not, his last, unfortunate moniker.

But that summer most of the drug stories were amusing, almost innocent. A month earlier, Phil had spent Independence Day in New York, watching Pink Floyd play at the Madison Square

Gardens. He'd been smoking a variety of spine-freezing sen-similia that was causing fearful havoc, even to his high tolerance level. Still, he was enjoying the sensory bend of the music and the smoke, when something weird happened. A punter in the balcony spilt some beer on Phil's head. But he wasn't aware of that. He just looked up and noticed one of Pink Floyd's famous props, a giant floating pig, far above. Outtasite . . .

'See that pig up there,' he burbled to Scott Graham. 'It's just pissed on me.'

Phil liked to sing about junkies and drug smugglers. He was fascinated with renegade figures and the rock and roll casualties like Jimi Hendrix and Duane Allman. 'It was a conscious thing,' he'd say. 'To go out and take the thing as far as it can go. To the limit.' But still he was outraged when the law harassed him for his own use. He'd been busted for possession of hash in the early days of Thin Lizzy and he'd ranted about it for months afterwards. How dare they? To listen to Phil, you'd think that rock and rollers had some kind of diplomatic immunity.

So when he saw the pages of the *Irish Independent* a few days after the Castletown bash, Phil was apoplectic. 'Six Held In Drugs Raid On Pop Party' said the headline of the Monday edition. It was another case of role playing, as the papers were responding to the police action, plus they were attempting to tell their readers about this new, rock aristo set, which they didn't fully comprehend. In addition, this was the era of the increasingly ruthless tabloid reporting in Britain, an additional role model to toy with. The *Independent* stated that the Gardai 'seized thousands of pounds' worth of cannabis and cocaine'; subsequently this error was distorted again by several other papers. Rock Babylon! The Lizzy homecoming was badly soured.

Phil piled into the newspaper offices with some of his mates. He headed for the news room, looking for the guy who wrote the story. He demanded retribution for the untruths and slurs and he bewailed the anguish which their story was causing his relatives, in particular, his ageing grandmother Sarah, who'd effectively reared him when his mother couldn't deal with the pressures of working and keeping a single-parent family together in Manchester. Fists were raised in anger. People were jumping behind their desks. It was like being in a Thin Lizzy song, as Phil shouted some more and then steamed out of the offices with an apology and a degree of personal satisfaction. The newspaper's correction ran four days later.

People used to talk about the Dalymount roar – the magnificent sound that the supporters of Bohemians FC would muster on special occasions at their home ground. But this concert was something else; the response of 11,000 pumped-up music fans to an almighty show. All through the day there had been revelations. Bob Geldof had finally found his niche; opinion-ating, posturing and bad-mouthing to the multitudes. He was undeniably a star. Afterwards, Graham Parker had summoned up his blues and his brass – an Englishman grooving to the Celtic swing that Van Morrison had adapted in turn from black Americans. 'Soul Shoes' was the greatest – maybe too great, since Parker would tour the States with Lizzy soon and he'd occasionally out-thrill the main act. But that was the Lizzy style, not scrimping on a support band. Get the crowd in good humour, then you'll completely bust them up afterwards.

Even the earlier bands had been apt. The Undertones were on the case with their raggedy speed-pop – one of many Ulster bands who'd been liberated by the accessible style of punk. The Radiators From Space were a Dublin group who'd likewise found their chance. However, the Radiators had been stymied at home by a fatal stabbing at one of their concerts, and the ensuing punk clamp-down obliged them to move to London to earn a living. Phil had personally insisted that they play Dalymount.

Fairport Convention may have seemed like a strange choice for the bill, with their sound of Olde England, but this Dalymount crowd had been raised on jigs and reels since they were kids, so they enthusiastically knew the score. Besides, this folksy style had actually been a key influence on Phil and many other Dubliners in the late 1960s. The Fairports had encouraged them to look back to their own roots, to take Irish traditional music and make it special again. One of Phil's last great recordings would be a lament for Sandy Denny, the Fairport's late singer.

Many other visiting bands would make savings on lighting rigs and PA systems. An Irish tour was normally treated as a cheap warm-up to the UK leg, a chance to experiment and make adjustments. It was a patronising and offensive practice, and

Lizzy had vowed to give the home crowd their very best. This was a good time to upgrade everything. When Phil left Ireland in 1971, there hadn't even been a proper phone system there, never mind a music biz infrastructure. Now they had managers, decent studios, rehearsal places, clued-up radio shows and a proper music mag, the recently published *Hot Press*. The cultural cringe was ending. The Irish were collectively pulling themselves out of the dark days, and it felt magnificent.

When Lizzy came onstage, their rapport with the crowd was beautiful. Phil wore his outlaw black and the leather pants which emphasised his long, lean legs. Like David Bowie's fictional creation Ziggy Stardust, he was the ultimate in sensual cool: well-hung, snow-white tan, taking it far beyond the old limits. And he was literally controlling the crowd with his fingers; calming them, uplifting their spirits, caressing them.

Phil had the ability to make the audience feel he was putting them in his confidence. He'd ask for everyone's helping hands, and maybe share a little story, like he was personally relating to every punter. And by the end of the show, they were all involved. He'd lunge towards the front of the stage on his left knee, holding the pose like a Marvel comic superhero. Then he'd smile, beaming the stagelights into the crowd with the mirrored scratch-plate of The Lone Ranger, his Fender Precision bass, picking out happy faces. He'd be crooking his left arm and balling up a fist, pushing out that great chin. Tonight, there was gonna be trouble, he assured them. Somewhere in this town. And the Dalymount roar would power up again in recognition of another fave tune.

The cider boys, the old Dublin heads and the weeping teenage girls, they all adored him. 'Still In Love With You' broke their hearts. The rampant passage of 'Emerald' – heavy boogaloo in a Celtic idiom – stirred their feelings in an intensely partisan way. The song's time signature was 6/8, which wasn't a common rock and roll figure, but one that was prevalent in Irish traditional music. Phil was naturally aware of this, and he'd developed the song's imagery along that same course – the fighting Celts, pikes glinting under the stars, massacres to avenge. The guitar triplets came faster and more piercing, alternating with power-chords and gigantic drumbeats – willing a new fervour out of the old ways.

And Lizzy built on these reactions with their dynamic

extremes; tour-hardened road-dogs who knew exactly how to move a show. Even a rain shower wasn't going to trouble this happy communion; Phil just gave them his new song, 'Dancing In The Moonlight', a jazz shuffle and a woozy story of a mid-summer bewitching. Perfect. They'd all sing these happy-sad lines on the way home. Scott and Robbo were spinning and meshing their guitar lines from right to left, two radically different personalities, harmonising tightly. Brian Downey was relaxing now behind the drums. He'd been under duress all day, trying to keep everyone sweet, to make sure his relations got the best seats and hospitality available. But now he was grinning. He looked up to the sky, and the moon was shining at last. It looked like being another great beaming addition to the lighting rig.

This was Lizzy's town, and Phil was their Elvis; down-home and yet wondrously different. The favourite songs were blasting out, the drink was flowing, even a little blood was spilt. It was just like the words that their hit record had promised. Them wild-eyed boys and a Dub encounter to stay forever in the city's folk memory.

'DUBLIN!! ARE YOU RE-AD-YYY TO ROCKKK???'

'YEEEEEAYYYYAHHHAHHHHUUUUGGGGGHH!!!!'

2

Mick Joyce eyeballed Phil in the school yard and he shouted out a line that he knew Lynott would never walk away from.

'Hey, Sambo, c'mere, your band's shit.'

Sure enough, Phil got violently upset. He told Mick if he ever said that again, he'd kill him. As a matter of fact, he'd not give him a second chance – he'd kill him anyway. Phil had taken his fill of Joyce and his mean, jealous comments. It was bad enough with the guy back-stabbing all the time, rubbishing his singing and the music that his band, The Black Eagles, played. But this racist name-calling was inexcusable. It was time for a fight. They'd have it out in the park opposite school, four days from now. Meet at five-thirty. No messing.

Everybody in Crumlin's Christian Brothers School was buzzing for the next few days. A lot of the big fights were over quickly. It was normally a spur-of-the-moment event – some pulling and slapping and then the teachers broke it up. But this Lynott versus Joyce event had the makings of a proper, bloody punch-up. Phil was fifteen, a big fella who could handle himself. Joyce was a bit younger, but vicious with it. A tough contest.

Two days before the confrontation, Brian Downey was sitting through a metalwork lesson. Unlike his classmate Joyce, Brian reckoned The Black Eagles were astonishing, and he really rated Phil's singing. The way Lynott stared up at the spotlight when he was on stage, ignoring the audience – tall, thin and impeccably dressed – totally into the music. And the pose he would strike, his hand over the microphone, his arm up high, it was unique.

Brian looked across the classroom and he noticed something was happening outside of the teacher's line of vision. Joyce was over there, grinding pieces of metal, making them as sharp as he could, obviously in preparation for the fight with Lynott. So

14

that's why he seemed so confident about the outcome. But as soon as he realised he was being watched by Brian, Joyce got anxious. He knew that Downey and Lynott were mates, so he aimed to silence this potential informer. 'If you mention to Lynott that I'm making a knife,' he said, 'I'll do ya.'

It was a terrible dilemma for Brian. If he said nothing to Phil, then maybe the fight would end in a stabbing. But if he passed on the information, then he'd risk the same treatment himself. Brian decided to forget about the last threat and when he saw Lynott the following day, he told him all he knew. Phil nodded in appreciation. But he didn't seem nervous about the prospect of confronting Joyce's nasty weaponry. He just pulled a thick, wooden ruler out of his pocket and he showed it to Downey.

'S'all right, I've got me own blade.'

Phil twisted the side of the ruler and two pieces of wood slid apart. Inside there was a knife. He'd already guessed that some dirty play might occur, so a friend had helped him out with the customised steel. Now they were both tooled up.

On the day of the confrontation, practically the whole school ran over the road to the playing pitches. There were so many of them there – pushing for the best view, rubber-necking like crazy – that it took a while to clear a place for the fight to begin. And then just before they started up, someone in the crowd – who was obviously in the know – shouted, 'No knives!' This shook Joyce up, and he looked at Downey to find out if the source of the leak was himself, but Brian said, 'No, I didn't tell anybody.' Whatever, Joyce threw away his blade in anger, and then Phil pulled out the ruler and chucked it away too, and they squared up for a regular fist-fight.

It was over quickly. Phil decked the guy with two clean punches. He knelt over Joyce and he held him down by the throat. He could choke the big-mouth now, people were thinking, do some real damage, and he'd be within his rights. But he stood up instead and told Joyce to do likewise. 'Now you see I can kill you,' he told the loser. Then he shook his combatant's hand and a big cheer went up from the hundreds of spectators. An honourable ending. But nobody ever again underestimated Philip Lynott and his awesome, black rage.

*

STUART BAILIE

Crumlin was planned as a tidy Corporation estate on the south side of town, ranged on the bottom slopes of the Dublin mountains. The foundations were laid in 1932 – the year the Catholic Church granted the International Eucharistic Congress to Ireland. So as the foreign visitors came to pay their respects to the Republic's emergent status as a land allied to the joint aims of Church and State, many of the streets of Crumlin – Kells, Armagh, Bangor, Clogher, Leighlin – were named after old monasteries and bishoprics.

Some of the early settlers there weren't so pious. The Behans arrived in 1937 – ejected from the tenement building of 14 Russell Street and bewailing the slum clearance policies of the Irish leader, Eamon de Valera. 'He built those great housing estates like something you'd see in Siberia,' Kathleen Behan moaned. She felt that this remote location would knock the carefree attitude out of the working-class people, leading to alienation and violence. She used to tell her old friends that the Crumlin kids 'played tip and tag with hatchets'. However, her own children, not all of them placid and law-abiding, would manage to enliven Crumlin, Dublin, and beyond for many years.

Their home at 70 Kildare Road was the location for many extreme incidents. Kathleen's son Brendan would become internationally famous as a playwright, a balladeer and a fierce drinker. An IRA activist, he once blew up the toilet of the house in Crumlin while experimenting with nitro-glycerine. He died in 1964 at the Meath Hospital, his innards ravaged by hepatitis and a series of diabetic comas, but still glugging a bottle of brandy to the last. Two other Behan boys, Sean and Brian, were Stalinists. Another, Dominic, would write books and beautiful folksy songs, including an anti-war ballad, 'The Patriot Game', which was later developed by Bob Dylan into 'With God On Our Side'.

Dominic also had a low opinion of the housing in Crumlin. He called the homes 'dolls' houses made by dwarfs with Lilliputians in mind'. He might have been more grateful; the Behans paid two shillings and sixpence extra for the luxury of a semi-detached place. They should have tried living around the corner in Leighlin Road.

The Lynotts lived there at number 85, second from the end of a terraced row. They were originally from the Liberties, Dublin's oldest inner-city quarter. There was Sarah, the mother, and her

16

husband, Frank. They had many children: Monica, Josephine, Betty, Irene, Marian, Philomena, John, Timmy and Peter. The last of these, Peter, was born when Sarah was fifty-one. A few of the sisters had moved away before the youngest arrived – thus allowing a turnover of space in the household. But in the late 1950s they welcomed in another family member, Philomena's son.

Philip, born in 1949, was athletic and handsome, with good skin and a half-caste complexion. Philomena was having difficulties bringing him up on her own in Manchester. She'd decided not to pursue her relationship with the boy's father, and felt that he'd stand a better chance in Dublin. So Sarah brought Philip into the household, while his mother stayed in Britain. Sarah first met Philip on a trip to see Philomena when he was three, and he came to stay a few years later. To save embarrassment, the family pretended that they'd adopted him. But as his face thinned out and his chin took on that powerful profile, it became manifest that Philip was a Lynott and they dropped this story.

While the Behans made a big issue of their situation, complaining that they had to feed a family of six on a single loaf, the Lynotts just got on with it. To everyone's distress, Frank died of a heart attack in 1964. Timmy became the chief earner of the house, and the money that Philomena sent over from Manchester became even more precious. Yet in spite of these tough economics, there was still some money left for a few luxuries, and thus Timmy put together a record collection: American rhythm and blues, soul, jazz stuff like Mose Allison, plus later on some of the English blues-rock bands.

The Christian Brothers School on Armagh Road was also built in the 1930s, a massive place designed to hold the many thousands of children from the new estates. Some of the kids were rough and so too were the priests who governed it. Brian Downey used to watch pupils jumping clean out of classroom windows rather than take a thrashing from one of the Fathers. He suffered a few beatings himself, but not as bad as some of the other guys.

Phil liked it there. Even if the school had an underprivileged status – the rich kids went to a better class of CBS – he found more stimulation there than he had across the Irish Sea at

Princess Road Junior, in Manchester's Moss Side. Back in England in 1957, coming up to the boy's eighth birthday, the examiners reported that he was an average pupil with poor conduct, time-keeping and attendance. His reading was substandard and he'd even missed three of his exams. But at the Armagh Road CBS, he started to come good.

The history lessons were weirdly fascinating. Part of the deal with de Valera's new Ireland was that the people should be brought up to enjoy native sports and culture. Therefore the Irish language was a mandatory subject, and so too was the teaching of the old myths of the Celtic past. But some of the priests were so cranky that they taught these legends of long ago like they'd definitely happened.

Brian thought this was odd, and he didn't care for it. But Phil was keen on such tales – especially the stories from the *Ulster Cycle*, the oldest vernacular epic in Western literature. They called it *The Tain*, or *The Cattle Raid Of Cooley*, and it dealt with provincial wars and bull rustlers and the boy hero Cúchulainn – a teenage prodigy who pole-axed the champion fighters of Ireland and waged guerrilla warfare on entire invading armies. He'd go breezing around the Boyne Valley in his chariot, caving in enemy heads with his hurley stick, doing his famous salmon leap to confuse the opposition. The boy also had this incredible feature called a warp spasm, when he would be transformed by his temper into a whirlwind of energy, when he'd devastate everything around him. People were even afraid to wake the warrior as the last one to do so got pulverised against a wall.

There was a sadness about the Cúchulainn legend too – the fact that his conception was the result of magical forces that left him without a true father, only foster parents. Also, the fighter had made a pact with the seers early on that while his name would live for ever, his life would be short. 'If I achieve fame,' he agreed, 'I am content, though I had only one day on earth.' The boy was grievously wounded after an immense fight with his old friend Ferdia. He lay on his sick-bed for days, his body pierced, his joints coming asunder. He eventually died after suffering a terrible disembowelling while defending his race against those who reviled it.

Phil's imagination was excited by all this. He was a big fan of cowboy movies too, watching Roy Rogers and Hopalong

Cassidy at the local picture houses, and he was equally roused by the superheroes in the Marvel comics he bought. He even drew his personal Superman cartoon strip, with Clark Kent's secret alias throwing shapes, trashing the baddies and always looking brilliant. In 1977, when Phil had got his own extravagant gig together, he recalled some of this. He found a comparison between his rich, childhood world and the particular style of warp spasm he lived through onstage with Thin Lizzy.

'Sometimes I go out there and I often go completely berserk – I'm often completely off me head. And it's got sweet fuck all to do with drugs. It's just that I get as heavily into what I'm doing as when I used to be a kid playing cowboys. When you'd be completely wrapped up in killing millions of Indians and just living this whole trip out, hiding in rocks and trees and just sneaking off to imaginary places.

'Anybody can be anybody in rock and roll. It allows for all these people to exist within it and live out their fantasies. I know; I certainly do.'

Phil got seriously into performing in 1964. He'd already watched his Uncle Peter in action at a community hall in Mount Argus called Father Browne's. It was hardly a rock and roll joint – the priest said a decade of the Rosary at the end of the night – but Uncle Peter would get up there and sing, and Phil thought it was the best. Peter, only a year older than Philip, was another of the Lynotts to be blessed with charming features and an easy way with the girls. He started singing with bands, and eventually cut his reputation with The Sundowners. But a nearby Crumlin band wanted him badly. They were called The Eagles, and they featured two brothers, Danny and Frankie Smith. Their dad, Joe, was the manager.

However, they discovered that there was another Irish band called The Eagles, so they looked through comic books for other ideas. Somebody remembered a cartoon figure called The Black Hawk, so they shifted this name around and arrived at The Black Eagles instead. Joe thought if he asked Philip in, then his uncle would join too. Brian Downey actually saw Peter perform with them and reckoned he was good. But the group ended up with Philip, who started wearing black polo necks and gloves on stage, already a flash young teenager. He sang 'Crying Time' by

Ray Charles, and the crowds at the local community halls were enchanted, especially so the girls.

Brian Downey used to cycle the mile down from his house at Cashel Avenue to Leighlin Road. He'd stay out until late with Phil, gassing about bands and football and records they liked. Sarah would be keen to bring Phil in off the street, so she'd invite his friend in for tea as well. Brian's dad got to know Sarah – they joked that his son was spending more time at her house than his own. Mr Downey was a jazz fan, so Brian would bring some of his records over to the Lynotts' – the West Coast blues 'n' bop of Eddie 'Cleanhead' Vinson and Chicago's Oscar Brown Junior, and Phil thought they were ace – especially Oscar's 'When I Was Cool'.

It wasn't just the music that bonded them. Brian looked up to Phil, two years older than himself, because he had a surefire attitude. If Lynott wanted to play football, he'd quickly muster half a dozen of the best players in school. He was an instigator who always knew where the parties were going, which dancehalls were the coolest, how to spin your evening out, and then how to soothe the family when you came home late and there were rows.

So when Brian finally got the drumming job with The Black Eagles in 1965, he knew who was the leader straight away. He played his audition to everyone's satisfaction, a version of The Kinks' 'You Really Got Me' with all the speedy fills that the other guy could never manage. Brian, whose dad played drums with a pipe band, had already gigged with a few small acts, The Liffey Beats and The Mod Con Cave Dwellers, and he was no slouch. But he always deferred to Phil. Even when Joe, the manager, got uptight and threatened to close them down, Brian allied with the singer and ignored the old man. Still, Joe was helpful too, taking the band on short holidays to the Butlin's camp in Mosney, where they'd battle to win the talent contests.

It was never boring with Phil. At school, everyone would remember the fight with Mick Joyce and they added this to their Hollywood image of the street-fighting black man, and figured that he was an invaluable gang member. So whenever trouble went off with a rival estate – Dolphin's Barn, Inchicore, Drimnagh – they'd bring Phil along. Sometimes, when the Crumlin boys were outnumbered, even Lynott couldn't save them. On one famous occasion, he simply put his head down, covered his eyes and charged into a crowd of hoods, and kept running when he was clear on the other side.

This tribal aggression even revealed itself during Black Eagles gigs. You'd get gangs pointing at Phil, threatening trouble later on. When they played at the skating rink in Aungier Street, a dangerous establishment at the best of times, it seemed like all of the Inchicore hardliners were there, waiting to get Lynott. As soon as the band had finished their repertoire of Stones, Beatles and Manfred numbers, Phil legged it into the dressing-room and stayed there until the dancefloor had cleared.

Dublin was a rockers' town, but by early 1966, The Black Eagles were heavily into the mod sound that was happening in England. Phil took Brian off to Manchester where the drummer found a cool barber who could give him a French crop. Phil got a smart cut as well, and they felt like they were in The Small Faces. The trip was made even more legendary by the fact that they stayed at Philomena's guest house in Whalley Range, and Brian set eyes on the latest residents, Viv Stanshall and The Bonzo Dog Doo-Dah Band. The wildest! They were getting closer to stardom all the time.

Nobody was going to dismiss them now. Phil wore button-down shirts, crisp ties and tonic suits. Even when he was short of cash, he'd pick a second-hand shirt off the racks in the market that everyone else had overlooked, and on Phil, it would look fabulous. And so they'd blast away at their Who songs, and slip in a thunderous version of 'Still I'm Sad' by The Yardbirds, ultimately pushing the music further into the mad avenues that were opening up in the US and the UK. Soon it would be 'Freak Out' by The Mothers Of Invention, and maybe even an Otis Redding song to keep the soul boys happy.

By the end of 1966 The Black Eagles had grown out of the local halls. Now they figured in the downtown Dublin clubs where the hip kids would beat the alcohol ban by necking pills and staying out until daybreak. As many as four nights a week, they'd be hammering a scene that was opened up by youngbloods like Bluesville, The Greenbeats, The Creatures and The Action. Dublin may never have fully enjoyed a teen spirit in the 1950s because of too much austerity and self-denial by all those abstainers with their pioneer pins, waiting for their kicks in the next world. But now the youth were compensating for all that, big style.

Phil became a performer and a participant in these fresh happenings at The Five Club, the Moulin Rouge, The Flamingo, the Club A Go-Go, Club Arthur and whatever new, funky cellar was in vogue. His name was featuring in the popularity charts in the Irish press. He meant something. And whenever his mother came over, or he visited her in Manchester, she'd see his confidence and stature rise by great increments.

The Black Eagles became Jigsaw, and then fizzled out. The manager, Joe Smith, was having trouble with his sons – one of them threatened to run off with his girlfriend – and eventually Joe lost heart. But it was never the end for Phil. He needed to find more people on his level, to fully tease out his talent. Already some guys had come to the house leaving notes, urging him to call them. He never got around to answering. Phil had been snatched away from rock and roll into a more mundane gig.

A neighbour got him a start as an apprentice fitter and turner at Tonge & Taggart's foundry, with a day-release course at Clogher Road Technical College. He hated it almost instantly, and he'd cycle up to the Grafton Street pubs and sit down for a pint in his greasy overalls, sick to his soul, too depressed to even get changed. All that clock-punching, supervision and regularity – he was nothing but a stranger in that world. He got paid two pounds and five shillings for his labour. A weekend's rock and roll earned him a tenner. So the only thing that cheered Phil was the prospect of measuring up to his Crumlin reveries.

Still, the Behans had got it wrong. Crumlin was a marvellous place to grow up. There were creative sparks flying all over the estate. You had Christy Brown as a neighbour, severely handicapped, but painting and writing with his toes, grooving to Handel and Chopin and reading Charles Dickens's tale of a lost boy made good, *David Copperfield*. Christy's autobiography, *My Left Foot*, was published in the year of Lizzy's first single, 1970. The film version of that story would be produced by another local boy, Noel Pearson, who'd once managed a beat group, The Chessmen, but later become prominent in The Abbey Theatre. He not only screened *My Left Foot*, but he produced *The Field* as well. And Crumlin would also be frequented in later years by

Paul McGrath, reunited with his ma on Keeper Road – Phil's equivalent in the football world. They called him The Black Pearl when he played centre-back for Manchester United and later Aston Villa. Raised in various Dublin orphanages as a kid, he was unique and tough, a star feature in the Irish international squad, a braveheart and a hell-raiser.

Phil never forgot Crumlin. He valued his accent, his education, the blood rites, the street savvy and the grain of Catholicism he picked up in those years. He remembered the tolerance and kindness of his grandmother and his uncles. He even sang fondly about the Crumlin boot-boys on a Radio Éireann session Thin Lizzy played in 1973, and later he brought a TV crew there when they were making a film about his glamorous career. Whenever other parts of his life were out of control, these thoughts, these deeply-set values helped to keep him centred.

'When I'm in Ireland, I say I'm from Dublin,' he'd say. 'When I'm in Dublin, I say I'm from Crumlin. When I'm in Crumlin, I say I'm from Leighlin Road and when I'm in Leighlin Road, I say I'm a Lynott.'

3

There she was up front, the famous Rose Tynan, all dolled up and yodelling like anybody's business. At the back of the stage was The Rangers' drummer, Dessie Reynolds, who was only twelve, but he battered out the waltz signatures as well as he might. Danny Ellis played trombone and, finally, there was Brendan 'Brush' Shiels, holding a shiny Kingsway guitar, knowing very little about the instrument, but grinning away fiercely at the paying customers.

That was Brush's job, smiling and faking it on guitar. 'Just wink at the audience and look presentable,' they told him when he got the gig – too young to know any better, too old to turn down the chance of making some handy cash. So Brush puckered and gave the glad-eye to the jivers and waltzers, playing a few rudimentary chords while Rose Tynan cruised though through the Slim Whitman songbook, her vocal cords all a-quiver with the tricks of the business: the melisma, the vibrato, the American twang and the tear-choked pay-off. Presently, the dancefloor was busy with starchy petticoats and Clery's three-button Sunday suits and the smell of chainstore perfume in the evening. Lovely.

But the weirdest thing of all was the sound that came from behind the curtains. It was reedy and a little arthritic, embellishing Rose's fatalistic croonings – it was like some phantom was getting in on the act. Or maybe, you'd have guessed, it was some old fella with his accordion, keeping low. Which, of course, was the exact deal. It was Rose's manager, also an important instrumentalist in the band. But he was old and ashamed. He thought his looks might spoil the dance, and so they hired these kids to sit up there and look cute while he played his squeeze box into a skull microphone behind the drapes. A strange practice, but it was best for business.

24

Brush never really had it in his mind to be in a band. He'd originally wanted to be a footballer, but they brought him in to make up the numbers. It was a shabby introduction to the music industry and he was never totally idealistic again – even though he became an accomplished player and a respected figure in Dublin's musical community, he never forgot those first lessons.

By 1966 he was playing with Brian Rock And The Boys. Brian was a fellow kid from Cabra West on Dublin's northside. They were following the acclaim of Brian's brother Dickie Rock, a star with The Miami Showband whose skinny frame and trembling ballads made him a huge draw across Ireland. Brush was making a good living at the country and western game, but he had more ambitious schemes. In 1967, he joined The Uptown Band and lashed out a soul revue that was less commercial but better for the self-respect.

Years after, when Brush saw *The Commitments*, he was severely annoyed. He felt that he recognised the music, the north Dublin manners and some of the characters in the film. Especially the scenes with Derek Scully, the bass player in his butcher's apron. Brush had worked as a meat packer when The Uptown Band were happening, and sure, didn't he play bass as well? When Roddy Doyle sent him the book to review, Brush vented his anger. He thought it was dreadful, and he especially hated the way Doyle was making capital out of the working-class accent from those parts.

The Uptown Band became a top act after nine months, and the music diversified. They got into the psychedelic thing near the end – throwing gladioli around the stage and letting off smoke bombs. Their manager, Ted Carroll, used to be in the Dramatic Society at school, so he knew how to employ flash powder and smoke bombs and to project weird slides on the sides of the stage. It was insane, but it was good for business. Meanwhile, Ted was getting famous for booking bands into the clubs and cellars and the tennis clubs around Dublin – he became so accomplished that the police hounded him for running public dances without a licence, obliging him to lie low for a few months.

Some time before, Ted had booked The Black Eagles into the Bastille Club in Dalkey. He'd realised that they weren't fantastic but that the singer was special. He thought he'd try and get him to play with the Uptowns, and since Philip Lynott wasn't on the phone, he journeyed down to Crumlin. The singer wasn't around so he left a message. However, Phil didn't call back, and the manager hired somebody else. Ted was so occupied getting gigs for lots of other bands that some of the Uptowns got restless. They brought in another manager, Larry Mooney, and Ted was edged out, followed shortly after by Brush. The two exiles began planning a supergroup – all the members hand-picked, the best Dublin had ever seen, and a real contender for acclaim across the water. 'Anyone can take off if you do this thing properly,' Brush used to say. 'Just give us three months.' He knew the business and now he was intensely impatient.

They approached Brian Downey, who was wary of Brush. He talked too much, the drummer felt – he was too dogmatic, and you'd never have a say in the running of the band. Besides, Downey was sick of playing The Kinks and The Troggs and all that stuff. He was getting his own thing together with Sugar Shack – doing some BB King, lots of great electric blues. Brian was taking lessons as well; a drummer called Jimmy Doyle had come back from playing the GI clubs in Hamburg and he was teaching him technique and how to read scores.

Phil was definitely into the idea of something ambitious though. Since Jigsaw, he'd been singing with Kama Sutra, a southside soul band who played numbers by Eddie Floyd and Sam And Dave. He'd given up his apprenticeship at the foundry to make a living in rock and roll, and when Brush called over one afternoon, he was intrigued. Brush hadn't even seen The Black Eagles, but he knew Phil from pictures in the papers and he was in a hurry. He'd previously considered getting in vocalist Peter Adler, who wore shades and the hippest clothes and whose dad, Larry, was the famous harmonica player. But that hadn't worked out. Therefore Brush asked Phil what music he liked. The singer said he was into The Velvet Underground, The Byrds, Simon And Garfunkel. 'Yeah,' said the band leader. 'You just go at it.'

They rehearsed that night and for the following six weeks straight at Mrs Quigley's at 10 Sinnot Place. Her son Pat was in a band called The Movement, so she was used to the noise. Ted Carroll wanted the band to play down-the-line rock and roll, the music he was passionate for, and which would become the mainstay of his record trading business later on. But the rest of the band liked the idea of acid rock – far-out and musically challenging. That was the form with many of the Dublin bands in 1967. Everything was getting visually and sonically strange, to the extent that the madcap act The Light once filled the entire cellar of The Scene club with smoke, causing a worried bystander to call for the fire engines.

In keeping with the times, somebody suggested calling the band My Father's Moustache. But right away they realised this was a ridiculous notion; Skid Row sounded better. Brush on bass, Bernard Cheevers on guitar, Noel Bridgeman on drums and Phil to throw the shapes and click the chicks. They even had a couple of roadies, Phil's mates Frank Murray and Paul Scully from nearby Walkinstown, the first in all of Ireland. Not that there was much need for a road crew, but Brush saw that they were good-looking boys. 'I'm not stupid,' said Brush grinning. 'They'll attract more women than the band. And if the girls come along, the guys will follow.' The old showband laws. Brush knew the form, that was for sure.

It went off in a terrifying fashion at the University College Dublin gig. It wasn't Skid Row's first show, but it was certainly the occasion when all the scheming and the theatre built into the band's make-up was realised. They were piling into Hendrix's 'Manic Depression' with immoderate noises and the hint of violence, just like The Who and The Creation were doing across the water in preparation for their stage-wrecking rituals. Except Brush didn't trash his gear. He took off his bass and threw it at Lynott, just missing him. Then he jumped on top of the singer, wrestling him down.

Phil was surprised by the attack, but he managed to push his colleague away. Then he laid a punch on to him. Brush fought back, and as the remaining two musicians kept the beat going, he took another swing at Lynott. They rucked some more and the audience got increasingly agitated. There was an awful ripping sound and you could see that Phil had the back of his shirt pulled right off him, revealing his sweat-streaked flesh. The bouncers couldn't tolerate any more of this primal behaviour. They dived in and separated the brawlers. Brush was laughing.

It was a classic stunt, and they'd been planning it for ages. Brush got the idea after watching *The Defiant Ones* at the cinema

– Stanley Kramer's 1958 film about a pair of escaped convicts who hated each other. What peppered the action was the fact that one of the runaways (Tony Curtis) was white and the other (Sidney Poitier) was black. Imagine, Brush figured, if you could replicate that tension on stage in Ireland. Aside from the students at the College Of Surgeons, Phil was the only black man in town. Loads of punters were driven to see him sing out of pure curiosity as it was. Guess how they'd react if he was rolling on the stage with another band member? Sure, he'd even put a little rip in Phil's shirt beforehand to make it tear easier.

Brush had big plans for his seventeen-year-old singer. But he had to learn his trade first. None of that gazing up at the ceiling for starters. Look at the girls in the audience, he told Phil. Make them feel welcome. And importantly, that girlfriend with the lovely red hair and the ringlets – that Carol Stevens from the northside – she wasn't to come to any Skid Row gigs again.

'We're not fucking having that,' Brush insisted. 'Your job is to attract all the nice girls. We're not interested in blokes – they'll come if the girls are there. Carol's banned. And make sure you talk to the girls at the end of the night. Make sure that they come to the next gig.'

'C'mon, Brush.'

'We'll fuck you out if you don't! We can get anybody just to stand there at the front. We haven't the time to be hanging around here. You look great, now let's get on with it.'

Since Phil lived on the other side of town from Brush and his mates, the natural thing was for them to meet up in the city centre. One favourite spot was the basement restaurant in Switzer's department store, where they'd buy a coffee or suck on an orange for hours, waiting for their fellow musicians to pass through. The waitresses were kind and never hassled anyone, so it became a regular drop-in for the upcoming rock and roll stars. If Phil had a long time to kill, he'd often walk into the Grafton cinema, which specialised in kids' shows. He hated the documentaries and travelogues, because the stories were so predictable, and he'd often call out a line before the narrator had spoken it. Cartoons were his thing – he adored the anarchy and the colour of it all.

Phil's close friend was a DJ from The Moulin Rouge club, John Hodges. When he learnt that the guy was dying of leukaemia, the singer helped him as well as he could. Since treatments were more advanced in the north, Phil would accompany John on the train to Belfast, where he'd get his blood transfusions to try and stall the illness. When John eventually died, they held a wake for him at Slattery's on Capel Street. Phil helped to organise this, and borrowed money to make sure his mate got a decent send-off. By the end of the evening, he was roaring and crying – a raw emotion that many people hadn't noticed in him before.

Meantime, Brush was mad for the American West Coast sound and the freaky musical ideas that were batting across the Atlantic. They learnt 'So You Want To Be (A Rock 'n' Roll Star)' plus 'Eight Miles High' by The Byrds, and The Animals' 'Sky Pilot', some Buffalo Springfield and a lot of the stranger Beatles tunes. They were good musicians, so they could handle songs which The Beatles, now studio-bound, wouldn't even perform themselves. And they were playing a couple of original songs too. 'Photograph Man' was definitely in the spirit of *Sgt Pepper*. It was about a groovy old guy who went around taking pictures. The chorus was:

'Click, click, click, click
Went the photograph maaaan!'

They recorded the song at the Eamonn Andrews studios in Dublin. Ted Carroll took the tapes to Liberty Records and then Apple, The Beatles' label in London, and another pal, Tony Boland, tried to get the people at Immediate Records interested. Everybody in the band was getting excited. Phil used to introduce the songs live as 'our next single'; but nobody wanted it.

There was an urgency about their efforts in 1968. Brush had reckoned they'd be kingpins in a couple of months, but other Dublin bands were getting the jump on them. Brian Downey's band, Sugar Shack, had started off on a purist blues vibe, but they stole a chance by recording a Tim Rose song, 'Morning Dew'. They played it like psychotic stoners: loose, warped and heavy with reverb – Haight-Ashbury relocated to Grafton Street – it had reached number seventeen in the Irish charts in February. Sugar Shack threw a reception to mark the release, and Phil was impressed. He started hanging around Brian's place, noting the mechanics of success, realising that a hit record got you better gigs, more money and increased kudos.

Phil was still quite shy on stage, but he was making a much

better job of it. His singing was developing too. Brush had read about Frank Sinatra's magnificent breath control – how he used to practise the pinhole technique that trumpet players used, and expand his lung capacity by swimming under water for impressive distances. So Brush would sit Phil down and hold his head in a basin of lukewarm water for as long as he could bear it.

Despite the lack of a record release, Skid Row was the biggest rock act in town. Blowing off their chief rivals, Granny's Intentions, at University College Dublin had been a significant moment. Their film projections were momentous as well, organised by Mick O'Flanagan, a mate of Phil's since The Black Eagles days. They'd experimented with 8mm projections back then, but it had backfired a little when the audience charged to the front of the stage, not to hail the band but to watch Mick's films of their local streets – an enthralling notion. But with Skid Row, the process was much cooler. They were now partaking in crazy scenes, just like Pink Floyd or The Velvet Underground. Phil also took to singing through an echo box, supplementing the instrumental breaks with dive-bombing noises and explosions as the girls smiled back and the liquid light show turned strawberry blonde.

This great multi-media gesture was designed to peak with their version of 'Sky Pilot'. Mick had spliced and mixed together home-movie shots that he'd bought in town: the Pope visiting the Holy Land and the assassination of US President John F Kennedy. It looked terrific on stage, and in the hip clubs it went down really well. However, they played a Catholic Young Men's Society hall one night, which was administered by prefects chosen by the local priest, and as the young men watched the images of His Holiness, which appeared to whirl over the deathly events of the Dallas shooting, they were outraged. The papers learnt of this happening, and editorialised about such rock and roll blasphemy – the *Evening Herald* even ran their account on the front page. Phil was made up. No other band had caused such a furore, never mind scamming a cover story.

He would sometimes bum a ride home on Mick's Honda scooter. They were a comical pair, since Mick was just five foot tall, and Phil's legs hung out like a stick insect's from the pillion seat. When he took taxis home, the singer liked to put on a show, telling the driver he was the son of a Nigerian chief, that he'd come over to Ireland to study medicine. He'd converse in pidgin English all the way home, but if the cabbie ever tried to overcharge him, he'd quickly revert to being a Crumlin hard man, and tell the guy that he was a robbing bastard. This resulted in deadlock one night, and Phil suggested that they drive to the police station to sort out the problem. The driver gave in, but as Lynott opened the front door at Leighlin Road, the taxi man delivered the nastiest line he could think of: 'I'll tell you this for nothin', I'm fuckin' glad they shot Martin Luther King.'

Brush Shiels was party to a strange parental rite in 1968. He'd arranged to meet Robert Moore, a ballroom owner from a town on the east side of Belfast Lough called Holywood. The Skid Row leader was promising to look after Robert's sixteen-year-old son, Gary, who was joining the band. He was replacing Bernard Cheevers, who'd just won an Apprentice Of The Year award at the Guinness plant, and didn't have so much time for rock and roll. Brush was still a teenager himself. Gary's father was thirty-six.

Robert Moore had hot-housed his son's abilities from the age of six, when Gary would walk onstage at his venue, The Queen's Hall, clamber on a chair and sing 'Sugar Time'. Soon after, he was picking out Shadows tunes on guitar and was billed as a solo act, Little Gary. Before he was even a teenager, he'd got a band together, The Beat Boys, who wore smart red shirts and rapped out anything from Beatles and Stones songs to versions of Baron Knights comedy skits. Back then, he was podgy with a pudding-bowl fringe and a sulky face. 'The group will play anything the public wants,' he told journalists, who were amazed at his accelerated talent.

He was after knowledge, and whenever bands visited The Queen's Hall, he'd quiz them about their technique and equipment. Gary spoke to the guitarist from The Deltones one night, Eric Bell, about the white plastic treble booster he was using. He'd never seen one before – could he try it out? Fine, Eric said, go ahead. They became mates, checking out groups at Belfast's Maritime Club together. Presently they'd follow each other in and out of bands on the local circuit.

By 1966, Gary had experienced the revolutionary power of John Mayall's *Blues Breakers* album, and he also copped licks from Jeff

Beck and Peter Green, cult British players. Two years later, his dexterity was heavily in demand. Davy Lewis, guitarist with Belfast blues band The Method, had been damaged in a car crash and they needed a replacement for a residency at the Club A Go-Go in Dublin. Gary had been arguing a lot with his dad at the time, and school wasn't an option any more. So sure, he'd take the gig.

As The Method played their show in Abbey Street, Skid Row were a few hundred yards away at The 72 Club. Brush had heard about the new boy and his dazzling ways, so he checked him out during his own interval. Gary kept his back to the audience, but he was striking out the most outlandish licks on his Telecaster. Brush asked him straight away to join Skid Row, but the guitarist said he just wanted to play the blues. However, Moore visited The 72 Club during his next intermission. He witnessed the lights, the back projections and Phil riffing out with the echo box and hitting the crowd with a startling version of 'Strawberry Fields Forever'. He liked this peculiar scheme. He was in.

Brush figured he knew the next way the business was turning. Bands like Cream, Taste and The Jimi Hendrix Experience were taking the blues format into unguessed-at areas: complicated, progressive, a virtuoso game. This was especially inspiring because Taste was fronted by Rory Gallagher, a Cork man, who was now famous all over the world. Brush was a smart player and Gary was certainly up for the challenge, so that's where they started aiming – they even performed a mini-opera about a hospital operation that ended in amputation and tragedy. All this was a contradiction of many of the aspects that Brush had previously established with Skid Row – the singer as a main attraction, the girl-pleasing routines, the thinly disguised showband laws. Phil would have to work at his end all the harder.

Brush got married on 11 January 1969. Phil invited him to spend his honeymoon at his mother's place in Manchester, The Clifton Grange Hotel. Brush and his new wife Margaret were delighted – after Brush working six nights a week for so many years it was a good opportunity to spend extra time with each other. However, a band staying at the hotel, The Ivy League, had lost a member due to the Hong Kong flu, and so Brush spent his honeymoon playing bass twice a night, earning his passage, bashing away at 'Tossing And Turning' while Phil danced at the front with newlywed Mar.

Skid Row released a single, on the local Song label, 'New Places, Old Faces', four months later. Brush had written a beautifully sad lyric about the effect of a repossession order on a tight-knit family pushed out of their old home to make way for the road developers. This had happened to Brush's own people when they'd left Phibsboro Road, even though the place was never actually developed. The music he wrote was a woozy pastiche of many styles, some of it age-old. The Rolling Stones had already touched on this ambience with songs like 'Lady Jane' and 'She's A Rainbow', where suddenly it was cool to experiment with descant recorders and Elizabethan madrigals in a pop format.

Phil recognised the value of Brush's forlorn story and thus he sang about Auntie Queenie and Uncle John walking away from the old place for the last time with aching intent. He gave you the particulars of the tale and the mood right away. It was a hard one to sing, with melodic frills and bits of stop-time and a tune that echoed the modal bleakness of Paul Simon's best. Brush thought Phil's singing was like Mick Jagger, and he was pleased. Johnny Moynihan, the tin-whistle player from the folk band Sweeney's Men, guested on the song, blowing forlornly, making the nostalgic theme all the more pressing. It was a good début.

But still the Skid Row boys weren't happy – they were losing themselves in jazz improvisation and difficult time signatures. They were a boys' band now, and it was debatable how much they needed Phil. Besides, his singing wasn't always great. This became manifest when they appeared at The Top Hat ballroom, filming their version of 'Strawberry Fields Forever' for the RTE pop show, *Like Now*. Phil looked like a star with his dark preacher's coat, but his vocals were strained. Everybody played along: Gary, Brush, Noel, a guy called Humphrey Weitham on sitar, and BP Fallon, the boy groover who hosted the Irish version of *Juke Box Jury*, on bongos. They managed pretty well.

But the playback revealed some of Phil's shortcomings. He was hitting bum notes. Noel was mad when he noticed it and the others weren't pleased. At one stage, Phil was toying with a balloon, and it seemed that the higher he bounced the balloon, the more out of key he sang. Maybe it was nerves, or the unflattering demands of TV recording – certainly it had some-thing to do with the inflammation in his throat that Brush had noticed. At the very least, he'd need to have his tonsils out.

In the summer of 1969, Phil travelled to Manchester, where Philomena fixed him up with some private medical treatment at St Joseph's. When he returned to Dublin later that summer, he found that Skid Row had managed without him. He was surplus. Gary could sing the high notes while Brush and Noel covered the rest. And they could jam endlessly without the embarrassment of somebody standing out front, doing nothing. As a consolation, Brush offered to teach him the bass guitar, to give him a better chance in another band. But the message was plain: Lynott just wasn't up to the job.

Years later, when Phil was irrefutably a star, Brush still wouldn't give him credit. It meant nothing to him. To Brush, Lynott was the same guy that he'd met on the doorstep of Leighlin Road for that first time – their relationship was still conducted on the old bandleader's abrupt terms. And when Lizzy played Dalymount Park in 1977 and the whole town loved him, Brush was unaffected. They played *pop* music, and he didn't enjoy it.

Brush never gave the singer the reassurance he always wanted. On occasions when the northsider thought back to the sacking from Skid Row in 1969, he rarely felt remorse. Maybe rejection made Phil work harder, or perhaps it fed on the singer's insecurity. Brush had his own philosophy: 'He was me best pal. Still, this had to be done.'

4

Eric Bell went to the east Belfast dole office and told them he was available for work. The clerk opened up a form and asked him what his previous occupation was. He told them he was a professional musician. The clerk wrote 'general labourer' on the form. Eric suggested that he might be useful as a plumber's helper. That's what the guys at the Maritime Jazz Club told him to say. Plumber's helpers did nothing all day and the money wasn't bad.

Eric was given a card with an address and a name written on it. He reckoned that he'd lucked it and would be carrying spanners and plungers around for a month until a good-paying band came up. So the next day he turned up at the address, a scruffy room like a working men's club, and met the boss, who said, 'Right, you're with him,' pointing to a sour-faced old boy wearing a hard peaked hat, wheeling out a bicycle with a ladder hooked on the side. He looked like Mr Magoo, and Eric grinned a little.

They strolled around to Jocelyn Avenue, near the Woodstock Road, the core of east Belfast. The old man took the ladder off the bike and raised it by a lamp post and then Eric realised what he was in for. He wasn't a plumber's mate at all – he was a teenage gas lamp lighter, the last of the breed. He climbed up the ladder and opened the glass door of the lamp and, as instructed, cleaned the panes of glass with a rag. But he never knew that the cloth was soaked in paraffin, or that there was a little bypass jet inside the mechanism that was always lit in order to get the mantle glowing. Eric touched the jet with the rag and suddenly he had a fireball in his hand.

It was snowing that day, and the cinders were falling on the white pavement. It looked incredible. The old man's face was covered in soot, and he wasn't amused. 'C'mon down, for Jeezus' sake! That's not the way to do it, son.' So the old man did it properly, making a big deal of the operation that a child of three could manage. And so by the end of the week, Eric was a pro. By the close of the second week, Mr Magoo was smiling more and confiding to the young lad, 'You know, there's nothing I like better in life than a nice clean lamp.' While Eric was thinking, *I've gotta get out of here . . .*

Eric must have quit a dozen jobs in the mid 1960s. He'd tried shifts in the ropeworks on the Newtownards Road and he'd been a window cleaner. He packed shirts in boxes and even worked in a pickle factory. And all the time he was practising guitar and working his way through local bands – woodshedding with The Bluebeats, The Earthdwellers, The Atlantics, The Jaguars, The Deltones, Shades Of Blue. In early 1967, he was nineteen years old and working in a line-up of Van Morrison's Them.

Van was virtually finished with beat music by then. He hated the constraints and the crummy politics of a group format. He'd spent time in California, shared a stage with Jim Morrison at the Whiskey A Go-Go and knew there were more creative ways of expressing himself. So Eric was sitting down with Van, listening to some of his new demos on a reel-to-reel. One of them was an amazing, freestyle rant, apparently about the shortcomings of the police force. Eric was puzzled, but happy to give it a run.

At showtime, Van took to the stage in a floral suit he'd bought in California and began making songs up on the spot – something that Eric hadn't been prepared for. The hard men in the Ulster clubs didn't care for this, especially when he started shouting abuse at them, so they threw coins back. A fiasco. A month later, Van had packed in the band and was recording 'Brown-eyed Girl' in New York, a solo act forever more. Some of the remaining guys kept going with Them, but Eric moved on.

By 1969, he was based in Dublin, playing in The Dreams showband. It was an ultra-straight situation, but they paid him a full £35 for six nights a week, fantastic wages then. The proviso was that if the managers ever caught him smoking any of that marijuana, he'd be out immediately. So Eric used to lock himself in a toilet cubicle before the shows and smoke a reefer, blowing the smoke down into the bowl. Then he'd pull out an air freshener that he carried around especially to kill the smell of his dope. Eric would then stroll on stage and play the old crowd-pleasers, suitably sedated, hoping that paranoia wouldn't kick in.

But it was soul-killing work. When The Dreams recorded their single, 'A Boy Needs A Girl', Eric put feedback down on his track, but the producer kept erasing it. He said Eric was making a mistake, that he had to do it 'properly'. Whenever he'd take a mad lead break on stage, they'd warn him off. 'Cool it, Ravi Shankar,' the singer John Farrell sneered. Eric hated the funny dances and the jokes and the skits and all that ridiculous, buck-leppin' behaviour. He wanted to cross over the fence again, to be somehow imaginative.

Monday was showband night off, but instead of hanging out in the usual bars, Eric began frequenting the rock and roll places – Neary's and The Bailey, The TV Club, and The Five – the last of which Brush Shiels ran on a Monday and renamed The Ghetto. You'd get the psychedelics and the folkies and the blues players all mixing there. Nobody had much money, but there was a more stimulating vibe and a degree of artistic pride. Eric started saving money, looking for a chance to better himself.

He met another Belfast musician in The Bailey, Eric Wrixon, who'd also played in Them; he'd been in the original line-up and took the credit for giving the band its name. More recently, he too had been playing with a showband – The Trixons – who worked hard and had even played dates in America. Together, they started planning an alternative, and put the word out. Wrixon approached Eric Kitteringham, the original bass player in Rory Gallagher's Taste, but with no success. They tried a drummer from Cork called Greg, but that didn't work either. In December 1969, Eric Bell had quit The Dreams altogether, and was running short of funds when he chanced on Phil Lynott and Orphanage at The Countdown Club.

There was a special significance in the name of Phil's new band. The Orphanage was the name of a Georgian house at 52 Mount Street, the premier hippie pad in Dublin. This was where the band Dr Strangeley Strange hung out, a place that blasted the mind and the senses. It was, after all, an era of idealised, groovy communities: The Grateful Dead had blossomed out of 710 Ashbury Street, San Francisco, while Bob Dylan and The Band were cooling their heels at Big Pink in West Saugerties, New

York. Also, British groups like Traffic were getting it together in the country, man. If there was a general aim in all this, it was to provide self-sustaining shelter for the misfits, a place to work up great hopes and unique music, to foster alternative ways.

The Strangeleys were Ivan Pawle and Tim Booth, students at Trinity College Dublin, and their friend Tim Goulding. The house was rented out by Annie Mohan, otherwise known as Orphan Annie, hence the name of the establishment. Phil Lynott was introduced to the scene by Annie Christmas, another teenager and a Mount Street regular. He liked it there. There was peculiar music and poetry, hash and hallucinogenics, wild styles and nursery rhymes.

Phil began to stop by The Orphanage during his Skid Row days. It was something different from the hustling and stroke-pulling of Brush's regime. The Strangeleys were a few years older, middle-class and less bloody-minded. Booth and Goulding had been raised away from the city, in Kildare and Wicklow. The latter's father even had the grand title of Sir Basil Goulding, and was a famous art collector and head of a lucrative fertiliser business. Ivan Pawle was English. They had back-grounds in graphic design, advertising and fine art.

They played a harmonium, acoustic guitars, whistles, fiddles and mandolins. Their music was joyful and child-like – a mixture of dream-babble, lines of James Joyce, myth and rampaging cartoon characters. On the song 'Donnybrook fair' they sang about unicorns, showbands and the 1916 Easter Rising while chopping between the pub ballad 'Waxie's Dargle' and church hymnals. A lot of the rock bands hated the Strangeleys. They resented the fact that the band had a deal with Island Records, and declared that their music was all pretentious pish.

But in 1968, Phil wanted ideas and information from every musical source around. The Strangeleys were friends with The Incredible String Band and Fairport Convention, bands from across the water that were adding fresh dimensions to traditional music. Phil was impressed by another feature of their art – the way they could write songs about themselves, their friends and little personal incidents and make it sound important and cool. Phil was there with Frank Murray one day when they first heard the expression 'Anyone fancy a joint?' They watched, gob-smacked, as someone unwrapped a scarf, revealing a block of dope the size of a cigarette block. Just then, Ivan Pawle came downstairs – he'd just co-written a song called 'Frosty Mornings' with Robin Williamson of The Incredible String Band. Wow . . .

When Tim Booth moved a few miles out to the lovely area of Sandymount, establishing a second Orphanage, Phil used to bring Gary Moore along with him. The guitarist may not have been particularly articulate at this point, but he had an amazing capacity for expressing himself through any instrument he picked up. He'd play bluegrass, country or Irish folk, executed on fiddle, mandolin or keyboards. So they'd all jam together, Phil batting ideas around, helping each other on their songs. Maybe afterwards, they'd have a smoke and listen to Zappa or the sound of Randy California riffing madly through a Spirit album.

By the end of the Skid Row days, Phil was dressing like a total star. He'd wear cricket trousers and gaberdines and started to cultivate the makings of an Afro hairstyle. He used to visit a girl called Jaffa Gill on Leeson Street, who'd studied fashion design in England. She opened Dublin's first ever boutique, The Happening, and she hired a proper tailor to make up these outrageous designs for anyone who had a few bob, which they all fortunately had. Trousers cut low on the hips, tight on the thighs and flared at the knees. Shortie T-shirts that left the midriff exposed. If Phil didn't turn heads on Grafton Street, something was badly wrong. Soon he was posing in fashion shoots for the Dublin papers: gloriously skinny, six foot two, the best looker in Ireland.

After Skid Row, Phil held Brush to his promise of giving him bass lessons. The old band leader had provided him with a Fender Jazz that had once belonged to Robert Ballagh from The Chessmen. Ballagh had despaired when his band had gradually moved from the beat scene to make money on the showband circuit, so he'd quit music to be an artist. Eventually, he'd become famous internationally as a painter, but he enjoyed watching Phil on television with his old bass.

Phil used to take the number 22 bus from Crumlin all the way across town, terminus to terminus, until he'd got to Brush's place at Cabra West. He managed this for a month, usually early in the mornings, learning scales and practising hard. But since the music he liked was practically all complicated, he would never manage his new trade quickly, especially if he planned on singing at the same time.

Therefore when he formed Orphanage in the summer of 1969 with his old mate Brian Downey, he wasn't going to play bass. That was Pat Quigley's job, the former member of The Movement, who'd already enjoyed a couple of hits in Ireland. The guitarist was Joe Staunton, who was nervous because this was his first band, although Phil always reassured him. Terry Woods, formerly with Sweeney's Men, was a floating player. The Sweeneys started in 1966 and broke up in 1969, and were another inspiration for Phil. They were breathtaking players, changing the shape of Irish folk music with their bouzoukis, keening voices and source material. They even went electric for a bit, enlisting Henry McCullough, the only Irishman who would manage to support Hendrix on tour and appear at Woodstock. Like the freewheelers in Greenwich Village, New York, the Sweeneys had made old music fascinating and relevant once more.

Phil aimed to use Orphanage to channel all of this musical traffic – acid, blues, folk, progressive – and to front it with an array of travelling musicians. Brian thought it was a great idea. Some nights there'd be half a dozen guests ripping it up with them. Alternately, many of the planned guests never turned up. Phil wanted to head for London, but Pat was about to become a dad, and Joe wasn't experienced enough. So it was Ireland or nothing.

Orphanage – the word – was charged with another meaning for Phil. He didn't know his father, and whenever he mentioned the subject to his mum, she just explained to him that he was a good man who'd offered to take care of his boy, but she'd decided otherwise. Phil had once written a letter to the guy, but Philomena, thinking it was for the best, never passed the note on.

When people asked Phil about his early days – as they would – he just laughed it off and changed the subject. He was Ireland's smallest ethnic minority and a lot of the time he worked it to his advantage. Whenever Thin Lizzy played Cork in 1970, the place practically came to a standstill when he walked down St Patrick's Street. A double-decker bus slowed down so that the driver could get a good look at him, not because he was a famous rocker, but because the population of the town had never seen a black man before. Everybody in the bus started waving out of the window at him, and Phil laughed and waved back. A black man with a Crumlin accent – no other musician on the island could ever compete with such outstanding features.

It had been upsetting when people called him Sambo at school, but Phil punched his way out of that kind of bigotry. Sure, it was humiliating in class when it was his turn to collect the charity money for the foreign missionaries – commonly termed 'the black babies'. And when the other kids remarked on his hair and his skin colour and called him an African boy, a *baluba*, he wasn't pleased.

Many girls were afraid of his unusual looks. Then again, a lot of other girls were curious. So he'd work it into his chat-up lines. He called himself 'a beauty spot all over'. He claimed he never knew he was black 'until I looked at the size of my mickey'. One summer night, Phil and his mates had been out clubbing in town. They'd missed the last bus home, so it was a long walk. Suddenly, they decided to jump in the canal, just for a laugh – requiring them to stop at a friend's place to dry out. Phil stripped off and covered himself with talcum powder. 'Look at me now!' he laughed. 'I'm a WHITE MAN!'

Philomena, however, had had to cope with prejudice from both barrels. An unmarried mother *and* the lover of a black man, she never publicly related the details of her son's arrival until the tenth anniversary of his death. Then she published *My Boy*, a distressing revelation of her ordeals. She'd met Cecil Parris, Phil's dad, at a Birmingham dancehall. Cecil moved south before Philomena knew she was pregnant. She gave birth on 20 August 1949 at Halham Hospital in the West Bromwich area of Birmingham. She'd resumed contact with Parris, who acknowledged his fathering the child, but they stopped seeing each other. Thereafter, Philomena was shunned by intolerant landlords, dismissed by cheap moralisers, and subjected to sordid lodgings and skivvying jobs until she decided to send Phil home to Leighlin Road.

Some kids may have viewed this as abandonment, but it seemed that Philip Parris Lynott accentuated the positive in his situation. Not only had he an extended family in Dublin who'd unconditionally welcomed him in, but he also had a mother who'd struggled against powerful circumstances to hold on to her boy, to keep him in the Lynott clan.

Phil may not have known all the details, but he was aware of the Catholic Church's attitude towards illegitimate children. It was normal to have such a baby adopted. And a half-caste baby without a father was total taboo. After giving birth, Philomena, then homeless, was moved to a Catholic institution in Birmingham, the Selly Oak Home For Unmarried Mothers. The figure in charge of this place, the Mother Superior, had begun the process to have the boy handed over to an appropriate new home. Philomena had refused this.

During the celebratory weekend of the Dalymount Park gig in 1977, Phil returned to these thoughts. The *Hot Press* journalist was asking about Phil's old band, Orphanage, but Phil was thinking of his mother and a different take on the word.

'I could have ended up in an orphanage. Having a kid when she wasn't married, a black kid in particular in the 1950s – keeping it was hard.'

Eric Bell knew nothing of this when he felt an epiphany coming on at the Countdown Club. He'd just taken his first tab of acid, and his sensory system was royally blasted. He clocked Phil jumping around at the front of the stage, singing 'Donnybrook Fair' in his white kaftan, and thought it was marvellous. He listened to Orphanage playing Dylan's 'It Takes A Lot To Laugh, It Takes A Train To Cry' as his nervous receptors flipped around and he realised he understood *everything*.

Occasionally the drug rush would fall away, and Eric noticed that Brian Downey was a classic drummer. The sound he was getting, the way he'd slap the snare like a veteran, was extraordinary for someone so young. Eric knew that he had to get going in a new venture, that he had no income and the situation was near critical; but even in the face of these emergencies, that this was a significant moment. 'I must get him for my new band,' Eric kept mumbling, as 'Lay, Lady, Lay' spun its slow, seductive trail.

When the gig was done, he walked backstage and saw Brian and Phil. The rest of the band weren't around, but that was fine, because these were the two guys that Eric wanted to meet. He spoke in his most polite tones, since he was incredibly conscious of the rampaging effects of the drugs. The last thing he needed was to come over like a gibbering idiot.

'Hello, I'm Eric Bell. I'm trying to form a group. Do you know any bass players and drummers?'

'I don't know any. Brian,' Phil said to his mate, grinning, 'do you?'

'I'm not too sure,' Brian answered, playing along with the game.

'Well, thanks very much, anyway,' Eric spluttered.

The acid kicked in again and the guitarist was swooning. Phil and Brian were impressed. They'd actually heard a lot about Eric – Gary Moore was always raving about his playing, and they'd seen him drinking in the bars a few times, looking shy but as if he wanted to get involved. Now here he was – utterly ripped on LSD, his showband haircut growing out, his former life falling away from him like old skin. He was ready to leave the room when they called him back.

'All right then,' Phil said. 'But only if I can play bass.'

Brian wasn't so sure about this notion, and he tried to stall them.

'Nah,' Eric gibbered. 'It'll be great. You'll look like Jimi Hendrix.'

A few nights later, Phil called around to Eric's flat in Manor Street, which he shared with the drummer and trumpet player from The Dreams. As agreed, Phil had with him a reel of quarter-inch tape, demos of the songs he'd been writing since the end of the Skid Row days. Eric borrowed a reel-to-reel machine from a friend and spooled the tape up. The recordings were basic – just an acoustic guitar, Phil's voice and the occasional rattle of percussion. It sounded folksy and downbeat. But the songs were remarkable.

One of the demo tracks that Eric remembered long after was called 'Saga Of The Ageing Orphan'. Phil's voice carried the same kind of mood that he'd brought to the first Skid Row single, an appreciation of life's awful fragility, of loved ones being torn apart by sad circumstances. He was singing about a future vision of his own family: Uncle Peter was writing a book and his grandmother was in the kitchen, getting a meal ready. But they were changed now, grown old, and he felt helpless watching on.

Phil had lifted the idea from an Irish myth that dealt with the wanderings of Oisín, a child abandoned by his mother and raised by the warrior race, the Fianna. But he'd fallen in love with Niam

Of The Golden Hair, whose father was king of Tír Na N-Og – the land of the young – away in the west. Oisín moved there with Niam but eventually felt a hankering for his homeland. Sadly, when he returned, he found that 300 years had elapsed in that place, and everyone he once knew had gone. Oisín fell off his horse, and when he touched the ground, he aged immediately and died.

'These songs are fucking brilliant,' Eric told him.

'You really think so?' Phil was pleased.

'I really do.' The guitarist could already hear his instrumental lines scrolling over the songs – real artistic liberation door-stepping his life for the first time, showing him the spaces between the words and signalling the new-found thrill of the Celtic crossroads blues. And *nobody* was going to tell him to cool it this time. It was Eric's second epiphany in the same week, and it felt utterly magical.

5

They raised the freak flag high on Castle Avenue, way up at Clontarf on the northern lip of Dublin bay. There was Philip and his business pal Larry Mooney, who'd somehow conspired to find this remarkable flat. They were joined by Eric Bell and Eric Wrixon, and they all marvelled at this hang-out. A huge living-room, a bedroom, a funky kitchen and – best of all – a glass conservatory that jutted out from the wall of the first floor. *This is like a palace*, Bell thought.

Phil grabbed the bedroom and decorated the walls with pictures of the comic-book character Pansy Potter, the strong-man's daughter. She was his pin-up at the time. The two Erics would have to sleep in the main room. But first, Eric Bell rolled a spliff. He'd spend the next three years completely stoned, all day, every day. And they'd be joined by people like Pete Eustace, who started working on Lizzy's stage equipment and stayed loyal to them for the next thirteen years. Most of the other kids in Dublin still lived with their parents, so this was a happening place to socialise.

Soon they'd be wakened at ridiculous hours by the sound of taxis, scooters and old transit vans, heralding the arrival of Skid Row, Granny's Intentions, Ditch Cassidy – whatever band had been playing late that night and wanted a few hours of recreation before bedtime. Word quickly spread. A visiting pair of American GIs, straight from Vietnam, staked out the Grafton Street pubs, hunting out this legendary band called Thin Lizzy who threw the wildest parties in Dublin. They approached Phil and asked if they could crash for a few days. The singer eyed them up, uneasy about these squaddies with their bullet heads. But when they flipped open the back of their camera and revealed an enormous block of dope – the stamp still freshly visible on the side – he agreed to let them come over.

Sometimes the parties were more formal. On 4 April 1970, they celebrated Gary Moore's eighteenth birthday by filling a huge plastic bin with the most heinous combinations of alcohol they could think of. After they got back from the pubs in town, they drank the contents of this bin and behaved like crazed animals. Eric Bell and Gary finished the night on the stairs, on their hands and knees, chasing each other, barking like dogs. Not surprisingly, the neighbours organised a petition to drive these long-hairs out of their beautiful road. But the trouble-makers stayed on regardless.

Phil loved the history of the place, the fact that Clontarf Castle was a two-minute walk away. This was the site where the famous chieftain Brian Boru had trashed the Norman invaders in 1014. He'd fought so well that the old musicians had remembered his deeds with a rousing march. Phil got into the spirit of the vibe and would presently write his own song, 'The Friendly Ranger At Clontarf Castle', strafed with visions of heroic acts, Western lawmen, intense love and the surreal effects of mind-torching drugs.

It was fun when they unpacked their record collections and began comparing tastes. Phil's current raves were Spooky Tooth, Free and Spirit. They all adored Hendrix, Zappa and Jeff Beck. Eric Bell had some bizarre stuff in his box: *Marty Robbins Sings Gunfighter Ballads*, some Wes Montgomery, The Chieftains, The Dubliners and The Nat King Cole Trio. Phil was tickled when he heard Nat singing 'Call The Police', eventually ripping off the title for one of his own ideas.

A steady favourite was Van Morrison's *Astral Weeks*. It was the strangest record: a jazzy, whirling testimony to one Irishman's travels, moving from his home in Belfast to Dublin and London, then across America and back again. All of his thoughts seemed random but rapturous. He was name-checking the streets where he'd experienced powerful emotions, flitting across time and place, seemingly entranced by the simple chord patterns and the sparks of his subconscious mind.

It was an especially valuable record since Van had recorded it in 1968, just before the Civil Rights marches and the subsequent riots and shootings in Northern Ireland, so the places and times he was evoking already felt like a lost state of innocence – life before 'The Troubles'. Phil and Eric would put the album on in the morning, just before they lit their first joint. The sun would come in through the conservatory window, making them feel entirely blissful.

The first practice session of the new band had been messy. Phil was still learning to play the bass, and when Eric Bell started to play some blues in the key of C, Phil was in a different key altogether. Wrixon was doing his best on keyboards, but the only star technician was Brian Downey. Still, it was an exciting prospect. Wrixon even offered to play bass on a few songs as part of his showband training had required him to cover for other musicians during their customary five-hour sets. So they muddled through, learning a few Hendrix numbers like 'If Six Was Nine' and 'Fire', plus Jeff Beck's 'Water Down The Drain', while giving shape to a few of Phil's new songs.

A regular face at band rehearsals was Terry O'Neill, a teenager who'd been helping out with Skid Row before working for their booking agency. He'd organise special bus trips when Skid Row played Belfast at Christmas – Brush called him the East Coast Promo Man. Terry was keen to get involved with Phil's new act, and Phil soon asked him to act as their manager. Thus, Terry sorted out a début show on 19 February 1970 at Cloughran National School, out near Dublin airport. A week before the gig, and they still hadn't a name for the band that *New Spotlight* magazine was already calling 'the Bell-Lynott supergroup'. One of the names they fooled with was Gulliver's Travels; but it was Eric Bell and his mimicry that gave them their identity.

He'd often talk in funny accents, making fun of the manners and pronunciation of the Dublin boys. Just as the deadline was coming down – the posters for the gig had to be out by five o'clock that evening and O'Neill was getting frantic – Bell began riffing on the name of a character from the *Dandy* comic, a female robot called Tin Lizzie. Phil picked up on the idea and gave it an extra spin by putting an 'h' in the first part of the name. Lots of people down south pronounced 'Tin' and 'Thin' exactly the same, so that would be their trick – a way of getting punters to remember them. Not everyone was sure about this, but they had no better option.

Phil appreciated that you needed an edge, a look and a

personality – he'd already figured that to be famous you had to attend to the totality of the band's presentation. Often he'd carry a plastic bag around town with a spare set of clothes in it. Around seven o'clock, he'd change into his extra-foxy evening gear. This puzzled Eric Wrixon. He'd got into this group to escape all of the superficial aspects of the showband scene. He wanted to be a musician, period. Also, he felt the band wasn't progressing fast enough. He couldn't understand why Phil was so hung up on popularity and acclaim – Wrixon would rather get personal satisfaction than bring in the crowds. Already there was friction.

There was a lifestyle to content with, too. While he worked hard, Phil was also enjoying his rock and roll pastimes. As well as smoking dope, the Clontarf set was ingesting lots of LSD, which had arrived just after the introduction of cannabis to Dublin. It was as if they were catching up with the pop drug culture of America and the UK all at once. While the US had celebrated their summer of love in 1967 and lost their wide-eyed freshness with the murder at the Rolling Stones' Altamont Speedway gig in 1969, Ireland's hip teenagers were still enthusiastic about the possibilities. Sometimes Lizzy took to Saint Stephen's Green in the centre of town for drug experiments, where it felt safe and beautiful; but the flat was just as handy. Terry O'Neill was curious; he wanted to give acid a try and so Phil arranged a time and a date.

The initiate arrived as planned at one o'clock in the afternoon. Phil gave him a tab of acid and he ate it, feeling excited and apprehensive. Phil was waiting on a dealer friend to bring some supplies for himself, but he later got the word that there was nothing around until the next day. Oh well, Terry would just have to trip on his own. But rather than just leave the guy to orbit and hallucinate, maybe even scaring the hell out of himself, Phil elected to look after him for the day. So he guided Terry through the trip, playing him records by The Fugs and The Velvet Underground. He fed him bits of dry bread, which to the day-tripper tasted like rubber and kept dropping out of his mouth. He took him for walks and advised him of the likely outcomes.

'So don't forget, Terry, when you get into town, you'll be seein' funny things. Men with no legs and stuff like that.'

When Terry got into the city centre sure enough there was a line of people on the footpath with not a foot or a leg between them. Phil then took him to a friend's house, but forewarned him of the possible dangers inside.

'Now before we go into this room, just remember that the carpet will be swirling round. Okay?'

And when Terry looked down he saw comet trails and Catherine wheels and whole galaxies pulsating from the weave. But it felt fine as he'd known that it was coming. Afterwards, O'Neill thanked his mate. It was a very considerate thing for Phil to do, and Terry never had a bad trip afterwards.

The early Lizzy gigs were shaky, with Phil constantly looking at his fretboard to check that he was hitting the right notes. Even though he was the singer, he never stood at the centre of the stage, which gave some people the impression that Thin Lizzy was a vehicle for Eric Bell, now playing his guitar with total freedom. He was a great guitarist and luckily his time with the showbands hadn't blunted his style at all. By June, the band was rated third in *New Spotlight*'s progressive group poll.

Sometimes they'd play society parties to bring in extra money. Phil's high-class connections got them a gig at Mulhuddart House, the great mansion that belonged to the Gallaghers, the cigarette people. It was their daughter's twenty-first birthday so they wanted something a bit groovy. However, part of the deal was that the band also had to play dumb party tunes like 'Simon Says'. They accepted that this humiliation was worth it, but what they hadn't anticipated was that the liquor would be so plentiful. After two hours of bumming free drinks off the waiters, they were all loaded on Guinness, chased down with double Scotches and blackcurrant.

Wrixon was slumped over his keyboards, smiling. Eric Bell had forgotten his guitar strap, so he wobbled on a stool for the duration. He kept turning the volume up and the guests in the monkey suits were getting annoyed. Phil told him to ease off – so Bell left the singer to play a solo set and went for a walk around the house. This was Eric's Belfast Cowboy period when he'd be crass and upfront just for the hell of it. As he met these attractive women on the stairs in their fancy dresses, he started leering. 'Hey, yer beautiful,' he'd say, before they shooed him off. 'Ah, ballacks to yez,' he'd slur in passing.

Eric locked himself in the bathroom as Phil kept it together downstairs. The guitarist felt sick as he lit a cigarette. Then he felt worse still. He couldn't move any part of his body. Ma Gallagher was banging on the door, demanding that he quit the room, but Eric ignored her. She returned with three bouncers, who forced the door open and hauled the drunkard outside. His parting words were, 'Do you know I used to be in The Dreams show-band? I used to earn £35 a week, you know.'

He came to several hours later in the band's VW van. The rest of the group were chuckling. They'd certainly made an impact. Phil had got into the spirit later on and had tried to seduce one of the younger guests. But instead of spoiling their reputation, after this Thin Lizzy were even more in demand amongst the party set and the ascendancy families. If your life was a little dull, then these boys could provide enough vicarious thrills for the whole town.

Some of those rides home were glorious. They'd be laughing and smoking, and Phil would be talking about the ladies he'd charmed – turning his romances into a sport, betting against the others' fortunes in love. If they'd been playing out of town, the sun might be coming up and they felt like the only people alive in the world. One time at daybreak, they were passing through the midlands when Eric Wrixon stopped the van. He'd brought his fishing rod with him and wanted to try his chances. So he threw a few casts by the river bank while they stood there, stoned, thinking it was just the job, wondering if they might rustle a sheep into the van for the evening meal.

Phil had moved in on another scene in town – a collection of poets and beatniks, centred around a band called Tara Telephone. This set-up was partly a response to the poet Roger McGough and his mates in the ensemble Liverpool scene, who'd brought a rock and roll influence to their verses. Irish heads like Eamon Carr and Peter Fallon decided to enliven their city in a similar style, so they'd hire out a room every other Tuesday night and hold workshops and open readings, playing bodhrans and bongo drums and rapping excitedly.

One of the down sides of the government's enforcement of learning Irish subjects at school was that many kids grew up hating the indigenous culture; they were taught in a boring way and therefore it didn't seem cool. But Eamon Carr and a few of his peers started to go back to the sources, to the poetry of WB Yeats right through to the old mythical tales. Hence the name of their band Tara Telephone, combining the site of the ancient Irish High Kings with a modern communication appliance. They wanted to be in tune with history, but blazing forwards. The local media got to hear of these hippie word-spinners, and soon they were doing their stuff on chat shows and pop programmes.

Phil turned up at one of the sessions on 11 November 1969, when he played some music with Brush and Gary Moore. Around that time, he was thinking of putting together a compilation album of Irish bands, and he wanted to use Eamon. Then Phil quizzed him about the poetry nights and revealed that he wrote some verses himself. Eamon Carr urged the singer to get involved in the readings, but he became very coy. Yet in the following spring, Phil made his move, arriving at the Arts Society behind Trinity College where they held the meetings. He looked funky, like Sly Stone, and the beat kids in their woolly jumpers thought he was the wildest. Phil read out some of his lyrics, which were well received. He seemed to have an extra pep to his stride afterwards – as if he'd found another dimension to his personality.

Carr and his friend Peter had also started an arts magazine called *Capella*, based on London's counter-culture publications like *Oz* and *International Times*. They'd get contributions from poets like Allen Ginsberg and Seamus Heaney. Meantime, Peter's brother, the journalist and scenester BP Fallon, asked Marc Bolan to contribute, and when he was covering John Lennon and Yoko Ono's bed-in in Amsterdam, he persuaded the Beatle to do them a drawing. Later when he met the pair again at *Top Of The Pops* for a performance of 'Instant Karma', he photographed them holding the mag.

Phil took all this in. One feature of the publication he especially liked was the illustrations by Dubliner Jim Fitzpatrick, who'd taken Irish themes and drawn them in the style of Marvel comics. Phil met him often in the Grafton Street pubs and they became friends. The red-haired Fitzpatrick would tell the singer more about the old Irish epics, refreshing his interests and giving him themes to riff around in his songs. He'd become another tight member of the gang, painting many of the Thin Lizzy album covers, emphasising the band's personality with Celtic knotwork, spirals, zoomorphic figures and superbad logos.

Phil was never a scholar – his metabolism was too fast to allow him time for old-fashioned study and contemplation. But he certainly took his writing seriously, and Peter Fallon would edit his two lyric/poetry books, *Songs For While I'm Away* in 1974 and *Philip* in 1977. And what the singer missed in deep learning, he made up for in diversity. He was at the nexus of Dublin's new artistic life – good friends with the folkies, the pastoral hippies and those beats who, like the writer Jack Kerouac, aimed to make their personal stories heroic. He understood the rockers, the psychedelics, the mods and the born-again Celts.

Phil was never going to be a mere volume merchant. He could boogie, sure, but he also liked to take the bus into town with Eric on a quiet night and play the folk clubs, using no microphones but just two acoustic guitars and a bagful of songs from Django Reinhardt, Paul Simon, The Dubliners or whatever trad song they could remember. Years later, you could still hear all this in his voice – he could take any influence and make it somehow relate.

Also, Phil had a unique take on Jimi Hendrix, the guitarist from Seattle who was part African-American, part Cherokee Indian. He was sexy, rebellious, poetical and brilliantly gifted – shattering for evermore any simple understanding of the imagination and impulses of the black man. When Jimi died of a drug misadventure on 18 September 1970, Thin Lizzy were devastated, and Phil and Eric Bell held a wake for him at The Bailey, drinking long, feeling lost. Bell, Lynott and Downey would later record a tribute to the definitive cosmic gypsy, 'Song For Jimi', revealing how much they owed to his music as Phil sang about the mysteries of death and the afterlife.

Lizzy's first single, 'The Farmer', was released on 31 July 1970. It was a feat of thrift and persuasion. They weren't ready for a major label deal, but they needed to make some kind of statement. They'd managed to get free studio time at Trend studios in Dublin because they promised to record a song by producer John d'Ardis called 'I Need You' on the flip-side. The latter was a jumping rhythm and blues tune and Phil sang it like Ray Charles or Georgie Fame – the producer later adding a brass section and crafting a personal showcase that wasn't at all bad.

'The Farmer' revealed another of the group's influences. In 1965, when Bob Dylan was trading folk music for mean-faced rock and roll, he hired a group of musicians who became known as The Band. When they all decamped to Woodstock in upstate New York, they mellowed and began experimenting with American old-time music. While the rest of the nation was wigging out on acid and making crazed soundtracks, The Band dressed like a nineteenth-century Puritan set and sang about the country's pioneer past. Their 1969 album *The Band* was a favourite for Thin Lizzy's skinning-up sessions at Clontarf, and Orphanage had performed many of their songs.

Thus 'The Farmer' sounded down-home and nostalgic. Phil was singing about a tough community in America's deep south, seemingly based on the outlaw family of Frank and Jesse James. But in his version, it was lonely at the old place since Ma died, and Pappa just sat there moaning. The boys had a barnful of whiskey, but there was nobody to help them drink it. So the main character headed north to Tennessee for some action – hardly the last time that one of Phil's fictional men would quit the homestead in favour of the wild life.

Musically, it was a smart début. Phil opened it up with a stoned, laughing invite to the party which was totally Hendrix. The remainder of the song shadowed The Band's 'Up On Cripple Creek', with Eric Wrixon's gospel piano, Bell's guitar swelling out the melancholy, and Downey's masterful, sloping beat. They released it on the Parlophone label, an imprint of EMI, which had previously handled The Beatles.

But Thin Lizzy were merely an experiment for the local subsidiary, EMI Ireland. They'd been given a one-off deal that allowed the band to use the company's mail-out system and provided them with complimentary records. There was no question of royalties being paid since just 500 copies were pressed. There was a verbal understanding between Terry O'Neill and EMI's Tony Hannah that if the single took off, then the latter would have the first option on a contract. But they sold less than 300 copies – with the band's name, still in a state of flux, spelt 'Thin Lizzie' on the label. Still, it was played on the radio and now they could start hustling for gigs in the country.

Prior to the single's release, the band decided to get rid of Eric Wrixon. Now that Phil was getting competent on the bass, there was less need for keyboards, and besides, money was tight and couldn't really stretch four ways. In any case Wrixon was losing interest. His father had just died, causing him to visit Belfast again. As an only child, this death was especially painful, and he started to reappraise his life. When Eric got back to Clontarf, he realised that there were lots of emotional upsets within the band: arguments about girlfriends and money, and anxiety about when and how the band would be discovered. He started writing to old musician friends in Europe, asking how the work was going out there, thinking out his alternatives.

The bust-up came during a particularly bad rehearsal at The Town And Country Club. Terry O'Neill was now acting as the band's manager, and he called a meeting to discuss finances.

'We can't survive the way we're going. We'll have to get rid of a member of the band. The only thing I can think of to keep the group together is to manage without Eric Bell. We don't really need a lead guitarist, do we?'

Lynott, Bell and Downey said nothing. They knew what O'Neill was getting at.

'No, that's a stupid idea,' Terry continued. 'Let's go acoustic and do without Brian. Would you mind?'

Silence.

'The only other thing is if Philip leaves. We could maybe survive without a bass, y'know?'

Wrixon wasn't stupid. He understood the drift.

'I get the message. If there's enough money for three, I'll leave.'

Three days later, Lynott and Bell returned to Clontarf to find Wrixon lying on the floor with a big map, sorting out his next destination. Shortly after, he headed for Sweden. When they met him a year later, he was totally straight and happy, working hard in Germany. He'd be written out of most of the Lizzy histories in future, but he didn't care. Wrixon would steer his own trail, back to blues music, which he loved and could relate to. Eventually he'd find himself working again with his Belfast colleagues from Them, home to the roots of it all.

Lizzy had several business advisers in the early days. Their flatmate Larry Mooney had been a help for a while, so had Ollie Byrne, who ran a booking agency. Terry O'Neill had worked for Byrne, but now he was out on his own – getting the band top publicity in the *Evening Herald* and organising photo shoots. He was still a teenager, and few people took him seriously, but soon he was securing the band gigs outside Dublin, where the money was often better.

Phil would try hard to excite the kids at these provincial shows. One of their most popular numbers was the soul-stirrer by Martha And The Vandellas 'Dancing In The Street', which name-checked a lot of the black cities in America. But Lynott would swap these for Irish towns – saluting the joys of Galway, Limerick, Cork or wherever the band was playing that night. While many Dublin bands viewed with distaste the country gigs, populated by ignorant 'culchies', this singer made them feel good about where they were coming from. The band was always asked back, and soon they were getting £40 per show.

Booking the band into these remote places the first time was always the challenge. But O'Neill was fearless, and he'd talk the bosses around. After one magnificent show in the middle of nowhere, Eric Bell was relaxing by the bar and the governor of the ballroom came over and congratulated him. He asked if Lizzy's manager was with them, since he wanted to bring the band back – even though it had cost him plenty for an act with no previous reputation. Eric pointed Terry out on the dancefloor; he was tripping a light fandango with some girl he'd just met – literally turning cartwheels across the floor. The old fella was dumbfounded.

'Fughin' hell – so *that's* the one that's taken me to the cleaners? Well . . . fair play to the little bastard.'

In August, Lizzy cracked the Associated Ballrooms chain – normally the preserve of the showbands. That was a huge result, because they could now pull in £150 a night. The straight guys who controlled the circuit had always shut out rock bands before, literally calling them dirty good-for-nothings. But greed got the better of the organisers and they wanted some of this new money. Ironically, Lizzy's involvement helped to shatter their scene. They'd be slotted in between the showband, who played from nine until eleven o'clock with their Elvis tunes and their amusing stunts, and then Lizzy would rock the hall for forty-five minutes, leaving the rest of the night to the other musicians. Some of the old-school jivers and waltzers walked out in disgust – Lizzy wasn't their style at all – but a significant number stayed on to have their expectations fried.

Back in Dublin, Eric made friends with Eimear Haughey. Her father, Charles, had recently been appointed Minister for Finance in the Irish Government, a course of promotion that would eventually make him Prime Minister. He was a self-made millionaire, and when Eric and Brian visited his place in the country, they were astonished. It looked like the White House, and was frequented by lots of highfalutin types. They were shown into the kitchen and Eric marked the occasion by dancing on the table. Here he was, a guy raised in a house with an outside toilet, now welcomed into one of the greatest mansions in the land. Mrs Haughey walked in just as he was bucking and winging like Gene Kelly, but she just stared through him like he wasn't there and then shut the door. Unbelievable.

After spending a night in a guest room, Eric went for a stroll around the grounds. He jumped in the swimming pool, and then headed out for the huge lake. There was a little island in the centre of it all with a tiny house built there. Eric was determined to go over – he wanted to stay the night in this amazing refuge, so he got a rowing boat and headed out. Just then, he noticed a figure by the shore. It was Charlie Haughey, putting in a spot of fishing before he resumed his political business. He didn't seem too bothered that a flame-haired hippie had commandeered one of his boats and was scaring all the fish.

'Howyeh,' said the future Taoiseach of Ireland. Eric returned the salute and steered out of harm's way.

There was another lodger at the Clontarf flat now. Gail Barber was eighteen, from Belfast, hoping to start a career in journalism. She'd come down to Dublin after her A-levels with two friends for a celebratory holiday. Shortly after, she left the north again, on her own, finding a place at Castle Lane in the glass conservatory that Wrixon had vacated. It was freezing cold there at night in the sleeping bag, but she toughed it out. For a while she'd be the unofficial housekeeper, cleaning and cooking for the boys. Then she got a job as an accounts clerk; hardly what she wanted, but it allowed her to consider her options while the band was on tour.

The party on 19 August 1970 was a special event. It was Phil's twenty-first birthday, so they invited masses of people around. Phil loved receiving presents and he threw a series of twenty-first celebrations for the next two years, partly because he enjoyed it so, and also because he took a couple of years off his official age when he moved to London. Phil seemed happy enough talking to everyone at the bash, but Gail thought he seemed lonely, and she noticed that he kept walking into the bedroom on his own. After the guests had left, she sat down with him on the conservatory floor, and they talked for hours, becoming friends. It was only later that she heard he'd had sex in his room with many of the girls at the party.

Gail soon came to notice unhappy aspects beneath the singer's glamorous front. He could be very paranoid and insecure at times, and there were parts of his childhood that he never discussed, even with close friends. It was as if he never completely trusted anyone. The fact that he didn't have a steady partner seemed to be part of this mind-set. So as she came to know him better and they developed a relationship, Gail hoped – naïvely and romantically as she later realised – that all Phil required was the love of a good woman. However, she experienced her first kick-back early on, when Philomena Lynott came visiting from Manchester, and Gail was asked to leave the flat for a few days while mother was introduced to Eimear and the socialite girls that the singer knew.

Businesswise, Terry O'Neill knew that the band needed more experienced help than he could offer. Even though Thin Lizzy was earning well, there was a large outlay for hiring equipment, and the VW van they always rented was a drain on funds. So Terry met a succession of people and offered them a cut if they'd advance enough money for transport and a PA system. Brian Tuite, who'd managed Limerick band Granny's Intentions, was interested and, as he ran a dealership service in town for Marshall amps and speakers, was a useful contact. Tuite spoke to Peter Bardon, who made his money with the showbands. But he would only come in if Terry gave up his share in the band. Phil insisted that his mate got a pay-off of £200. Since the average wage then was £25 a week, O'Neill agreed.

Phil wasn't desperate for a deal at this stage – he knew that the band had to improve if they were to register in Britain. But they were party to an amazing stroke of luck. Brian Tuite also managed a soul act called Ditch Cassidy, in whom he'd interested a former business friend at Decca Records in London,

Frank Rodgers. The latter was Irish-born – his sister was the pop singer Clodagh Rodgers. Frank was due to come over to see Ditch play at Zhivago's nightclub in Dublin.

Just before the audition, Ditch had a fall-out with his band. Would Thin Lizzy do the honours instead? Sure, they would back him up, realising that they might get some attention themselves. Which was the exact scenario when Frank arrived at the half-empty club, fresh from a talent contest in the country. He'd come along with a house producer at Decca, Neil Slaven, who'd previously worked with the likes of Savoy Brown. Cassidy wasn't at his best and Frank was more impressed with Phil, who looked remarkable.

'Do the band play on their own?' Frank asked Tuite.

'Yeah, they do.'

After hearing three numbers by Lizzy, the visitor was enthralled. He wanted to sign them on the spot but instead he went back to London and raved about them, getting them the deal he felt they deserved.

Frank came back for a second gig at the Peacock Theatre in November, bringing the American producer and songwriter Scott English with him. The latter had co-written a song called 'Brandy', which later became 'Mandy' and was a huge hit for Barry Manilow. He'd also co-written 'Hi-Ho Silver Lining' for Jeff Beck, so he already had form, and Frank wanted him to produce the band's début album. They were both excited by this 'proper' gig and Thin Lizzy got a major contract and started fixing up their first album, getting ready to head over to the land of Phil's birth for a recording session.

They took the mailboat over on 2 January 1971. By chance, they met the Radio 1 DJ John Peel, returning back to London from a holiday break. The singer introduced himself and Peel was encouraging, telling him to keep in touch. Maybe they'd even fix up a session with the band if they were as good as they said they were. Wasn't that the perfect way to cap off an incredible twelve months? Weren't they totally on the pig's back?

6

Phil was smoking hard and laughing plenty as the tour van battered down the M1 through another long night. He was touching his new-grown moustache – glad that people remarked upon it, saying he looked even more like Hendrix. That was an obvious benefit, but as well as adding a rakish aspect to his looks, the facial hair also made his chin seem less prominent. Now that his Afro hairstyle was also handsomely grown, Phil seemed even more cool, a funky nomad from another place entirely.

Earlier, they'd stopped at a transport café, and after scoffing up some greasy nutrients, the singer had bought a wad of American comics – the *Green Lantern*, the *Silver Surfer*, *Spiderman* and the *Fantastic Four*. Every few minutes, he'd point to one of the drawings and shout, trying to involve some of the other band members in the fun. But Brian was dozing off at the back, tired from the gig – his new beard looking fuzzy and strange – so he wasn't interested. This time it was Eric who had to share in Phil's entertainment.

'Hey, Er, look at this guy in the picture! Look at the shapes he's throwin'.'

The guitarist, his hair also frizzed up and spectacular, leant over the magazine to take in the view. He knew basically what Phil was going to show him. Spiderman climbing a skyscraper, his sinews flexed and bulging. Or Silver Surfer on his gravity-free board, his stance frozen, throwing all his weight on his front knee. Or maybe even Superman, his arm bent, the light catching the musculature of his forearm. Eric glanced at the latest favourite. It was the Green Lantern, his legs apart, his upper body upright so that he took on the outline of a letter A. Eric nodded. That was a good one, all right.

The best part of this game was that Phil had started trying to copy the poses on stage. They'd be in the middle of some tiny club in England, and Eric would turn sideways to see Phil throwing one of the shapes he'd seen in the comic. It looked bizarre at first – and the singer would quickly get embarrassed and pull out of it – but it was happening more often. When it worked, he looked awesome, so no one commented much and just hoped that he'd muster the confidence to try it more often.

Certainly they'd been hoping for a transformation. Phil still wasn't talkative on stage, and in desperation the management had actually scripted lines for him to memorise and then repeat to his audience. Eric was happy chatting to the punters, but that only made the singer's shyness seem all the more problematic. But generally they were progressing well and gaining fans. They had radio DJs who were plugging the band and their profile was rising.

To brighten their long hours on the road, they played tapes that Ted Carroll made up. He was the old Skid Row manager who was now working hard on Thin Lizzy, a partner with Tuite and Bardon. He'd sat through a month of band rehearsals in Dublin through February 1971 – just before the permanent move to London – suggesting changes to the set and advising them of the kind of music that went down best across the water. His passion was rhythm and blues and many of the old sources of rock and roll, so he'd record rootsy compilations for the band, dropping in offbeat songs from Sarah Vaughan or Frank Sinatra just to twist Phil's imagination.

And he was rarely disappointed; the singer listened to everything and stole from the more unusual sources. Any cute lines or observations would be scribbled down in his hard-backed notebook that he kept in his travel bag, along with his Brendan Behan books, his comics and spare clothes. Words could always be recycled and the hint of inspiration was usually enough. As Phil would say, 'Give me half an idea and I'm away . . .'

Touring was good because it allowed them to socialise and kept them away from their rotten accommodation in London. They were surviving on less than £10 a week, which meant that fancy lifestyles in the capital were denied to them. Sometimes Frank from Decca Records would take Phil to The Speakeasy and introduce him to music biz figures, but that was exceptional. Spare time in London was spent at home with their girlfriends, trying not to feel depressed with the reality of a small reputation in a country full of rock notables.

They'd settled in the West Hampstead area after Easter 1971 – near the Decca recording studios and also conveniently close to the M1 motorway that would take them off touring the northern towns. Eric was in a miserable little room in Belsize Avenue. Brian stayed in Greencroft Gardens, which was slightly more upmarket. But Phil had the meanest deal of all – a tiny bedsit he shared with Gail on Hillfield Road. He had the worst accommodation because he was black.

Finding the singer a place had been problematic. Landlords didn't care for rock and rollers at the best of times, but in Phil's case, they were completely intolerant. The fact that he was living with Gail – who'd packed in her job to join the adventure – didn't help any. The only lodgings they could get belonged to an old Italian couple, who rented their front room, three flights up, for £7 a week. The house was covered in little signs, telling the tenants not to make any noise, not to use the bathroom at certain hours and not to leave the lights on. Phil and Gail survived on mince and potatoes, rarely going out together, sometimes wondering what the hell they were doing in this city.

Phil was glad that the band's début album, *Thin Lizzy*, had been kindly received. They'd recorded it in January 1971 while they were still living in Dublin, and had to travel to London, lodge at a bed and breakfast in Paddington, and commute to the Decca studios over four days. The sessions had been fuelled, as ever, by lots of dope smoking, but even Lizzy had been staggered by the strength of the weed they found in London.

Still, they'd managed well, recording Phil's pocket odysseys like 'Saga Of The Ageing Orphan' and 'Diddy Levine'. The latter song was also about single-parent families – in this case, the mother and her daughter both decided to rear their kids alone, passing on a scorn for male partners down through the generations. On 'Honesty Is No Excuse', Phil viewed the other side of such a relationship, as the guy felt compromised by love and responsibility and walked out. Phil didn't sing it in a macho way though; his pained style suggested that even the playboy had his moments of desperation.

He wrote a coded lyric about Gail on 'Look What The Wind Blew In', seemingly amazed at the strength of feeling she'd provoked in him. Elsewhere, Phil mentioned his uncle and gran, an old flame and the scenes back at Clontarf. And in 'Clifton Grange Hotel' he put a romantic aspect on his mother's boarding house in Manchester. That was his style for the rest of his career – embellishing real stories, name-checking friends, his whole life a throbbing diversion from plain existence.

Eric played some inspired lines on the album, riffing and vamping and riding the wah-wah pedal like Jimi on 'Ray Gun', while keeping the tone delicate on Phil's saddest confessions. Brian was fairly happy with his own work, even though the sound of the record was rushed and a few tunes were so perversely complicated that he struggled to carry the groove. That was a hang-up from the era of progressive rock, and they were moving out of there. But what hurt Eric most was when he heard the final mix and discovered that lots of his finished solos had been swapped around or lost. Eric was prone to brooding and melancholia, and often there was cause to feel bad.

British rock seemed unassailable at the time – The Stones, The Who, Eric Clapton, Led Zeppelin, Fleetwood Mac, Deep Purple and newcomers like Free and The Faces were internationally famous, so it was hard for Thin Lizzy to compete. Many British critics didn't care for this Dublin band, and they felt that songs like 'Eire' – in which Phil summoned up the dead Irish warriors and remembered the old ways – were odd. But the band had another extraordinary break from a DJ. Their new champion was David 'Kid' Jensen, who worked for Radio Luxembourg, and was a big fan of Van Morrison. Jensen understood some of the nuances and sentiments in Lizzy that his peers had missed.

He played the album a lot on its release in April, and his *Dimensions* show had a hip cachet across Europe. He even put the LP at the top of his personal chart for three weeks, above Paul McCartney's *Ram*. The band would listen in to the show on their way back from a gig as it wafted and distorted over the medium-wave band. Whenever he played one of their songs, the band would bang the sides of the van and holler with joy. Thin Lizzy was now arguably bigger than a Beatle!

Clifton Grange Hotel was sometimes called The Showbiz, or even The Biz. In Phil's song about the place, he termed it 'a refuge of mercy'. When the band steered there after a gig – often travelling out of their way for free lodgings and unique hospitality – they simply called it 'Me Ma's'. It was just at the corner of Wellington Road in Whalley Range, Manchester, and from the outside it looked overgrown and decrepit. Its hulking nineteenth-century frame actually seemed to lean over, as if empathising with the residents inside.

'We only take show-business people,' Philomena Lynott once told Allan Jones, a *Melody Maker* journalist who'd come up to see this legendary place. 'No normals. I couldn't stand having to put up with toffee-nosed commercial travellers with silk pyjamas demanding their breakfast at eight and their dinner at five. We don't get to bed before eight in the morning when we've got the people here.'

The people who stayed with 'Aunty Phyllis' included ventriloquists, conjurors, magicians, strippers, Maori dancers, lounge singers – many flavours of entertainment and burlesque. She gave shelter to a transsexual ventriloquist, a former sailor who'd undergone one of the first operations of that nature in the UK. This guest was happy and liberated at the hotel – although Dennis Keeley, Philomena's partner, sometimes felt embarrassed when the artist's dummy started making eyes at him.

George Best was another regular; the footballer sometimes liked to relax away from the more public Manchester clubs, drinking straight vodka by the bar, surrounded by the décor of dolls, flowers, elegant bowls and sundry Victoriana. When Thin Lizzy became famous, lots of Manchester United players came to The Biz for the parties that only ended well into the morning, when Philomena pulled open the curtains, causing the hangovers to kick in, forcing the revellers to slink away to their darkened rooms like something out of a Dracula movie.

When Philomena took over the place in 1966, there was already a clientele of nightlife people. The big stars who played in Manchester, like Val Doonican and Frank Ifield, could afford luxurious hotels in town, but their backing bands headed for Whalley Range. Rock and roll bands followed suit, and mixed freely with the old-time shakers like Nils, the Swedish magician who was continually pulling cotton balls out of his mouth and was discovered one day doing a runner, owing three months' rent. Philomena brought him back and tried to restore his fortunes, but he fled again without paying her the money.

As a kid, Phil used to spend his summer holidays here. He'd meet the failed cabaret acts, grieving about their disastrous shows and their cancelled bookings. There were lots of artefacts in the house to interest him, like the signed pictures of Gregory Peck and Sammy Davis Jr, the latter inscribed 'To Phyllis – thanks for a wonderful week'. His mother and Dennis had signed the photos themselves. And later, there were crazy-head rockers like Viv Stanshall to watch.

Phil would meet a bunch of men who were known as the Quality Street Gang. There was Jimmy The Weazel, Joe and Tiny – who was of course huge – and many other such characters. These guys took care of business. Somehow, they always had the best seats for the football games, and could get served in pubs at any time of the night. They were highly protective of Philomena, so her son thought they were great. But his real mentor at the hotel was a musician called Percy Gibbons who played with an all-black Canadian act called The Other Brothers.

Percy was well educated but gloriously unconventional. He read a lot and smoked a bit. He was into comparative religion, astrology, the I Ching – a store of great quotes and useful philosophies. Gail loved him – she reckoned he was the only musician she'd ever met who was interested in the entire universe. So as well as giving Phil advice about playing in a band, Percy gave the boy knowledge relating to life, relationships, enlightenment and the experiences of a black man in the entertainment business.

Gail and Philomena became friends. The Belfast girl would stay up at the hotel sometimes, and she'd find herself helping out, serving breakfast some mornings to maybe half a dozen strippers and The Tremeloes. Sometimes Philomena would help the band out when they were short of rent money or needed cash to keep the van on the road. She was extremely kind that way, and clearly adored her son.

It was a unique relationship. While the hierarchy in many families made the parents responsible for discipline and tough love, letting the grandparents do the pampering, in this case it was the other way round. Philomena and her boy never had a major argument. Also, she was only a teenager when she'd given birth, so the generational difference wasn't so huge either. It wasn't like a brother–sister vibe, but neither was it a conventional mother–son rapport. It was just different.

Phil tried to articulate all of this Manchester life in his song 'Clifton Grange Hotel' – another touchstone in his life, something that no other kid had experienced. He sketched a few of the regular features: old Lou, the Jewish attendant who carried the bags, plus Percy in residence at the top of the stairs in his funky bedroom. He described the mina bird who'd mimic the guests, and of course he included his mother, keeping this unruly house together, protecting them all from the dreaded 'normals' who prevailed outside. It was a decent song, but probably the only instance when Phil's art was less remarkable than the subject he'd based it on.

Phil celebrated his twenty-second birthday in 1971 by releasing the 'New Day' EP. On the title track, the singer was cutting loose from a shady, experienced woman. This was the year that Rod Stewart topped the UK and US charts with 'Maggie May', and it was unfortunate that Lynott was taking the same theme and that his vocals were derivative of Rod. He was better on the ballad 'Dublin', bidding goodbye to the old streets and squares that now seemed so poetic in exile.

Thin Lizzy played an Irish tour that same month, making a big night of their return show at Dublin's National Stadium. These excursions home became critical to the band's finances. They would run up debts in London, borrowing from Ted Carroll's mail-order record business, and then play a tour of Irish ballrooms that would leave them flush for another six months. It was also lovely for their feelings of self-worth to see people who rated you highly and wanted you to do well.

Over at West Hampstead, they returned to mince and potato dinners and the band's uncertain future. After some hesitation, Decca Records agreed to finance a second album, even allowing them to work away from the company's own studio. The management plan was to record with Martin Birch, who'd been prolific with Deep Purple and Fleetwood Mac. So they booked De Lane Lea Studios in Wembley – brand new, with the best gear inside. Except there were loads of teething problems and Birch wasn't available. It was a costly mistake: the bill for *Shades Of A Blue Orphanage* was £6,000 – more than ten times the price for the previous job.

Ted eventually shaved two grand off the invoice, citing all of the problems and stoppages at the Wembley site. But it was still disappointing because the record sounded so flimsy and disconnected. There was also a shortage of material – this was a time when serious rockers rarely released singles, and certainly they wouldn't put any such tracks on an album. So Lizzy ignored the 'New Day' songs for the LP, and were obliged to go back to numbers like 'Chatting Today', which Phil had performed with Orphanage. Some of the titles had been made ready for the record sleeve before they were actually written – and they made do with riffs and musical jams instead of true songs.

Eric tried his best – he was bringing his broad record collection to bear on his playing, jumping octaves in his solos just like the jazz man Wes Montgomery. But there was little he could do on tracks like 'I Don't Want To Forget How To Jive'. That was Phil's boogie tribute to Elvis, the first of his Presley trilogy that finished with 'King's Call' and 'Do Anything You Want To'. He sang it in the style of his hero and obviously had fun doing so, but again it confused the issue of what Thin Lizzy meant and who was going to listen to them.

There was a powerful indigo mood over the record – certainly living in London had given them the blues, and the band's situation didn't allow for too much optimism. In 'Buffalo Girl' Phil was telling his partner that the old ways had gone for ever, and they needed to push on to the next stage of their lives. 'Brought Down' was another pregnancy drama, forcing the couple to evaluate their roles. But it was the album's title track that caught the power of this maudlin spirit best.

Phil had combined the name of Eric's old band, Shades Of Blue, with his own former act, Orphanage, for the title. 'Shades Of A Blue Orphanage' was a beautiful song, starting with his childhood reveries: sneaking into Dan's old scrapyard, visiting the snooker hall and losing himself in the picture house, watching the cowboy stars and imagining he was a friend of theirs. In the second verse, he was looking at an old photo of Dan, realising he was involved in the 1916 Easter Rising in Dublin – fighting for the country's independence.

The singer mused on the possibilities Dan must have had ahead of him when he was young; his life must have been a thrill. But now he was just wandering around in a shabby coat, thinking of lost loves, forgetting his favourite songs, the freedom dream now realised as a mocking joke. As Phil intoned this sad drama, the music dropped into a rickety waltz – like something you'd hear across an empty old ballroom, the life gone out of it.

This was the greatest poem Lynott would ever write and he obviously rated it enough himself to print the words on the album sleeve. And he sang it well too. In the middle part of his career, Phil would be artful about his sad songs, playing a role. But on his second album, he sounded vulnerable and unaffected. You felt party to some of his inner thoughts.

Shades Of A Blue Orphanage touched on many themes that had already become familiar in Irish literature: the backwards glance, sentimentality, a strong awareness of place and time, a fear of adult life, the flight into fantasy, the evocative power of half-forgotten secrets. Importantly, Phil was able to bring much of this into the country's pop music. He gave his fellow rockers a new colour. True blue, Irish blue.

7

Upstairs at The Duke of York, Phil was feeling dejected. The pub was sited on a cheerless stretch of York Way, near London's King's Cross area. There wasn't much to occupy him outside, and besides, this was supposed to be a band practice, so he was obliged to spend this summer afternoon writing new songs, finding a way out of Thin Lizzy's commercial impasse.

Brian and Eric were reading books, too demoralised to want to play much. The first part of 1972 had been a grind. They'd toured the colleges and promoted the *Shades Of A Blue Orphanage* album on its release on 10 March. Some of the reviews were kind, but also patronising. *Melody Maker* reckoned, 'It's very hard for second division bands to make an impact with an album when there is so much competition, so it is to their credit that they have attempted to put down their own thing and experiment.'

Kid Jensen had been ever encouraging, making *Thin Lizzy* his album of the year, and he placed the follow-up at the top of his weekly chart. Phil flew over to Luxemburg in April for an interview on the show. They were good friends now, and the band had been invited to play at Jensen's local club, Blow Up, which was then transmitted on the programme. On this latest visit, Ted Carroll had urged Phil to describe the unhappy circumstances that went into the making of the second LP.

But this was hardly positive action. Meanwhile, Decca Records weren't going to bankroll another album until they knew they could recoup some of their money. They would promote a single if they heard something with hit potential, but the band had to come up with something special. This was the cause of the band's low spirits at the pub practice.

Since there was nothing better to do, Phil picked up the microphone and started singing tunes that he'd heard in the folk clubs of Dublin. He ran through Brendan Behan's 'The Auld Triangle', and Ewan MacColl's 'Dirty Old Town'. He was enjoying himself now, strumming the chords on a Fender Telecaster and singing another standard, 'Whisky In The Jar'. This song had been resurrected in the ballad boom of the 1960s – when The Clancy Brothers came back from America, having wowed New York with their hearty come-all-ye songs and their *báinin* jumpers. They'd even performed on *The Ed Sullivan Show* over there. This astonished the people at home, most of whom didn't much value Irish music.

The band that benefited most from this new era was The Dubliners. They were more dangerous than the Clancys – hard-living, lewd and sometimes political in their music. Their single 'Seven Drunken Nights' was a hit in Britain in 1967 and got them on *Top Of The Pops*, but Irish radio banned it because the lyrics were supposedly offensive. The band's most visible member was Luke Kelly, with his beard and huge bush of red curls. He was a regular around town, and Phil met him several times in the bars and coffee shops. He was always helpful and unaffected. Somebody once shouted over, 'Hey, you with the woolly head,' and Luke answered, 'At least mine is only woolly on the outside.' He was true Dub, all right.

Luke had recorded 'Whisky In The Jar' on the band's *More Of The Hard Stuff* album in 1967. The song had been sold on a ballad sheet at the turn of the century, and was well known. But it wasn't one of The Dubliners' best tracks. They'd missed the drama in the words – a gallant young bandit steals from an army officer to keep his girl happy, only to be betrayed by her and locked in jail. But when Phil started singing this song at The Duke Of York, he got the sadness and romance of the tale straight off. He understood the mind-set of the outlaw who loved his life and his beautiful Molly. When Phil sang it, you knew the character was a dashing figure with his pistol and his rapier, lying drunk in Molly's chamber – a picture The Dubliners could never evoke.

Eric was intrigued by this performance. He could hear melodic line in his head, so he grabbed his guitar and started experimenting. He found a tender riff that underlined the pathos of the story. So they jammed together, just for their own amusement. Phil was enjoying the lyrics about getting ambushed in his girl's room by Captain Farrell, jumping up and firing both barrels at the man. He left out the part where the guns misfire because Molly had soaked them in water, leading to his imprisonment at the jailhouse in County Offaly called Phillipstown.

When they'd finished messing about, the band looked around and noticed that Ted Carroll had arrived. He'd actually been standing on the stairs outside for a few minutes, marvelling at what he'd heard.

'What was that?'

'Oh, we were just fucking around,' Eric said.

'So what do you think?' Phil asked.

'I think it's a hit.'

'You're joking.'

'No, it's really good. That's a hit record if you do it in the studio exactly like that.'

Phil was peeved because he wanted to release 'Black Boys On The Corner' as a single. This was brash and slamming, as the singer dealt with the prejudices and stereotypes enforced on the black man. In Lynott's version he had the option of being subservient, or he could reinvent himself as a superfly boy – dressing flash, playing poker, betting on the horses, hot with the girls, always chasing the instantaneous thrill. It was a confrontational idea – pushing an aspect of the singer's personality like never before.

Ted wasn't convinced though. In July, prior to an Irish tour and months before the single was even due to be recorded, he was telling *New Spotlight* magazine about his plans: 'We must have a crack at getting a single into the Irish charts, and we reckon we'll do it this time. Originally we were going to bring this old Irish ballad out as the A-side in Ireland and flip it as the B-side in England. But we're so happy with the arrangements that it's going to be the A-side here as well.'

Eric was upset a lot of the time now. He felt that the artistic freedom he'd envisioned finding with Lizzy was now being denied. Money and survival seemed paramount. The band had even recorded an album of Deep Purple cover versions – under the alias Funky Junction – for a German businessman. They had to bring in a vocalist, Benny White, and a keyboard player called Dave Lennox from another Dublin band, Elmer Fudd, to duplicate the English act's style. When they found they were short of material, Eric had even played the Irish air 'Danny Boy' on his feedbacking guitar – just like Hendrix had done with 'The Star Spangled Banner'. It was a bit silly, and although they were paid £1,000 for their work on *Funky Junction Pay Tribute To Deep Purple*, it was also hurtful to the morale.

Ironically, Phil had been approached by the former Deep Purple guitarist, Richie Blackmore, who wanted them to form a band together called Baby Face. Lynott was tempted, and they tried writing together, but finally he reckoned he'd be wiser earning his success with Thin Lizzy. All this made Eric more agitated, so when they toured abroad, he drank a lot. And while Brian got jarred and had a laugh, and Phil did likewise and hardly changed his manner, Eric got maudlin and twisted. Sometimes he'd get into arguments with Phil, and they'd punch each other over trivial issues.

The band's management was changing as well. Ted's old partners Brian Tuite and Peter Bardon had been replaced by an Englishman, Chris Morrison, who'd formerly booked the band's gigs. The newcomer was well connected and sensed that there were chances to popularise the band well beyond the current limits. To this end, he secured them as tour support to Slade in the winter of 1972.

Newcastle City Hall was more like a bear pit than a concert venue. The crowd was rowdy and intolerant – waving scarves around, raising their mob chants, booing anything that distracted from the main event. They wanted to hear Slade, with their rampant rhythm and blues – choruses that translated straight over from the football terraces, populist hit singles and ever-gurning faces.

They wanted Noddy Holder with his Midlands accent, tartan trews and the top hat with the mirrors all over the sides. Dave Hill was a favourite with his gold platform boots and the body of his guitar carved into a legend that read 'Super Yob'. Dave Powell, the drummer, would chew gum and twirl the sticks around his fingers at the same time. Jimmy Lea played a metallic fiddle on their first big hit 'Coz I Luv You', and the fans thought that was brilliant.

Slade was a former skinhead band that had capitalised on Glam Rock. While originators like David Bowie and Marc Bolan combined sexual confusion with fringe theatre and decadent art, Slade slung on some lamé and bellowed about girls grabbing boys. They became huge stars, only rivalled in their field by Gary Glitter and The Sweet. They weren't dazzling musicians – guitar solos were never part of this deal – but they could inflame the masses with terrifying skill, as witnessed on their current hit album *Slade Alive*.

As the tour kicked off on 3 November, nobody else wanted to walk on that Newcastle stage. Support act Suzi Quatro wore a leather catsuit and wailed like a tomboy, but even she took abuse from the punters, and she ran off after her set, practically in tears. Thin Lizzy couldn't expect any better treatment, but if they wanted to get more famous, then here was a howling constituency who might help them along.

When Phil walked out there, they were calling him 'Darkie' and telling him to get back to Africa, throwing bottles at the stage and demanding to see Slade instead of this weird-looking band. And Lizzy incensed them even more by playing 'Slow Blues', followed by more downbeat material. Ted and Chris had begged Phil not to play this combination, but the singer had insisted, and now he realised his mistake, and became even more introverted and sad. Those four minutes felt like four hours. Utter hatred was coming off the crowd during that song; it was like watching the prelude to a lynching.

The band was devastated afterwards. The management tried to talk them up, offering to help in changing the set-list around, promising better nights ahead. But then another figure came in and told it straight. It was Chas Chandler, Slade's manager. He'd previously played bass with The Animals, and had managed Jimi Hendrix, encouraging the guitarist to become a showman. Right now, Chandler was furious that Thin Lizzy had ruined the mood of the evening. Slade would have to perform even harder now, to restore the fans' good humour.

He told Phil that if he didn't get it together, he was off the tour. His job was to rouse the audience, not send them to sleep. He'd better talk to the crowd next time – and make confident gestures with his arms instead of giving off all those fear-stricken signals. Chas even suggested that he should start wearing more colourful clothes so that the punters at the back could make him out better. This was the man who'd discovered the star potential in Jimi, and now he was rubbishing Phil. It was a depressing moment.

For the next few dates, Lizzy watched Slade from the side of the stage, working out how Noddy Holder managed to project his personality – the degree of trust and humour he directed at his fans, the exaggeration and vitality he stuffed into his act. And so Lynott tried some of that as well, chatting to the audience like everyone was his best mate, asking for understanding and support. Halfway through the tour, they took a break and played a few gigs on their own, at Southampton University and The Marquee. Lizzy had already changed a lot. It was like a new band, and they just walloped it.

'Whisky In The Jar' – with 'Black Boys On The Corner' as the flip-side – was released on the first day of the Slade tour, but Radio 1 didn't play it for the first six weeks. In Ireland, it topped the charts in time for their customary homecoming shows, just as Ted had predicted. Many of the people there thought it was a fresh, sexy take on folk music. Phil was singing just like Rod Stewart again – all those days listening to his *Gasoline Alley* LP hadn't been wasted. And loads of people saw the good in Eric's guitar lines – those woeful, sustaining notes at the beginning and the way he worked the whole way around the guitar neck, neither flash nor flaccid, uniquely Irish but not stagy.

Yet Brush Shiels and a few of the serious rockers were disgusted. They'd spent years trying to fracture the image of Poor Paddy – to give the music from those parts a kind of integrity that didn't rely on green-tinted associations. How could Phil revive this hoary song, and not even have a bass guitar on the track? Where was the proof of Downey's drumming skills? How could you tell from such a record that Eric was a cosmic blues explorer? The old guys didn't get it, but the kids understood all right.

Thin Lizzy's reading of 'Whisky In The Jar' quickly became the new standard – people sang it Phil's way in pubs across the country, and the buskers followed suit. Whenever a tune became popular like that in Ireland, loved by a critical mass of people, it would become ageless. They'd say that it was now 'in the tradition', staying there for decades, maybe centuries, crossing continents and languages. The record took off in Europe, where Irish music was often favourably received, and Germany in particular would provide another good source of tour funds. But even the band wasn't aware of the widespread nature of their first hit. Far off in Rhodesia, guitarist Bigge Tembo – later to become famous with The Bhundu Boys – discovered that 'Whisky In The Jar' played in the local *jit* style, but still recognisable as Phil's creation, would tear up every bar and shabeen in Salisbury.

Lizzy's management re-promoted the record in the UK after Christmas, when the market was normally slower and easier to access. They bought loads of baby bottles of Power's whiskey and removed the labels, replacing these with special designs that Phil's mate Tim Booth had dreamed up. They sent these to DJs, who were thus prompted to give the record a spin. The ploy was totally right, and soon the band was appearing on *Top Of The Pops*. The record reached number six in the charts on 20 January 1973. The press finally wanted to know them, and they even appeared on the kids' TV show *Crackerjack*, presented by the ever-smiling Leslie Crowther. It was both exciting and disorientating.

Phil would wear mascara for photo sessions, and when he made TV appearances, he would act feminine, almost camp. He hung a little budgie mirror from the machine heads of his bass to reflect the stage lights, later adding a reflective scratch-plate around the pick-ups – his very own gimmick. Brian's concession to the glam age was to bleach a streak in his hair. Eric was encouraged to wear a waistcoat, chainmailed with large silver discs. He really disliked that outfit, and was glad when fans ripped bits off for souvenirs. When it finally disintegrated, he felt unusually happy.

Now they were playing for more money, but many of the people who came just wanted to hear the hit. When Lizzy rocked wildly on their songs like 'Suicide' or Jeff Beck's 'The Nazz Are Blue' the newcomers felt confused. Where were all the cute folk songs? But Phil never gave up on a crowd now. He flattered and talked them over, making them realise that the soft tunes and the heavy riffs were different aspects of the same act. His persuasive powers became essential; Lizzy wouldn't have another hit for three years.

In May, they released a single, 'Randolph's Tango', with a snappy Latin groove and a storyline about great romancers. Phil was writing intelligent lines, but the music was just too contrary to advance their pop success. People started to panic and talk about recording another folk song – why not 'The Spanish Lady' or 'Waxie's Dargle'? That tiny moment of success was already giving way to confusion.

Two rational ideas came up. Phil had to be presented as a star, and the band should break away from the pop gigs that were killing their souls. One of the people who seemed most sure of this was Chris O'Donnell, a twenty-two-year-old who knew Chris Morrison from the times that they'd worked together at the Rik Gunnell Agency during the UK blues boom. Since management was having some trouble finding gigs for Lizzy, and O'Donnell was such an enthusiast, they offered him a desk in the office, the chance of booking the band as a solo agent for a 10 per cent commission, and some creative input into the direction of the project.

O'Donnell found gigs that paid less, but placed the band in more prestigious settings. Even if it meant playing on a quiet night, at least they were at The Marquee in London or The Winning Post in Twickenham, and when you opened the *Melody Maker* gig guide every week, the band's name was always featured in the coolest places. The two Chrises agreed that Phil had to move to the centre of the stage instead of hanging to the left. And they weren't happy with Eric's style, his long solos and improvisation. But Eric wouldn't give in. Maybe, they thought, he was just set in his ways.

The guitarist's last work as a member of Thin Lizzy was completed at the Tollington Park studios which Decca had built for the Moody Blues. They had recorded 'Whisky In The Jar' there and felt good about the place. So as they laboured through July, many fine songs were produced, the makings of the *Vagabonds Of The Western World* LP. They even involved their old DJ friend Kid Jensen, who read out the bizarre narration for 'The Hero And The Madman'. Since he'd mostly seen Lynott at play, the DJ was surprised at the singer's perfectionist style in putting a record together.

Eric was also working hard, scoring bottleneck blues on the ecology-conscious 'Mama Nature Said' and overdubbing his guitar lines on 'Little Girl In Bloom', so that he harmonised with himself. That was a precious song, as Phil imagined a teenage girl preparing to tell her father the news she's getting married the next day and is also expecting a baby. But she's hardly worried – she's deeply in love, it's a lovely summer afternoon and the men are batting a cricket ball across the green outside her room.

There was no such delicacy on 'The Rocker', as Lynott revived his Wild One archetype – bonding with the guys, kissing the girls, riding his motorcycle and booting out trouble-makers. Importantly, this boy also knew where to buy the ace records, and he crooned his song with the lascivious style of Elvis or Jerry Lee.

The album was released on 21 September, bearing a sleeve illustration by Phil's old Dublin friend Jim Fitzpatrick. He pictured the three musicians towering over the landscape of some rocky planet as space-shuttles buzzed around them in the purple sky. In the foreground was a drawing of the famous megalithic entrance stone to the passage grave at Newgrange in Ireland's Boyne Valley – its front carved with spirals, lozenges and solar calculations, even older than the pyramids of Egypt. Just as Phil would accommodate sci-fi and ancient history in his songs, so Fitzpatrick was able to merge these ideas in Lizzy's artwork. A perfect alliance.

Eric was less compatible with the band now. He was drinking often, and getting upset when the band's advisers criticised him. *Thin Lizzy's finished*, he kept thinking. *We've taken what we had and changed it, and we can't get it back together*. He remembered how proud he'd felt before, but all this pop business – flying off to Paris to mime for a TV show and then jetting back – was destroying him. His health was bad and he despised London. Yet when Eric returned to Belfast that Christmas, his first visit home in a long while, he was freaked by the mess of the place. The paramilitaries had been waging a civilian bombing campaign and the town was wrecked.

Thin Lizzy played Queen's University Belfast on New Year's Eve, 1973. Eric had spent the day looking up old friends, drinking toasts and getting twisted. Three years of daily dope smoking hadn't done his constitution much good either, and by the time he got on to the stage, he was hallucinating, seeing phantoms waiting for him in the wings. There was an awful crackling sound from his speaker – it sounded like he was picking up radio signals from a taxi cab. He looked into the front row, noticing the faces of people he knew, feeling rotten. Then he trashed his gear and walked off.

Backstage, he drank some more stuff that a fan handed him. He realised that the punters thought the whole thing had been a terrific act, so Eric decided to rejoin the band, who were jamming on desperately without him. Brian was a little squiffy himself – his hands were raw with infected blisters and they were using a second drummer on stage to help him cope. But even Brian noticed how shocking the guitarist was, his instrument totally out of tune for the closing songs. It was a sad way to play out a resignation message. Eric was formally sacked the next day. But he was glad, really.

8

Black satin breeches, thigh boots with square toes and four-inch cork heels, a little crocheted waistcoat and a crucifix pendant – Gary Moore was back again with his old mate Phil. And as he faced up to the Birmingham audience at Barbarella's club, nobody was going to miss the fact that a new guitar-slinger was in the band.

He was taking his solos on his knees, shaking his greasy hair, pulling ecstatic expressions, jumping up and stomping at the colony of effects pedals by the lip of the stage. He'd perform yelping harmonies, and on his own song, 'Crawlin', he sang and played like some maladjusted Chicago bluesman. It was 10 February 1974, and Moore had been working with Lizzy for almost six weeks, pulled in with a day's notice when Eric had left. There was little point in caring about finesse and tidy arrangements. He was just getting loaded and having a good time.

Moore had quit Skid Row in December 1971. He'd recorded two albums with the band: *Skid* in 1970 and *34 Hours* the following year. They'd played a lot in America – even getting on a bill at The Filmore West with Frank Zappa. But he'd become frustrated with the leader Brush and his flash moves – tearing off his shirt and bouncing his bass off the stage, playing twenty-minute versions of 'Johnny B Goode' – all those old habits coming back.

So he formed The Gary Moore Band, and cut an LP, *Grinding Stone*, in 1973. He was still being managed by Clifford Davis, the boss of Fleetwood Mac, who had seen him play Dublin's National Stadium back in 1969, when he'd excited both Clifford and Fleetwood's legendary guitarist Peter Green. They'd recognised a teenage prodigy, and so Davis got Skid Row a deal with CBS, and then he stuck with Gary after he'd left.

But Gary didn't realise how much trouble it was being the prime mover in a band. There were business decisions to make, and administration and discipline to enforce. He was just nineteen, and he found himself staying practically sober for two years just to get things done. So when his album didn't sell so well and Chris Morrison asked him to play with Thin Lizzy on the last dates of their Irish tour in January, he felt like he was going on holiday. He learnt as much of the set as he could, and then busked the rest.

Sometimes he'd get so wasted in the following weeks that the Lizzy crew had to carry him to the door of his London place like a little kid, leave him on the doorstep, ring the bell and then drive off when the bedroom lights went on. When he went down on his knees for solos on stage, there were times when he wasn't able to get back up again. Taking him out socially was a liability; when Joni Mitchell played a gig at the Rainbow in London, Moore and his girlfriend kept shouting at the singer throughout the performance.

'JONI, WE LOVE YOU!' Gary repeated constantly.

'GARY LOVES YOU, JONI!' his girl added.

This commentary became even stranger as Joni played a few songs with erratic and complicated time signatures. Gary didn't care for this.

'HEY, JONI! GET BACK TO 4/4!!'

The Canadian singer had taken enough from these hecklers. She stopped the show and looked over in the direction of Moore's entourage.

'Hey, buster,' she snarled. 'Take five.'

But when Moore struck form on stage, the band forgave him just about everything. His playing was faster than ever. He used to practise in the garden outside his bedsit, playing Ten Years After albums, working out the intricate breaks that guitarist Alvin Lee would spin off. Eventually, Moore got up to speed – another technique mastered. But there were many other aspects to his style. He would amaze visitors by casually playing a traditional Irish tune. Out of nowhere, you'd hear him summon 'The March Of The King Of Laois' or something equally grand.

Gary reflected these disparate sounds during the gig at Barbarella's. He was slamming through 'Black Boys On The Corner', but then cooling to evoke the delicate heart of 'Little Girl

In Bloom'. Phil liked this extroverted company, and was talking to his fans a lot more now, dedicating tunes to particular friends, urging to hot-heads to wait a bit before they played 'The Rocker'. Just before 'Showdown', he told the audience that this new song was about a Dublin boot-boy called Johnny and his girl Miss Lucy, and immediately Moore took the funky beat and made the story groove along.

They were nurturing another extraordinary new tune called 'Sítamoia', in which Phil tried to combine his mixed ancestry in one voice. It was like an African war chant, but also resembled Celtic mouth music, as the sound of the phrases locked into this common 6/8 rhythm. Phil alternated between the spiel of an African-American shoeshine boy and a Gaelic rap – using words like the Irish for money (*airgead*) to imply that greed was the cause of suffering everywhere. The song was also a magnificent showcase for Downey's drumming, and so Brian followed it home at the Birmingham show with a thunderous solo.

Gary had his own party piece. As a preface to 'Whiskey In The Jar', he performed a rich musical quest – starting with some classical Spanish picking, then hounding through 'The Mason's Apron' before breezing into a slow air, 'The Limerick Lamentation'. The latter was old and beautiful – it had first been noted way back in 1676. This was no clumsy gesture; Gary knew his stuff and he wouldn't play out with some corny crowd-pleaser.

The band's management used to watch these shows and thrill to the possibilities. Chris O'Donnell turned to tour manager Frank Murray during one such moment. 'Fucking hell – you can take on the world with this,' he wowed. But Gary wasn't committed. He knew Lizzy wanted a new record deal, and if he stayed, he'd have to contract himself both as a band member and a future solo act. Also, he was too headstrong to work within Phil's remit. So he told Ted Carroll he was leaving. He recorded the single 'Little Darling' for them – it was released on 11 April – but soon after, he joined Colosseum II. It was time to sober up and to kick up those four-inch cork heels in a jazz-rock fusion kind of thing . . .

Back at the ranch, Pippin The Friendly Ranger had jumped on to the record deck, scoring another of Phil's precious records. The singer shooed the adventurous cat away, and then cued up a relatively scratch-free Stevie Wonder album. He rolled up a joint and listened to the fine music, his troubles easing for a while. Pippin – the area around her eyes marked by a patch of black fur – wandered off in search of some new fun.

Gail had brought the pet home as a kitten when they'd moved out of the bedsit to a new flat in Welbeck Mansions on Inglewood Road, West Hampstead. There was more room here, and it felt more homely, so it was nice to have Pippin around. Phil named his new song publishing company after the feline guest. Gail was glad of the company since her boyfriend was either touring or rehearsing much of the time.

She was happy when Pippin became a mother after a while, giving birth to five kittens in the cupboard at the end of the hall. Since the windows of this Georgian building were long and tall, the animals used to entertain themselves by climbing to the top of the curtains and sliding down the back, ripping the linings to shreds.

They shared a flat with Desmond, a sound engineer who worked at De Lane Lea Studios in Wembley. He was from Lagos, Nigeria, and his surname was Matchadoume, but the Lizzy people just called him Magic Des. He used to take Phil out to see acts like Fela Kuti, and he introduced him to new friends who'd socialise at places like The Q Club at Paddington. Phil's empathy with African and reggae music had been prompted by these connections – his song 'Sítamoia' was an expression of this. Des even had an Irish girlfriend called Moira, so the cultural mix was accented even more.

Gail was working as a social worker, specialising in drug abuse. All day, she'd deal with people addicted to heroin and barbiturates, and then come home, wanting to forget her hassles. On a bad night, the flat was either empty or full of rockers, all discussing music and their tribulations in the business. That's why Gail liked to meet Phil's artist friend Jim Fitzpatrick – he was fun to engage in conversation, full of stimulating theories about culture, painting and esoteric books. He didn't only discuss PA systems and support acts.

She'd occasionally get mad when Phil came back from a European tour. When she asked him what he'd enjoyed about the countries he'd seen, he just shrugged, like there wasn't much to say. He was often uptight when he'd been away. He wanted to know what she'd been up to, and sometimes accused her of having affairs. It was like he didn't trust anybody, not even his long-standing girlfriend. She began to lose her confidence. She wasn't encouraged to go to Thin Lizzy gigs since Phil's image was that of the dashing bachelor. She began to classify people Phil mentioned according to her relationship with them: those who knew she existed, and those who didn't. *It's like being shut up in a cupboard*, she thought.

Presently, the band was heading off to Germany again. Moore's departure had left them with a financial poser. To keep the band solvent, they had agreed to tour Germany. Chris O'Donnell had flown out there in advance and had picked up 50 per cent of the money from the promoter, Klaus Schmidt. When they realised that they had no guitarist to tour with, they had to make up an excuse and postpone.

They quickly found two guitarists: John Cann from Atomic Rooster, and Andy Gee, who'd been working with The Steve Ellis Band. After some rushed rehearsals, they conceded that it was rough, but there was at least some energy there. Ted Carroll flew out to watch them play some early dates in the south of the country, and was pleased to see that they were going down well. Brian was feeling disgruntled, though, and there were some peculiar scenes when John Cann expected the star treatment – to have his guitar and bags carried around for him – but they made him understand that Thin Lizzy was a step down from his glory days with the Rooster.

Just before Carroll returned to London from Germany, he spent a spare Saturday with the band. The hotel where they'd spent their Friday night didn't want to put them up for another day as there'd been too much uproarious behaviour. There were a couple of girls hanging out with the band who suggested they visit a pretty valley nearby. So they drove off in the van, playing tapes on a portable Sony machine, taking in the sights. One of Phil's favourite tapes was a parody of the Sherlock Holmes detective stories. Phil was a big fan of Sir Arthur Conan Doyle, and so when he listened to the Firesign Theatre narrate 'The Tale Of The Giant Rat Of Sumatra' he would laugh and roar.

A friend had scored some acid, so they lay up in the fields and waited for it to work. But it must have been a dud lot because nothing happened, so they just played some football instead. They packed up and found a little village that had been recommended to them – the hotel was about twelve storeys high, right in the middle of this quiet scene, so they couldn't miss their destination. A Turkish band was playing instrumentals in the lobby, like The Shadows, only weirder.

As they sat drinking and listening to this cacophony, a bunch of strippers arrived and began to gyrate. This was odd, since it was only six-thirty in the evening, but Phil had noticed on something even more sensational. He kept looking at this one girl, and as she peeled off her clothes, he gave a shout of recognition. Why, she was one of the girls who used to stay at Me Ma's in Manchester! Everyone thought this was funny. Was there no place in the Western world that hadn't been somehow touched by the Lynotts?

Ted arrived back in the UK and told the two Chrises that everything was cool and the band was improving over the tour. Yet two days later, there was a call from Frank Murray in Germany. He told them that Brian Downey had quit the band and was demanding to come back before the tour was over. It seemed that he hated at least one of the new guitarists, and that the precarious position of the band and this absurd money-making tour was driving him literally mad. They had to put him on a ferry and pull out of a big festival date in Holland.

Now there was just one member of Thin Lizzy who wanted to carry on – and even Phil was hesitating. The only positive aspect of the story was that *Vagabonds Of The Western World* was selling quite well in America, meaning that some money and possible fame could still be accessed. The management urged Brian to stay around at least until they could audition new guitarists. They even agreed to pay him a better wage. So Downey – who didn't even own his own drum kit at this stage – consented to stick it out for a few months.

The situation at Welbeck Mansions was also gloomy. Phil had been ringing Gail from the tour, asking her where she'd been the night before when he said he'd called. Gail told him she hadn't been anywhere and that was the absolute truth, but he was so insistent that she began to doubt herself. What made this worse was that they were now engaged, and when he was in a good mood, Phil was even talking about them starting a family. He really wanted a little boy, he told her.

But the singer's motives seemed all twisted up. Phil had suggested they buy a ring just before Gail's parents came over to London on a visit. It was a highly romantic gesture, but was he really signalling long-term intentions? And was he being faithful when he was on tour? Gail was also uncomfortable about his desire for a son. To hear him talk, you'd feel that he imagined his child as a replica of himself, not a living, breathing individual. So Gail wouldn't agree to this.

They still had some happy times, and she liked it when they were alone and he'd produce some lyrics and ask her to read them and to say what she thought. She was a forthright person, and they'd have lively arguments about Ireland, and what the country meant to them both. She accused him of looking back with a rosy glow and that he wore his patriotism like a badge. Her home town of Belfast was being blown apart. She didn't feel so nostalgic about the south of the island either. 'Dublin's a dump,' she'd say. 'Isn't that why you left in the first place?'

And while he was sentimental in his songs, there was an aspect of Phil's personality that always seemed to lock her out. He never brought his guard down. Maybe he was masking insecurity by control. He would freak out at the strangest times. Even though he was a much-loved joker, he couldn't stand being laughed at himself. And on occasions when he seemed to be losing his grip, he could be mentally and physically frightening. When they holidayed in Ibiza with Phyllis and Dennis, he sang on-stage at a local club one night. She had been sitting there for hours and so she decided to dance by herself. When Phil discovered this, he got so angry that he punched her face. The next day, Gail had to tell Phyllis that she'd tripped on a kerb.

She stayed a bit longer – while Phil found two new guitarists in Brian Robertson and Scott Gorham, and Thin Lizzy became an even more exciting prospect. And she still listened to the words of the songs, trying to discover a few windows into Phil's deepest personality. By the time she heard 'Still In Love With You', their relationship was practically over, and she wondered if – by any chance – he was singing the words to her. But if he was, it simply made her more angry. *How can he write it but not say it? Why can't he say the words, 'I love you'? And then he uses his experiences to sell records?*

THE BALLAD OF THE THIN MAN

Thin Lizzy was touring Europe again when she got her last phone call – yet another 'where were you?' accusation. He sounded even more cruel than before.

'Well, you'd better be out by the time I get back,' he said, before hanging up.

Gail thought about this for a second.

Sod you, I will.

9

A big hammer and a bag of six-inch nails: Brian Robertson was at work. He'd already hauled his speaker cabinet to the back of the town hall, now he was making sure that nobody was going to shift it. He found the wooden bevel at the bottom of the cabinet, angled the nail inwards, and then banged it home. He repeated this along the sides until his equipment was immovable.

He'd come early to the hall – just north of Glasgow – to mark out his territory on stage. Nobody had specified who the headliners were going to be, but if Robbo had his way, it was going to be his band, Heidi. And if you'd got your gear stacked up at the very back of the stage, then there was no conceivable way another act on the bill could presume to come on after you. The rival band was called The Bay City Rollers. Robbo hated them.

The Rollers' manager was trying to smarten them up, although he wasn't yet having much success. They had long hair and jeans, and they played really badly. But they carried themselves like they were something special, and so when they arrived at the hall much later, there was a lot of moaning about the arrangements on stage. The Rollers figured that since they were the bigger band, they should play last.

'Move the fuckin' gear if you can, then,' said Robbo.

There was an altercation in the dressing-room. Certain people got battered. Later on, Robbo finalised his victory on stage, playing the blues with fearsome skill in both major and minor keys, squaring the shuffles and the rockers and the boogie grooves with a finesse that would have seemed unlikely for a fifteen-year-old. When Heidi played The Who's 'Won't Get Fooled Again', Robbo started the song on a crummy Farfisa organ, booting the notes through a wah-wah pedal – replicating

Townsend's famous intro as best he could. Then he switched to guitar in mid-song, mastering the power chords, loving his confident hold on the situation. He was a cocky wee bastard, but unarguably good.

Robbo most definitely had The Rage. Permanently wired, ever-cussing, fighting and drinking. You could never separate his emotions and the music, and that's why he related to the blues. Like his elders from Glasgow, Frankie Miller and Maggie Bell – people he'd befriended and jammed with – Robbo found his temperamental home in the blues. There was no neutral feeling in the boy or the sounds he created.

People wrongly assumed that there was little behind the rough-house personality. But Robbo knew his stuff. His dad was a jazzer, playing clarinet and alto sax, and he'd performed with Art Blakey. There was a great library of records in the house – Mose Allison, Django Reinhardt, Joe Pass and Louis Stewart. When he was seven, his mother got an upright piano in the house, and she booked lessons for herself, Brian and his brother Glen. After the boys had learnt their classical stuff to his satisfaction, the teacher Fred Purvis would end the lesson with some boogie-woogie.

At the age of twelve Robbo started sprouting facial hair. He didn't mind this, because if he didn't shave on the Thursday, he had a little beard by the weekend. Thus he could lie about his age, and play cabaret in the hard-nut hotel gigs. He'd be thumping at the bass pedals of an ancient organ while the old girl sang to the drunks. The money he got for this paid for an amp and a Gibson SG guitar.

Brian and Glen joined Rue Morgue around 1969. They played Hendrix's 'Red House', Argent's 'Hold Your Head Up' and loads of twelve-bar songs – anything to knock the classical edge off Robbo's style. During school hours, he provoked havoc, causing one of the teachers at Eastwood High to burst into tears because of his heavy manners. This same behaviour cost him a place at music academy and at art school; on the latter count, he was admittedly 'arsy' when he hit a superior on the head. So he got a job in Cuthbertson's music store in town. He was in the records section and his pal Freddie Mayo looked after the instruments department. They'd jam at lunchtime and it was Freddie who recommended that he should join Heidi. Which was just as well, because he got the sack from Cuthbertson's soon after, when they found he'd been ripping albums off on the sly.

Even though he was underage, Brian's local drinking spot in the Clarkston area was The Redhurst Hotel. He was there one evening near the end of 1973 when Thin Lizzy walked in. Phil was wearing a white, double-breasted jacket. He also sported a huge pearl earring, a clip-on job like your mother would wear. The regular drinkers at the bar started growling – they didn't care for this sort of thing at all – but Brian went over and had a word. He was a big Lizzy fan. He could play all of the *Vagabonds* album, and was looking forward to hearing the band perform at the hotel later that night.

After the show, Robbo hung around. He finished up in Downey's room with his girlfriend, drunk, but still managing to play guitar. The drummer listened bemused as Robbo tore into one Lizzy song after another, throwing in a few blues tunes to keep it lively. Downey thought this was the weirdest thing, but he could hardly believe the conversation that followed.

'So do you think I have a chance?' Robbo asked him.

'For what?'

'For joining Thin Lizzy?'

Downey explained that they already had a guitarist and there was no need for a fourth member. But it was a hell of a thing to ask, and the drummer never forgot this brassy introduction. Robbo remembered it too. It was fun being cocky; it gave you the breaks that never came to the shy, retiring souls. His close mate was Charlie McLennan, who lived 200 yards further along Ayr Road. He was a couple of years older, but they liked the same kind of stuff. When he started working as a roadie, he'd get Brian involved when acts such as David Bowie came up to Scotland to play. Then Charlie moved to London, where he got work humping gear for Lizzy. In May 1974 Charlie told Robbo that there was a job going in the band.

Brian figured that loads of people would be trying for the Lizzy place, so he brought both his guitar and a set of drumsticks down on the train, along with his £25 savings. Since he was a passable drummer as well, he figured that if the gig fell through, then at least he could try his chances elsewhere. In fact, when he checked the classified ads that week in *Melody Maker*, he noticed that a band called Slack Alice were looking for a drummer, so maybe he'd give that a blast first.

Slack Alice were holding auditions in Denmark Street, in London's West End. There were masses of people queuing outside, including the old drummer from Heidi. When it came to the latter's turn, Brian's friend clearly didn't have what Slack Alice were after, and he left five minutes later. Robbo, however, was in there for about forty-five minutes, bashing away, and it seemed like they wanted him in. He stopped off that night at 55 Elsham Road, where the Lizzy roadies had their squat. Robbo was relieved that now there was something to fall back on.

The Lizzy people were pretty despondent by then. The money they'd raised on the German tour was virtually gone, and their overdraft was more scary than ever. They couldn't earn more money until they toured and recorded, but there was no chance of this until there was a permanent band behind them. Downey's heart wasn't really in it – he was still thinking of walking away from it all. But still, they'd set up auditions at The Iroquo Club, just by the Belsize Park tube station on Haverstock Hill. Charlie kept badgering the band to give Robbo a try, and eventually they agreed.

The Iroquo belonged to Ginger Johnson, an African drummer, and there were posters of his Nigerian homeland on the walls. There were rolled-up mattresses on the floor and the place had the musty aroma of late-night sessions. As he was walking in, Brian noticed a Teac recording machine inside a doorway – the band were obviously taping the sessions, so they could review each of the many hopefuls who'd tried for the job. And there'd been loads of these.

The depressing thing about such auditions was that many of the applicants were totally unsuitable. Either they looked terrible or they weren't able to cover all of the musical areas that the band wanted. Some of them had learnt the Lizzy albums off by rote, but they played the stuff mechanically, with little feeling. But all of these people had taken the time to come to The Iroquo, so they deserved a little courtesy, a couple of jam sessions, even though they were all plainly useless. The band's gear was stacked up on the little stage in the main room. Phil wasn't so friendly to the Glaswegian hopeful, but Brian said hello, recognising Robbo, even though his hair was longer now and he looked less like a kid. There were two guitarists already in the room – Andy Gee

and an Irish guy, Mike Cox, from Eire Apparent, the Ulster act
who'd toured with Hendrix and had even gotten Jimi to produce
their album *Sunrise*.

Robbo couldn't understand the scenario. It seemed like these
people were already on a wage – so why were they still
auditioning guitarists? And why was the Irish bloke doing so
little, just hanging around and rolling joints on his Strat? Robbo
didn't feel intimidated. If this was the level of competition, then
he'd easily get the job.

Phil kept asking Brian if he knew such-and-such a Lizzy song.
Robbo said 'yep' every time, and he plugged in and played them
all, no bother. When they'd established this aspect, they started
playing a few blues tunes. Downey was brightening up now, and
they kept at it for hours, playing for the joy of it. There was
Robbo, seventeen years old, tireless and confident, hammering it
out better than anyone. And he was thinking to himself, *We're off*.

Scott Gorham had also financed his career by stealing records.
His particular gig was at the ABC record warehouse on San
Fernando Road in Glendale, California. His job was filling
orders, but since he needed the money for a passage to England,
he had developed a side business, supplying the smaller stores
with the most in-demand vinyl.

It was a cool system. Scott would first check the LP charts for
the highest sellers, then he'd take a box containing twenty-five
copies of the album he'd identified and drop it in a bin. He'd
cover the bin with rubbish and then take it outside and throw the
contents into the large dumpster. After repeating this operation
three times, he would go home and take a shower. At nine
o'clock in the evening, he returned to his workplace, rummaged
in the dumpster, and retrieved his cache. During the weekend,
he'd find a record dealer who was up for the idea of some illicit
trading. He'd give Scott a dollar-fifty each for his contraband,
and everyone was happy.

Scott's father was a master builder and had earned plenty of
money in the past, but some of his investments had come out
badly. When Scott was twelve the family left the mansion on the
hill and shifted to a more modest home. The old man was a
World War II kind of guy, and it upset him to realise that his boy
wanted to be a rock and roller, so they were always at

△ Thin Lizzy before they swapped moustaches. Eric Bell, Brian Downey and Phil Lynott.

△ Breakfast at me Ma's. Phil and Phylis at Clifton Grange Hotel.

△ The Famous Four, 1975. Scott Gorham, Brian Robertson, Phil Lynott and Brian Downey.

△ Solo in Dublin, August 1977.

△ Live, and quite possibly, dangerous, 1978.

△ The Crumlin Vagabond and the Belfast Cowboy. Phil and Van Morrison sidle up.

▽ Philomena and her mother, Sarah, 1972

△ The Greedy Bastards at London's Electric Ballroom. Chris Spedding, Gary Moore (hidden), Steve Jones, Phil Lynott, Jimmy Bain, Brian Downey (hidden), Paul Cook.

▽ Stars in their eyes. Philomena, Phil, Caroline, Leslie Crowther.

△ Promoting 'Black Rose' on a
Parisian walkway. Brian Downey,
Phil Lynott, Gary Moore, Scott
Gorham.

▷ Midge Ure, left, beams down
from Planet Pop.

△ Entering 'Chinatown' with Snowy White, left.

MERRY CHRISTMAS
AND A HAPPY NEW YEAR

philip, caro, sarah, cathleen, gnasher

△ Happy times at Howth with Cathleen, Caroline and Sarah.

▽ Grand Slam's first season

loggerheads. Mother was more encouraging about his music, but she was often laid up with illness and various problems. So leaving home wasn't a wrench. Scott was cutting his own groove and taking the initiative in a series of moves that would utterly change his life. But to the parents, he was just another juvenile law-breaker.

The worst instance of this was in Yuma, down by the Colorado River in Arizona. The teenager had been strung out on downers for a while, and didn't have the money to get home, so when he was approached by a hippie guy with a beard, shorts and sandals, he figured that salvation was at hand.

'Hey, listen,' the hippie said. 'I got this party going down on the beach. I wondered if there was anything you could sell me.'

'Sure, man.' Scott took him over to the car and pulled the stash out of the exhaust pipe. He told the guy to take his pick and pocketed the money. Ten dollars for a gram of hash. Enough to buy gas for the car and to get him home. Great, he naïvely thought, preparing to set off the next day. However, the drugs squad surprised him sleeping on the beach at three in the morning. Two guys grabbed his arms, another pair held on to his legs. Flashlights, badges and a ride to the jailhouse. 'You're under arrest for sale of marijuana,' they said. He'd sold the deal to an undercover cop.

Scott wasn't so worried. He'd already been busted seven times. Normally he got off with a weekend in the slammer and a slap on the wrist. Yet on the Sunday, when all the other petty offenders were walking out, he didn't hear his name being called. Then he realised that his charge was a felony in Arizona. He was facing a two- to five-year sentence in the State Penitentiary. The cell had a dirt floor, and there was no glass in the windows, only bars. It was 100 degrees outside. This was alarming. He gave the jailer the number of Bill Gorham, his dad, and asked him to call. A while later, Scott got his reply.

'Your old man says you can rot.'

Scott's father took some persuading before he'd do anything. Eventually, Bill flew down with Scott's uncle, a lawyer. They went to court and struck a deal with the judge. The general drift of the conversation was this: Arizona didn't really want this kid in its state and they'd like to take him out of the state's way. If there was any possibility that the judge and the public defender could see fit to put him on inter-state probation, then they'd be extremely grateful. Scott would even write to the judge on a regular basis and inform him of his reformed ways. They'd compensate everyone for their trouble, of course. A deal was arrived at. It had been an expensive trip, and the teenager was very aware of the fact that they'd never oblige him again.

His life was getting more perilous. His friend Steve Schrage, the guitarist out of his first band, The Jesters, was knocked off his Bonneville 650 and killed. Scott also did a spell in the LA County Jail. While the Arizona slammer had been filled with drunk and disorderly cases, he was now passing murderers in the corridors. Some of the inmates had their arms broken and their faces were swollen from beatings. It was time to pull himself together.

It was better now for Scott to forswear the drugs and to get the music side of his life in shape. Thus far it had been an easygoing venture. With The Jesters, he had played surf music by the likes of Dick Dale and the Surfaris – just a bunch of kids, showing off in the mid-1960s at weddings and friends' parties. With later acts he played gigs on The Strip in Hollywood. His most serious band, The Ilford Subway, had featured the son of English parents, hence the Anglo-sounding name. The drummer in that act was Bob C Benberg, who would later become Scott's brother-in-law.

The Ilford Subway rehearsed constantly for three years. They only played one gig – at an all-girls school – although they were managed by a couple of rich guys in Beverly Hills who bankrolled much of their outgoings. They got a singles deal with producer Terry Melcher, Doris Day's son. This was exciting because Melcher had hung out with people like Dennis Wilson from The Beach Boys.

What Scott never realised at the time was that Charles Manson and his followers, The Family, had a vendetta against Melcher for not giving him a record contract. The murders of August 1969, when actress Sharon Tate and four others died, were carried out at Melcher's old Hollywood home at 10050 Cielo Drive. The Family were still causing havoc long after Manson was found guilty of murder in 1971. In later years, Scott shivered to think that he was unknowingly close to such a vibe.

Bob the drummer married Vicky, Scott's sister, and they moved to London. Unfortunately they had visa problems which caused them to return temporarily to Los Angeles, but when Bob called, he was happy and excited. He'd just joined a band in Britain called Supertramp. They'd been recording demos for the album that was to become *Crime Of The Century*, and even though they were still playing the pubs, Bob reckoned they'd be huge. He passed on a tape of their songs, and Scott liked it.

There was a vacancy in the band for a guitarist, and Bob figured that Scott should give it a try. So Gorham spent all his savings on a flight to London, only to realise that the band's multi-instrumentalist, Roger Hogson, had decided to keep playing guitar as well as keyboards. Bummer. Yet unlucky circumstances actually worked in his favour. Before, Scott could have relied on family and friends. Now he was directly responsible for his own fortunes, and he realised that being in a strange country was inspiring. Nobody knew his history, so he could become this different person – outgoing and pushy. He became a hustler, getting up on stage with bands he didn't know, jamming and making connections.

He formed his own band, Fast Buck. He'd walk into any pub, demand to see the manager and deliver his spiel. He'd tell them he was from Los Angeles, and that his fellow members were from Louisville and Cleveland – big contenders. Inevitably it worked, and Scott would be playing five nights a week around the London circuit. They put the word out that anybody could get on stage and jam, and soon they'd liberated this mass of part-time axe-heroes – frustrated clerks and schoolteachers who didn't have time to form a band, but loved their five minutes of blamming away up there.

Scott was pulling in £12 a week and drinking a lot of that, and so he signed on a government Manpower scheme for some extra revenue. He'd wash and cook for old ladies, cleaning toilets and windows. One task involved clearing out an infested building. He had to pick up dead rats, bag them and dispose of the remains. People from Glendale would have freaked if they'd known, but he persisted, rehearsing the band at the hairdressing salon where the singer, Charlie Harper, worked. The latter would become famous in the punk era as the frontman of The UK Subs.

A regular visitor to the Fast Buck jam sessions was Ruan O'Lochlann, the sax player with Bees Make Honey. For a time,

Bob had played drums with this band, and they'd pioneered the use of pubs around the capital as rock and roll venues. There was a heavy Irish involvement in this flourishing pub rock scene – the makings of a network of friends and fixers who were jokingly called The Murphia. Ruan had heard via these channels that Thin Lizzy needed a guitarist. He suggested Scott.

The Californian had never heard of them, and he thought it was a stupid name for a band anyway. So when he arrived at The Iroquo, lost, late and rain-soaked, he wasn't terrifically impressed. When he saw Phil sulking around inside, he couldn't be sure if he was in the band or just worked at the club. Downey and Robbo looked equally pissed off. It was more than a week since Robertson joined, and nobody except Phil knew exactly what they were looking for now.

Scott was wearing a green checked lumberjack shirt, and his flared jeans hung down at the crotch. The jeans were also – as Robbo noted despondently – pressed like a pair of slacks. The only thing going for him at this stage was his unfeasibly long hair, which Robbo envied. Then he pulled out his guitar, a cheap Japanese copy of a Les Paul, and they all groaned.

'Show him "The Rocker", Brian,' Phil mumbled.

Robbo took him reluctantly through the chord shapes. They played it straight through, and since Scott wasn't really familiar with the song, he played around the spaces, improvising like he did in the pub gigs. He had a completely different approach from Robbo, who normally played tight little chords. Scott hit all six strings, making a much richer sound. And his rhythm was on the case, underlining that strong American style.

Nobody said as much to him. They'd seen so many people now that they were case-hardened. But occasionally they went into the back room and listened to playbacks of the recordings they'd made of the session. Scott couldn't even figure this out. He didn't know the tape was rolling and he assumed that they were smoking joints and making tea. Which they were, too, but that wasn't the point of it.

It was a clash of disinterested parties. Scott didn't care whether they hired him or not, and the other three were low on enthusiasm. He gave them his number and Phil returned the gesture by tearing a tiny scrap of paper off an envelope and writing his phone number, really small, in the corner. *You prick,*

Scott thought to himself as he walked out.

The rest of the band reconvened at Phil's place and listened to the tapes again. They all agreed Scott was the best they'd heard. He added to Robbo's playing instead of grinding against it, which was a thrill. Phil rang him the same night and asked Gorham to join the band. They'd pay him £30 per week. The singer's tone was completely different this time – he was friendly and welcoming. Nobody could second-guess the future but it had a dazzling international aspect to it now. Thin Lizzy: Dublin, Glasgow, Los Angeles.

10

Scott was amazed when Phil took him out shopping. He'd never cared about clothes before, but now he was getting educated. It became a ritual over the years. Before a tour, a photo session or a special party, the singer would grab a wad of cash and take his pals out to places they'd never imagined visiting: Granny Takes A Trip on the King's Road, the most outlandish corners of Kensington Market, chichi boutiques in the West End. Phil would fuss and spend hours choosing his accessories. He'd worry over a tiny detail on a shoe, or take an entire afternoon trying to find the exact pair he'd seen in a magazine. He'd walk into a shop and pick out an extravagant silk shirt and hold it up, gasping, 'I gorra have this!' Meanwhile, Scott was standing behind him, feeling embarrassed, checking his watch, wanting out. *This guy lives to shop*, the guitarist was thinking. *He's like a chick.*

But it was also part of the business. Phil wanted his greenhorn guitarist to understand that Thin Lizzy wasn't purely about standing on stage and hitting a chord. You had to be memorable – walking, talking and looking just so. He'd take them to parties and record company receptions and demonstrate the art of the schmooze: cutting into conversations, making contacts, ensuring they all knew who you were and what you were up to. And they'd watch him talking to women and appreciate another of Phil's arts. Often he'd play shy, making the girls want to take the initiative – to mother this little lost boy. That was one of the reasons he pulled his shirt collar up. The girls would try and straighten it for him, and he'd thank them sincerely. Or he'd stare somebody out in a room, making her feel special. And he'd compliment his new friend on her hairstyle, or an item of clothing she'd obviously taken some care with. Phil would say,

'You have beautiful eyes' to a female without a molecule of embarrassment. He encouraged Scott and Brian to compete with him, turning the whole routine into a kind of game. Scott had a different kind of admiration for him now. *He's a mastermind*, the guitarist figured.

Phil had a vision of how the new band would look, and he used a failsafe trick in photo sessions. Hendrix was his marker here, and Phil wanted to capture that mixture of sensitivity and rebel allure. So he'd make sure that everyone was stoned before a shoot – which was no difficult thing – and then let a photographer mate do his stuff. Their eyelids would start drooping and the facial muscles were relaxing. They smiled like bad boys. Afterwards, he'd look at the contact sheet and score off the ones he didn't approve of. But he'd normally find loads that he liked, and would pass them around excitedly.

'Some of these are very funky. Look at that – totally grassed! Knowarrimean?'

But when the public wasn't around, Phil was the drill sergeant. He rehearsed the new band for two weeks straight, twelve hours a day. Suggestions were allowed, but not all were tolerated. He was three albums down the line now. Thin Lizzy had featured nine different members. There wasn't any time left for diversions or misfiring personalities. On one occasion, Phil learnt from a roadie that Robbo had been talking about him behind his back. It was nothing heavy, but the singer knew that he had to stop this. He waited until the band were in full rehearsal – lights, monitors, the lot. And he got his point over, making sure that all of the crew could hear his barracking.

'You little Scottish bastard! If you've got something to say – say it to my face, right?'

Robbo held on to that advice for the rest of his life – to the extent that he'd be as upfront as Phil. There were many screaming matches after this, and opinions were fired around between Lynott and Robertson in hysterical bouts. It lessened the back-stabbing, but Downey and Gorham realised they had two volcanic personalities in the band now.

Their first gig with the new line-up was at Wolverhampton's Lafayette club, near the end of June 1974. The audience was outnumbered by the bouncers and the bar staff. The venue was ridiculously small but there were expanses of space everywhere.

Scott and Robbo flanked the little stage with their shiny new Les
Pauls, waiting to be blooded. Scott hadn't even seen Lizzy play
live before, so he didn't know how he was expected to behave.
The only clear direction so far was that the old Thin Lizzy was
over. They wouldn't play 'Whisky In The Jar' on stage, even
though the change might lose them some of the old fans. Scott
had taken home *Vagabonds* and a few singles when he joined, but
he didn't like the sound at all. He thought it was hippie music. So
they junked much of the back catalogue, sticking with upbeat
numbers like 'The Rocker' and 'Little Darling'. They even tried
one of Scott's songs from Fast Buck, 'Bottle Of Red Wine'.

It hardly seemed worth the bother to Scott when he looked
around The Lafayette. Downey counted the band in as expected,
but suddenly – whoosh – Phil was rocketing into his act,
dropping poses, working his beanpole frame, bellowing and
beckoning at the six punters, who were already feeling energised
in return. Robbo looked to Scott and their faces registered mutual
shock: *Is this what we're supposed to do?* Phil kept glancing over,
giving them the nod, urging them to pile in. So Robbo started
shaking his hair and slamming his right arm, enjoying the play.
Scott watched this jumping and screaming and decided to
abstain. He backed up in the corner, happy to be out of it; there
was a lot to remember and he didn't want the distraction of
having to make a show. But when Phil got off the mike, he
cornered Scott by his Marshall cabinet, grabbed him by the jacket
and led him to the front of the stage, saying, 'You're staying
there.'

Afterwards, when they'd sat down and gone through the post-
mortem – pulling out songs that didn't work, thinking up new
orders for the set list, Phil remarked on Scott's coy behaviour on
stage. It was a similar lecture that Phil had received from Chas
Chandler during the Slade tour in 1972, but Phil was kinder with
his words. 'You can't let the audience know you're afraid of
them,' he explained. 'If they do, they'll eat you alive . . .'

There was an added pressure on the band to shimmy and blast
when they played London's Marquee, a month later, on 9 July.
Thin Lizzy had actually been dropped by Decca. Instead of
receiving a fresh £10,000 advance when the contract was up for
renewal, the label decided not to pick up their option. The band

was already £7,000 in debt. Chris Morrison used to joke – half in panic – that they were going to bankrupt the local branch of their bank. Prior to this, the management had been talking to other labels, keen to walk away from the old deal if they could. They'd spoken to people at RCA, who'd meandered on the idea. There was a very strong bid from a friend of Morrison's, Chris Bedfordshire at Island Records, but when the company's head of Sales And Marketing saw them at The Marquee, he decided that they were the 'antithesis' of an Island band. Luckily, there were other parties at that London gig, including Nigel Grainge from Vertigo.

Nigel's involvement started with a Saturday visit to Ted Carroll's Rock On record stall at the Golborne Road market, west London. Grainge was an obsessive collector, and knew more about American imports than anyone else at Vertigo – hence his promotion to Head of A&R. He'd liaised with many of the American acts, including the mega-crooner Andy Williams. But he was also keen to sign stuff from the London office, to make an impression. As he stacked up on rarities from Ted's stall, Nigel asked the vendor what he did during the week.

'Well, I manage a band, Thin Lizzy.'

'So why don't you come to a real company?'

Nigel couldn't believe he'd just said that. He actually liked Thin Lizzy – he'd bought the old albums. But that was such a corny, music biz thing to come out with.

'Make me an offer,' Ted replied.

'Pardon?'

'We're not with Decca any more.'

On Monday morning, Ted sent over a quarter-inch tape of 'Still In Love With You', which Lizzy had recorded with Gary Moore in the spring. This part of the affair was never mentioned until two years later – as far as Grainge was concerned, he was hearing the new line-up. Again, it was seat-of-the-pants management, but it worked fantastically well. Nigel thought the tape was staggering, and The Marquee show thrilled him even more. He advanced the band £15,000 and they were safe again.

It was Ted's last great service to the band. His Rock On stall was going well, and on his trips to America, he'd noticed a similar trend – that old records were becoming a premium. Rock and roll had never been taken altogether seriously in the early days, with the result that few people had worried about its history. But now there was an affection for this heritage, and Ted had been able to help this along, introducing fans to vintage rhythm and blues and soul records, and all the curious offshoots of the story. Phil had already advertised his friend's trade on 'The Rocker' when he sang about the Rock On stall, and concluded, 'Teddy boy, he knows the score.' Now Carroll wanted to set up in a proper shop and run a label – and thus he said adieu.

That left the two Chrises in charge. Morrison was the cool dealer, holding the main office together, keenly aware of the business angles. O'Donnell liked travelling with the band and riffing off their ideas – understanding the warp of Phil's rich imagination and passing this to the record companies in a presentable manner. It was also necessary to have someone close by when the band went on tour, to sweet-talk the cops and hotel managers and indignant townsfolk when the Lizzy operation got messy. And they were all only just learning to deal with Robbo and his outspoken ways. The first time the guitarist walked into the band's Dean Street office, he looked at a poster on the wall of one of their other acts – Iron Virgin – who wore American football helmets for some reason. 'You manage them?' he asked. 'They're fuckin' shite!' There was a new aspect to the group and the wider organisation, and it was hardly ever boring.

Scott was amazed when they toured Ireland. It felt like they were finally on the road, and any worries about being shunned by the original fans were unfounded. The new guitarists were immediately hailed as friends. Nobody made an issue out of Eric Bell and Gary Moore leaving, and some of the Dubliners even felt flattered that an American and a Scotsman should have wanted to join with their homeboys. Very early on, Scott and Robbo appreciated a special vibe about the island that had succoured Phil in the bad times: you can always go home and it will be all right. As they motored through Antrim, Kilkenny, Galway and Dublin, Phil was a fascinating tour guide – telling Scott about the history, politics, topography and myths of each particular region. The American was humbled because he knew nothing about his own nation and nor had he cared. It was Phil revealing another part of his self. He could be *this guy*, and then he'd do a 180-degree turn and be *that guy*.

But if the song 'Philomena', released as a single on 25 October 1974, was the expression of that Celtic awareness, then maybe it wasn't an entirely valuable allegiance. It was the strangest idea – Phil singing in a blarney accent about wanderlust taking him over the seas, leaving his old ma back home. The reborn Thin Lizzy was gearing up to be a premium rock and roll band, and here they were firing off with a sea shanty as the inaugural single from the new line-up. The guitarists didn't care for it, but they were new recruits and had to defer to the boss. Even the Irish fans felt uncomfortable, some accusing Phil of shamrockery. Phil was still aiming to write the modern Celtic standard but the quest was misdirected here.

There was hope that producer Ron Nevison would define the possibilities within the fresh set-up. He'd been the engineer on The Who's monumental song cycle *Quadrophenia* and had conspired in the international launch of Bad Company. Yet when he turned up at the recording sessions for Lizzy's *Night Life* album with his Rolls-Royce and a fur coat Robbo was instantly aggrieved. And when Nevison wouldn't let the Scotsman play through his Marshall cabinet in the studio – loud and impassioned – there was trouble. So Robbo tore into the control room and demonstrated just what he wanted to play, as opposed to all that nonsense on the recording floor with a wimpy Fender Twin amp and a stupid Pig Nose speaker for sustain. He wanted deep, passionate blues on the solo for the 'Night Life' track. He picked up a Stratocaster and first-timed his part straight through the mixing desk. The engineer taped this, even though it was spontaneous madness and Nevison was shaking his head. But Downey was there, and when the Quiet Man uttered an opinion, you'd be stupid to dismiss it.

'That's brilliant, keep it on.'

There were few such victories. The band didn't have strong enough convictions, and Nevison was working to his own agenda; his other main job in 1974 was engineering parts of Led Zeppelin's *Physical Graffiti* – thunderous drums and extremes of sound – but it seemed like he was giving the Lizzy record a mushy, adult presentation. Strings and swooning backing vocals were obliterating the street-punk spirit. He'd turned them into lightweights.

Two songs surpassed the experience. 'Frankie Carroll' was

Phil back in his songwriter mode, sketching out a picture of a fragmenting family; with simple piano arpeggios for backing, he told of the man's alcohol binges, the wife-beating, the child abuse. He held back on the sentimentality – which was unusual for Phil – and so the tone of the lyric was all the more disturbing.

For 'Still In Love With You', they kept the Gary Moore recording of the song. The band returned to Saturn Sound Studios in Worthing where it was originally done and added some vocals with Frankie Miller. There was no point changing the guitar lines; Robbo listened hard and felt that he couldn't top it. It took a long while and a deal of maturity before Brian could work his own signature into that.

Moore, like his mentor Peter Green, had understood that the blues played slow in a minor key was the saddest thing ever. And when you allied this to Phil singing about unplanned pregnancies – always a significant theme to this man – you'd have the most grievous creation. They would carry 'Still In Love With You' with them always, a sad talisman. This kind of thing happened to the best rock and roll bands – the songs growing old with the artist and taking on a different mood over the years: Bob Dylan's most cruel lyric, 'Like A Rolling Stone', changed from gratuitous scorn to self-criticism of the hardest kind, and Marianne Faithfull ageing into 'As Time Goes By', living the sadness in the song. And now Lizzy had chanced upon their epitaph.

Initially, they used it as a critical downswing in the mood of the set – a chance for Phil's tender-hearted side to reveal itself before they revved up for a noisy conclusion. On the *Live And Dangerous* album it became a showcase for Robbo's raw glory, a guide to the deep, despondent places the music could send you to. By 1983, 'Still In Love With You' was the emblem of the band's relationship with their fans and the mutual pain of their finale. After Phil's death it felt more desperate still.

When Lizzy set off for America in March 1975, the mood was joyous. They'd been playing constantly, learning each other's ways and finding a collective buzz in the music. Scott and Robbo could anticipate which song suited the other, and how to share riffs and spin lead breaks across the stage. They'd play a variation on a line together, a melodic interface that surprised even themselves. Soon, the lines were diversifying, using thirds, fifths and seventh harmonies, according to the mood of the song. This was unique. So now they had a fun chance to hone their method – five weeks Stateside with Bachman-Turner Overdrive, ZZ Top and Bob Seger. As they assembled at the airport, they were like kids. Some of the entourage had even packed their clothes away in their parents' suitcases.

Phil expected Scott to be his host for the tour – after all, it was his homeland. But the Californian had never seen most of these far-out places. The second gig was Louisville, Kentucky, and on the way to the hotel, they passed through the downtown area. There were hustlers hanging out the windows screaming, music blasting from the housing projects, old guys busking a twelve-bar tune on the corner. The band asked the driver to stop the car and they sat there, slurping in the atmosphere. They were acting like uncool tourists – but the Crumlin posse didn't care. Saint Patrick's Day – unbelievably Scott's birthday too – was two nights away, and the green beer was already on tap.

In Chicago, they discovered Rush Street and its blues clubs and felt utterly satisfied. Robbo had just been introduced to tequila and he liked it plenty. So as the house band gave it their best and the punters were clapping and stomping, the guitarist's chair slowly toppled over and they all belly-laughed at the lucky circumstances that had brought them here. The down side of the American trip was noticing the racist attitudes that were practically unchallenged in some parts, and Phil was pulled into that sometimes. But when the locals heard him talk – a black guy with an Irish accent – they declared it was the craziest thing, and the singer swayed many bigots and mistrusters with his Celtic jive.

In New York, Scott decided to treat the boys to a famous deli sandwich. He'd been obliged to chow down on British motorway food for the past year, so he was ready for some decent sustenance. He sat them down and put through an order. Phil looked at the plates suspiciously.

'So what's that?'

'Roast beef on rye.'

'Oh *no*! And what's this other stuff?'

'That's pastrami.'

'*Nooh!*'

'And this is coleslaw and that's potato salad. Want some?'

'*Noooooh!* D'ya reckon they do beans on toast?'

Phil enjoyed his American food after a time, but there was never a question of him getting into the fine wine and foods which many bands investigate to stave off boredom and to get some cultural value from touring. But expensive restaurants were never the Lizzy ideal. Phil was happy with the fundamentals: clubs and women and drinking and smoking dope.

Bachman-Turner Overdrive weren't the hedonist sort. They were a family operation from Winnipeg, Canada, and most of them belonged to the Mormon faith. That meant no tea or coffee, never mind the Bacchanalian lifestyle Thin Lizzy were mustering up. Randy Bachman was appalled at their behaviour, and ordered his boys to keep away from the support band. BTO had topped the American charts with 'You Ain't Seen Nothin' Yet' the previous autumn, after being turned down by twenty-five record companies. Randy Bachman didn't want to squander anything. But the young drummer Robbie, you could tell that he was busting to hang out with these hell-raisers. They practically had to lock him up.

Brian Downey got drunk one night and gatecrashed their hospitality room. He glugged down everything he could find and then fell asleep. When the BTO crew woke him, he got abusive and started calling them 'Morons', which wasn't particularly clever. He later realised he was lucky to get out without a beating. The tempers finally ripped when Lizzy were playing it casual in the dressing-room, not worrying about their on-stage time. They didn't know about the American system of curfews and unions, and when the BTO manager, Steve Allen, walked in, he collared Chris O'Donnell and forcefully explained the rules. Showtime meant precisely that. Following this lesson, Thin Lizzy actually went on early, so they could play more songs and enjoy the vibe and freedom of an 18,000-seater hall.

Normal, Illinois, was the setting for the Star episode. Lizzy were astonished at the manners of the girls they met on tour – upfront and uninhibited. Robbo came across such a person in the Midwest. Phil had sensed a bad scene and warned him off, but the Scotsman brought her back to the hotel room that he shared with Downey. The drummer was watching the Mohammed Ali fight on the television and was annoyed at the disturbance beside him, but Robbo wasn't put off. He'd just discovered why she was called Star. There was a pentangle tattooed around her vagina.

'Put your arse down,' Downey moaned. 'I'm trying to watch the fight.'

There was a different kind of combat going on by the bed. Star had bitten Robbo's tongue. Then she took a lump out of his forehead. There was blood everywhere. Downey took the girl and led her to the door, throwing her clothes after her. Scott came out of his room to see what the ruckus was about. He tried to pacify Star and she bit him as well. So they set her by the balcony, but she was unsteady, and for a terrible moment, it seemed like she was going to fall way down to the pathway below. Fortunately, she collapsed and they all went to bed. They thought nothing of it until the sheriff arrived; Star was accusing Robertson of assault and rape. Chris O'Donnell persuaded him otherwise, suggesting that in fact this woman had harassed an artist who merely wanted to get his much-needed sleep. Robbo couldn't eat hot food for weeks. During photo sessions, he was obliged to comb his hair down over his forehead to hide the teeth marks.

Los Angeles was Phil's town, especially so the myth and the actuality of West Hollywood. He wanted to find the spot where the television show about an LA club, 77 *Sunset Strip*, was filmed, but when he got there, all he saw was a little velour-furnished diner called Dino's. He lunched out at Barney's Beanery, just below The Strip, where Jim Morrison and Janis Joplin used to hang out and play pool. But Phil's ultimate was The Rainbow Bar And Grill on 9015 Sunset Boulevard, just up from the Whisky A Go-Go. That's where all the rockers convened, and Phil was keen to measure himself up to the competition, getting himself known.

He caused a huge commotion there one night. He'd chanced upon Mitch Mitchell and Noel Redding, formerly with The Jimi Hendrix Experience, who were old friends with Chris O'Donnell. So they all sat down together around the little banquette. Since Phil's legs were so long, they suggested he sat in the middle. They were all having a beer, gassing about music – Phil looking great in his red jacket – when they realised they were being watched. This guy was dosed up on Quaaludes and was in a bad way, but he was freaking and pointing in their direction. He looked like he was having a heart attack. It took a while to register what he was shouting about.

'He's alive! I'm telling you! JIMI FUCKIN' HENDRIX!! Over there!!!'

Phil reckoned he could produce the *Fighting* album himself. So many of his past efforts had been damaged by unsympathetic ears, and he felt he'd learnt enough during the *Night Life* sessions to master it. Therefore he hired Keith Harwood, who'd engineered The Rolling Stones and Led Zeppelin, and they played for hours at Olympic Studios in Barnes, London. America had stimulated them to write loads of new songs, and the guitar parts were roaringly sweet.

When they'd supported Bob Seger on tour, they couldn't believe that the Michigan rocker could leave his song 'Rosalie' out of many of the gigs. So they recorded it themselves – a more pacey salute to the record-spinning teen queen. They put it out as a single in June, and many people started to cotton on to this freshly enlivened band. As for his own stuff, Phil wasn't forcing the myth in his songs now; he could write about the hard man and the freedom fighter without the strained posturing of before.

During his visits to Clifton Grange, Phil had become friendly with George Best, his footballing hero. But Best was a more harassed man of late – his soccer playing had deteriorated and his drinking made him a stock feature in the tabloids. The most nasty example of this was when George was accused of theft by Marjorie Wallace, a Miss World with whom he'd had a casual affair. The police arrested him at his Manchester club, Slack Alice, and put him in jail. George's cousin was shot in Belfast during this period and he was in bits. The case was eventually dismissed and the judge exonerated the footballer, but he'd been wrecked by the media attention. Phil wrote 'For Those Who Love To Live' in Bestie's honour, demanding a cooler attitude towards society's stars and mavericks.

Phil's case study for 'Wild One' was the clash in Ireland between the Catholic James II and the new Protestant king, William III, resulting in the surrender of James's army in 1691. The defeated soldiers chose to leave their country and serve abroad under the French king, Louis XIV, becoming known as The Wild Geese. As with many of Phil's songs, he used the story in its loosest sense, but the drama, emotion and Lizzy's crossfire guitar were all in place. It was a folk song for the modern Irish diaspora – a culture that regarded emigration as a fact of life and took homesickness as a given.

Phil hadn't reckoned on the terrible demands of writing, playing, singing, producing and editing the album. While everyone else went home, he was reviewing alternate takes well into the morning. He actually worked for four days without sleep until it was finished, and then he bailed out on holiday. Maybe this fatigue affected his judgement when it came to the shoot for the record sleeve, for which they posed in an alleyway with weapons – a baseball bat, lead piping and knife. They looked silly.

'The most upsetting thing about the *Fighting* album is the cover,' Phil moaned afterwards. 'Because it made us look too punkish, too dumb. I didn't mind being punky, but dumb and punky was too much to take.'

What pleased the Lizzy camp though was the new perception of the band. They'd been viewed by some as a loser act since 'Whisky In The Jar', making critical mistakes and never knowing how to present themselves. But that opinion was being revised. They could now fill The Hammersmith Odeon. The Marquee was a cinch, and even the gigs away from the reach of the music industry like The Winning Post at Twickenham couldn't contain their now rampant audience. That was the other exciting issue – there was a new understanding between the band and their crowd, a groovy, inspiring consensus.

Scott found it hard to put all of these feelings into words. There he was, barrelling around Britain, still very much a foreign country, then jumping on a plane to some frenzied overseas expedition, recording, getting wrecked and all the time copping ideas from mastermind Lynott. So how do you describe the good times, the tumult, the nerves and the accelerated blur of your life? He was speaking to a journalist from *Melody Maker* just before Christmas and he found his line: 'I think this last twelve months has aged me . . . about ten years.'

11

Phil was twenty-six and he was about to meet his father – their first encounter since he was a baby. He was hunkered down in Studio Four of the BBC complex in Maida Vale, preparing some new tracks for a John Peel radio session. Everyone's concentration was shot and nobody really wanted to be around when the meeting happened. The other band members offered to leave – to allow the singer some privacy at such a personal time, but Phil insisted they stay. He didn't want to meet Cecil Parris on his own.

Phil had actually gone out looking for his dad on previous occasions. In 1970, just after his twenty-first birthday, he'd travelled down to London with a couple of friends, including Terry O'Neill. They'd walked along some of the main roads of west London, checking the barber shops, since he'd heard that was his father's profession. Nobody they met had heard of the man. At one stage, they gazed down the main drag, and every shop along there seemed to be a gents' hairdressers. It was like a psychedelic trip, because they were exhausted, disorientated, and the road seemed endless. This was so sadly absurd that they burst out laughing and gave up the search.

Four years later, when the singer had moved to West Hampstead, he persuaded his pal Frank Murray to go out looking with him again. They tried Ladbroke Grove and Portobello Road, to see if there was any sign of him there. Phil's only lead was the fact that his dad's nickname was The Duke – supposedly on account of his good looks, stylish dress sense and a capacity to charm the ladies. But again, there was no recognition in any of the shops they went in. Publicly at least, Phil admired the man – he pretended that Cecil was a Brazilian sailor who'd just shipped out to Rio before he was born, a swashbuckler who wouldn't be tied down. There was no point telling the reporters that you heard he was living around the Shepherd's Bush area and that your mother had met him at a dance.

Phil steered this curiosity into his songs. Lyrics such as 'Little Girl In Bloom' and 'Still In Love With You' imagined the drama of an unplanned pregnancy – how the two people reacted and how they managed to resolve the birth of a child they weren't ready for. When the band released 'Randolph's Tango', Phil was pleased with the cartoon that his friend Tim Booth sketched for the release showing a Latin romancer, who met with Phil's raffish vision of his dad, in full party mode. He even dedicated his first collection of lyrics – *Songs For While I'm Away* – to his father in 1974.

In Lynott's songs, there were two roles to picture: the nurturing, maternal soul and the father who moved on. And so this became a kind of schism in Phil's own personality. He was the boy with endless mother-love, respectful of family and home. He used the images of the farm, the orphanage and Ireland itself to represent a feeling of shelter and belonging. But Phil's other archetype was the vagabond, the cowboy, the carefree Valentino, loyal to none. When the situation got tough for this figure, he just headed out towards the old sundown.

It was *Titbits* magazine that brought father and son together. In its issue dated 22 January 1976, the publication ran a feature on Phil with the headline, 'The Lizzy In A Tizzy About His Dad'. During the interview for this, Phil realised that he'd need to give the paper some fascinating detail or otherwise they wouldn't run the story. This wasn't a rock mag and you really had to sell yourself to get across to a readership hungry for sensation. So Phil opened up a bit about his parentage, talking about Sarah, his grandmother, and his uncommon childhood. He mentioned his dad and how he hadn't seen him since he was four years old, and how he was called The Duke. Even though Phil said his mother rarely spoke about him, as a boy he had learnt that 'I've got most of his looks – he was fairly tall and a good dancer . . . she said he was a good geezer and I should be proud of him.'

Cecil Parris's wife read this story, and brought it to her husband's attention. This was his son in the paper, and she urged him to get in touch. So a few calls were made, and presently Cecil was in the band's management office, wanting to sort out a meeting. Philomena was contacted, and she vouched that he was for real. She wasn't exactly happy about the notion, but she was resigned to it happening. She spoke to Phil and they arranged a date: Maida Vale, 12 February.

When Cecil walked into the studio, everyone tensed up. Inevitably, he didn't look as Phil had imagined him to be. He was wearing a white three-piece suit with wide lapels. He sported a creamy Fedora hat and gold chains. It was a kind of Superfly look, but he didn't quite carry it off. Robbo couldn't help noticing that the sleeves of his jacket were riding up his arms. Nobody said much. It was an awkward scene. Cecil said something about wanting Phil to meet his wife, his daughters and some other family members. But there was no point trying to have a conversation here. Phil invited the guy to step outside for a chat. He returned alone, less than an hour later. He'd got his look, but the recording session fell apart soon after.

It was a bleak moment in an otherwise magnificent season. Lizzy were making their best-ever music now. Just before Christmas, they'd stopped off at a rehearsal place, The Farmyard in Buckinghamshire, to knock the songs into shape. Chris O'Donnell had introduced them to the new producer, John Alcock, an extremely tall man who didn't seem at all intimidated by Phil. He'd been working closely with The Who and then on John Entwhistle's solo albums, while Scott's brother-in-law Bob Benberg was also enthusing about the way he'd handled Supertramp's *Crime of the Century* LP. Early on, Alcock told Phil he was writing too many riffs, and not enough songs. He needed to arrange things more, to give definition to his work. Phil rang the management, enraged.

'Get rid of this guy! I'm not gonna walk into a studio with him. He told me I couldn't write a *song!*'

But the singer eventually saw the sense in the criticism, and in January they started working at Ramport studios in Battersea, London. It was a converted church in a desolate area, and Phil was weirded out by the pulpit that was still intact by the wall. The rest of the band were having fun with the aquarium, chasing the tiger fish around the tank, and playing darts. But they were confident and road-drilled, so soon they were putting down the songs that Phil believed were the makings of a classic record: 'Jailbreak', 'Romeo and The Lonely Girl', 'Emerald' and 'Fight Or Fall'. The latter was another message to Phil's mixed ancestry – a call for the 'brothers' to unite and sort out their poor situations.

Robbo wouldn't be pacified, though, and he was clashing with Alcock, cranking up his amplifier, demanding that the music was strong and rowdy. The guitarist completely refused to play on 'Running Back' – he wanted to record it as a slow blues, like something Little Feat would do. Robbo was playing his piano lines in the studio, suggesting a likely adaptation. But the others settled for a mid-tempo style, with a simple keyboard line played by session man Tim Hinkley. 'It sounds like the Bay City fuckin' Rollers,' Robbo announced before sulking off.

But Phil's imagination was fizzing now. He wanted to give the album a science-fiction theme – influenced by HG Wells's *The War Of The Worlds*, and by related comic-book characters such as Kilraven and Deathlock The Demolisher. He was also working up an idea for the sleeve with his mate Jim Fitzpatrick, to present an evil Overmaster dominating his subjects, with Thin Lizzy busting out of this totalitarian nightmare. Phil wanted the public to appreciate that his boys would never capitulate to The Man.

Part of Lynott's libertarian beliefs involved the freedom to take drugs. Hence the song 'Warriors', with its echoes of Jimi Hendrix's 'Are You Experienced'. That was an international reference, because Phil based the lyrics on the fast-burning lives of the rock and roll dead – people like Hendrix and Duane Allman, drug-users and artists who'd run perilous courses. He felt there was something noble about their decision to wing it high overhead, bringing back freaky reports from what they'd encountered – before they took a burning.

Lynott was always absorbed in the image of the cowboy figure – on 1972's *Shades Of A Blue Orphanage*, he'd remembered his childhood days at the cinema, following the adventures of Roy Rogers and Hopalong Cassidy. And on 'Cowboy Song', Phil put himself into the head of such a loner figure: self-reliant, remorseless, ever-moving. He clearly saw parallels between this lifestyle and his own career, illustrated by a quote afterwards. 'We're a dying breed,' he reckoned. 'All we got is rock and roll and the road. We got no wives, no family, no homes, just this.' With a spooky kind of resonance, Lynott's grave was

111

temporarily marked out with rocks in 1986, just like a cowboy's burial – upstanding headstones being banned from the Irish cemetery where he was placed.

The band's liberal use of minor chords helped to underline the pathos in Phil's lyrics. Most rock groups kept their music straight and upfront – there was no mystery or insecurity in their style. But just as Phil sang the last word of the line 'I am just a cowboy', the guitars picked out a minor chord. It sounded vulnerable and unresolved, just like the guy in the song. This wasn't a complicated idea and most of the Lizzy's writing was bright and accessible, which is why so many beginners start off playing the band's songs in their sets. But it took skill to make these basic ideas swing so brilliantly. That was their special forte in 1976.

'The Boys Are Back In Town' was the capstone of the *Jailbreak* album, a highlight from Thin Lizzy's career, the essence of premium rock and roll. It became a staple with bar bands, karaoke acts and with more famous turns like Bon Jovi and Def Leppard. And as with all good poetry, no one could be sure of the song's origin. Phil was certainly inspired by the comic book hero GI Joe, who returns home from combat to raise hell with his pals. But he was also thinking of Manchester United supporters, and The Quality Street Gang, who frequented his mum's hotel. His friend Frank Murray also recognised the mood which the Crumlin boys would muster just before a return visit to Dublin. They'd make sure to be duded up in their fancy London clothes – real Mickey Dazzlers – ready to sway the old city.

Much of the song's energy related to Phil's discovery of Los Angeles. He was thinking of The Rainbow Bar And Grill as well as Barney's Beanery. He even used the name of Dino's, the sad little place he'd accidentally discovered on Sunset Strip. He pictured a young kid in such a town, watching the return of the old gang – immediately bringing vigour, music and sexual thrills back to the place. The kid runs to tell the news to the pretty girl who used to hang with the gang. She's presently down on her luck – an early lyric had her 'working downtown' – enduring the lecherous attentions of the old men. But the kid realises that she'll soon be reinstated as the boys sweep away the killjoys and dead spirits with their prodigal charge.

Phil knew he'd written a definitive rite of summer, something with universal power. 'Every street gang in the world can relate to "The Boys Are Back In Town",' he figured later. *Rolling Stone* critic Greil Marcus went even further, recognising that this song was pure tribalism, representing a fertility ritual, the renewal of the land and the deposing of the ageing chiefs. He quoted a famous work of comparative anthropology, Sir J G Frazer's *The Golden Bough*, as a pointer to the song's great power. It was deep myth, it sounded ace on the radio and was blazingly great live. The best.

Phil, of course, had been writing story songs since the beginning. One of his models was Van Morrison, who could relate a little happening in his life and spin this out into a beguiling yarn. Van would import the brassy refrains of Stax soul and the call-and-response choruses of gospel music and make the words sound inspirational. He also had the ability to sound Irish without stressing the point – you'd hear it in the lilt, in the riffs and the melodic intervals to his tunes. But Phil wasn't the only one who'd been working this source to his advantage. In 1973, the word went around Dublin that there was a remarkable album out called *The Wild, The Innocent & The E Street Shuffle* by a kid from Asbury Park, New Jersey, called Bruce Springsteen. The Dublin music fans were unanimous: 'He sounds like our Phil. But sure, with a name like that, he'll never get anywhere.'

It was a comparison that would hound both singers through the 1970s. Bruce got so fed up with the name-checking that he ordered up the Thin Lizzy albums. He liked them. Phil was bemused – he knew that they were both Van Morrison fans, that they'd been drinking from the same well. But it was frustrating too. Years later, when Lizzy's management tried to find the multitrack tape for 'The Boys Are Back In Town', they were baffled that it was missing. Finally, they came across a mislabelled box. A waggish engineer from Ramport Studios had written 'Kitty's Back' on the label – suggesting that Phil had been copying ideas from the Springsteen song of 1973.

The two parties actually met by the pool of The Sunset Marquis in Los Angeles. They made eye contact and Phil was about to start singing a Bruce song just for the laugh of it. But Chris O'Donnell checked him: 'Sing him one of your songs, Phil.' So that's what he did, and then Springsteen came over. 'I've always wanted to meet you,' Bruce gushed.

*

One of John Alcock's specialities was creating a sound that excited music fans in both America and the UK. This trans-atlantic savvy was evident enough at the recording stage, but everyone who'd been working on the record had heard the songs so many times that they'd become deadened to their effect. It was only when the management took the finished master – with the tracks sequenced up – to Chicago that they realised they were in possession of a glorious album. Every time they spooled out the tapes at a boardroom playback, the Americans were in raptures. It got better every time you listened and there was something about hearing it on this continent that made so much more sense. For O'Donnell and Morrison, it was a revelation.

San Francisco DJs picked up on 'The Boys Are Back In Town' first, blasting it out relentlessly on the FM shows throughout the spring as the Bay area wowed to its power. Soon it was lighting up stations across America, and when the band arrived for a tour in April, they realised that finally they had their hit record. The tour was due to last six weeks, but promoters were calling back – bumping up prices, urging the band to stay out and enjoy the massive status that was looming. The asking price for Lizzy went from $500 to $10,000 per show. The single was number twelve in the charts as they rushed the continent, piggy-backing tours – playing with Aerosmith, The Tubes, Be Bop Deluxe, ZZ Top, REO Speedwagon, Styx and Rush – outclassing many of the soft-rock headliners.

In May, Chris O'Donnell was walking along Sunset Strip, exhausted by the demands of this new situation. The money still wasn't coming in fast enough to cover the band's debts. Somebody had stolen Phil's bass after a gig at the Santa Monica Civic, so he had to get a loan from Mercury Records to buy a replacement. Just then, he noticed an uncomfortable sensation in his foot. He'd worn a hole right through his shoe, and didn't have the cash to buy another pair. So he sat in a heel bar while it was patched, figuring out the next stage of this extended tour, anxious that the UK record company could match the euphoria that was surrounding them stateside.

Back at The Sunset Marquis, Phil was celebrating in his own style. The band motto had been established and lived out: 'If it's fun, it's done.' At one stage, the band's sound engineer, Pete Eustace, turned to Lynott and asked him how he was. The singer

114

replied that he'd been up for four days straight and that he felt fine. Peter eyed him over. He still looked fantastic. This was Phil's moment, and there was no point squandering it on something as trivial as sleep.

When he did take to his room, he had another agenda. His bedroom was party central, overlooking the pool. As the others lounged by the water below, sipping cocktails and enjoying the life, they noticed a string of beautiful girls leaving by the entrance near Phil's place. Each one walked off with a signed copy of *Jailbreak* under her arm, looking happy. After several hours of this, the curtains opened and Phil peered out: 'Hey, guys, c'mon up!'

His room was like a war zone. Beer bottles and room service meals on the floor. Lipstick and sweaty clothes. Unclean bedsheets and the overpowering funk of sex. He laughed as they viewed the scene. 'Well . . . it's the lifestyle.' A visiting friend noticed a box of Lizzy albums in the corner and asked if he could have one. Phil nodded and started unzipping his flies, making like he was pulling his jeans down. 'All right – but you know I gorra do this first,' as he suggested how previous visitors to his room had earned their free albums. Everyone just fell about the place . . .

By the start of June, though, Phil started complaining of tiredness. Whenever he came off stage, the sweat was literally pooling around his feet. This wasn't normal, and the band suggested that he should temper his lifestyle. But Phil hammered on, showing his face at The Rainbow Bar And Grill with Scott and cornering Richie Blackmore. The former Deep Purple guitarist had tried to steal Phil for one of his own projects in 1972, but he'd since become famous with his own band, co-incidentally called Rainbow. Now here was Phil telling him that Lizzy were going to totally destroy his band on the upcoming tour they were sharing.

Richie was getting unsettled – he was starting to consider such a possibility. It was like Mohammed Ali gearing up for a big championship, messing with the opponent's head before the fight even started. Another regular to the club, Led Zeppelin's John Bonham, was watching this with approval, roaring with laughter that the challenger should have so much front.

The tour with Blackmore's Rainbow was due to start on 8 June, at Columbus, Ohio. The opening night was looking problematic from the start, since there was a power cut in town, and the hotel was lit by candlelight. The venue organised a generator, thus saving the concert. But when Chris O'Donnell called Phil, the singer sounded awful. When the manager went up to his room, he noticed that his friend had turned a livid shade of yellow. Even his eyes were banana-coloured. He could hardly get out of bed, but still was insisting that the gig should continue. Chris took him to the hospital and learnt that Phil had infectious hepatitis and should be quarantined straight away.

O'Donnell felt he couldn't leave him in America, away from people who could really care for him. So he smuggled Phil out of the ward on to a series of flights: Columbus to New York, New York to London, London to Manchester. Then he travelled to the venue to break the news to everyone. He had one last piece of brinkmanship to execute. Rainbow had promised the best of tour facilities to Lizzy during an earlier production meeting in New York. Now it seemed that the headliners had reneged on much of the deal. This of course was irrelevant, since Phil was sick, but Chris got his say anyhow. He told the Rainbow people that if his band didn't get all that was promised, he'd pull out of the tour. They laughed at him, daring him to execute the bluff. He walked out of the office, leaving them in utter panic.

The remainder of the party flew back to Heathrow. It was a beautiful June day when they arrived. 'The Boys Are Back In Town' was hitting in the UK charts now – on its way to number eight – and as they drove down the M4, they listened to Radio 1's Johnny Walker cueing it up. It was massively satisfying, their 'tee-hee' moment, when they realised they had made an impression everywhere. Chris O'Donnell got dropped off at his parents' house, where he sat in the garden eating cornflakes and strawberries – a custom he'd learnt in America. The record seemed to be on the radio every half-hour, the soundtrack to the greatest heatwave anyone could remember.

At the office on the Monday morning, they learnt of the fortunes of the *Jailbreak* album. That was doing fantastically well too as it reached number ten in the UK charts, and would eventually feature in the bestsellers for fifty weeks. In America, it would reach number eighteen. O'Donnell felt like throwing himself out of the window. He'd never felt such a charge of emotions. Everything was coming together, he thought, and he couldn't contain the feelings. After years of crap and people telling you that you're wrong, now you felt vindicated. You'd suppressed all of the criticisms in the past and held on by a sense of naïvety. You never argued the point, you just moved on. Then you have this semblance of success and you become even more aware of the backbiters and critics who bothered you in the past. It struck O'Donnell in waves . . . *so that's what he was saying . . . that's what they meant . . . what the fuck did he know?*

Back in Manchester, Phyllis had the chance to look after her boy. She nagged him at the hospital for three weeks about his unhealthy ways, his eating habits, the terrible state of his teeth. He lay there, defenceless, obliged to listen. The singer wasn't to drink alcohol for at least a year as his liver was severely damaged and any misbehaviour might kill him. But Phil recovered quickly, he didn't want to lose the momentum of the chase. He'd brought an acoustic guitar into the hospital and he started writing songs. He was more driven than ever. By 11 July, he was back on stage, playing a thank-you gig to the fans at The Hammersmith Odeon.

Some of his new songs had a more philosophical drift. The song 'Massacre' had been prompted by a hospital visit from a Protestant clergyman. He was a nice guy, but Phil's Catholic upbringing made him defensive and uptight towards the reverend. Later, Phil realised he had been stupid, and so wrote a lyric that condemned religious prejudice and holy wars. Meanwhile, 'Fool's Gold' was Phil's take on the Irish potato famine, the period 1845–9 when a million died of starvation and as many emigrated. Phil followed the story west to imagine the prospectors and frontiersmen making a life of it in the New World.

In August, they began recording the *Johnny The Fox* album at the Musicland Studios in Munich, living in the Arabella Hotel above the complex, excited that David Bowie had also chosen to work there. But while Bowie and his producer, Brian Eno, managed to evoke a spacious, modern sound, Thin Lizzy were continually frustrated. They'd spend hours in the basement room getting Downey's drum sound the way they wanted, and then return the following day to find that everything had deteriorated. John Alcock hated the recording console and the monitor speakers, and was having many difficulties with Robbo. Alcock's style involved sitting in the control room, smoking cigars, letting the engineer work the desk. He was a director more than a technician – he constantly gave out orders, which was intolerable for a twenty-one-year-old Scotsman with a gutful of whisky.

It got to the stage that Robbo wouldn't even listen to the playback of his solos, many of which were his best ever, and ten years later would be sampled as breaks by the emergent hip-hop culture. But his attitude was trying. Phil was enraged by this, and he started talking about chucking him out of the band. They decided to go back to Ramport Studios in south London. As they packed up, Alcock noticed that the oxide was falling off the tape – everything they'd done in Germany was literally falling apart. The big man was losing his composure, and in the cab back from Heathrow he was ranting about his many problems to Brian Downey. The drummer told him to shut up. There were too many drama queens in this outfit already.

Downey was more valuable than ever in this second session. 'Don't Believe A Word' was originally written as a slow blues, but didn't sound ideal. In the studio, Brian suggested a more vibrant beat. The two guitarists then piled in as Phil outlined his most jarring lyric thus far. He was confessing to the public that his charm and romantic ways were perhaps a screen for lust and manipulation. It was a hit record, reaching number twelve in the UK charts, but the untouchable sound of the track actually masked a terribly sad idea. Phil had spent a dozen years rooting for success, but now he had his moment, he recognised the ruthless side of the man who'd gotten this far. And this same impulse couldn't resist a swagger as he told the tale. While later songs were often sensitive and self-critical, Phil chose to balance this out with his laddish demeanour. From this point onwards, it was more revealing to trust the song and not the singer.

Johnny The Fox was Phil's most personal character: his senses ever wired, mistrustful and resourceful, keeping to the dark side of the street. In the title track, he meets Jimmy The Weed – a character based on a gangland figure Phil knew from his mother's hotel in Manchester. Johnny prevails on his instincts, but as the drummer and guitarists take up an exemplary, riffing funk, the singer recognises that the victory is inconclusive, the hustle unending.

Lizzy's seventh album – and their second of 1976 – was proof of the band's resilience in a fearsome year. But the tone and the energy of the record were better than the actual songs, bar the occasional bonus like Robbo's ballad-writing abilities on 'Borderline'. Not even Phil could manage his best when he was always checking out skid row, surviving on the lam.

The only consolation Phil got from his hepatitis was that he didn't have to share his spliffs with anyone. So he'd get slowly stoned while the after-show parties raged on the autumn tour, watching the debauchery with interest. Next day, he'd meet everyone in reception, salute the hungover entourage and then relate to them all – in wicked detail – just what they said and did, and to whom, on the previous night. It was a mean habit. People couldn't wait until he'd start drinking again, which he did when his year was up. For a time he'd only sip white wine and champagne – he said it was less harmful to his innards, but the cynics in the crew figured it was an affectation.

The support act on that tour was Clover, a country-rock band with a vocalist called Huey Lewis. Phil coached him through the dates – demonstrating the dynamics of a good set-list, how to work your audience best, and even how to survive the politics of leading a band. One Clover song involved a dance called the Chicken Strut – and Phil would come on stage during this tune and do his best funky routines, which was a very generous thing to do. He'd also bring Huey up for the Lizzy song 'Baby Drives Me Crazy', and let him play mouth harp. Huey would take a solo and watch the crowd go mad. He'd look at Phil to see if he could do even more, and sometimes he got that indulgence too. But it was so addictive that they practically had to haul him away from the mike some nights.

They also had a dog on board for the tour. Derek was a three-foot-long, floppy-eared beagle with sad eyes and a seen-it-all smile. Robbo bought him at a petrol station on a German autobahn, and now they were inseparable. It was a total ploy to attract more women. The guitarist thought he might look cute with his stuffed dog in one arm and a bottle of Johnny Walker Black Label in the other. 'But Christ,' he'd say, 'you have to have some kind of a gimmick to compete with Lynott.'

If anyone saw a girl at a club holding Derek, that meant she was spoken for, and nobody should talk to her unless they wanted to get battered. It was such a successful system that Derek became a good-luck charm – an over-sized rabbit's foot. Robbo would even bring the dog on stage with him, and sometimes Phil would give him a credit at the end of the show: 'On guitar, from Glasgow, Scotland . . . Brian Robertson! And all the way from Germany . . . Derek the Dog!'

Robbo's other indulgence was a flash Cadillac with a Scottish flag billowing from the aerial. He'd be gunning through the streets of London in this machine with his pal Charlie McLennan, scaring the natives and hunting out havoc. They used to throw the car up on the pavement whenever they stopped anywhere. The cops never booked them – they were only too happy to know of their whereabouts. Since Thin Lizzy were rock stars now, a whole new aspect of the capital was opening up. They'd be welcomed into The Speakeasy, where all the big acts socialised, or maybe they'd try La Chasse in Wardour Street, an exclusive little *boîte* where the rock fraternity would throw tenners into the kitty and Frank the boss would set them up with chilled champagne and vodka. But on 23 November 1976, Robbo's destination was The Speak.

The next day Lizzy were scheduled to fly back to the States on a three-week tour, compensating for the emergency cancellation in June. Many people reckoned these were the critical dates, giving Lizzy the opportunity to move up on to that elusive next level to rival bands like Led Zeppelin and The Who for the attentions of the American youth. Already they'd shamed Rod Stewart during his TV show, *A Night On The Town*, in October. He'd chosen to mime, and the LWT director suggested that Lizzy do likewise, since their great volume was shaking the cameras. But the band just turned the speakers round to face themselves, and virtually hijacked the programme, causing a big rush of ticket orders for their three November shows at The Hammersmith Odeon. Rod later told the band he'd been so excited by their performance that he started playing with a regular group again soon after.

Robbo was planning to behave on his night out – he wanted to grab some nosh and say goodbye to a few of his mates. He wasn't

THE BALLAD OF THE THIN MAN

even drinking heavily – just a few whiskies – but when he got to The Speak, he noticed that his mate Frankie Miller was fighting drunk. Robbo got on stage and jammed a bit with the reggae band Gonzales and, unfortunately, Miller followed him up, singing badly and making a scene in front of the crowd. Afterwards, the guitarist from Gonzales wanted to punish Frankie, and lashed out with a bottle. But Robbo put his hand out and caught the blow instead. His skin was slashed, an artery was cut and his guitar-playing tendons were damaged.

Lizzy's perilous year finished in busted glass, disappointment and blood.

12

The producer Tony Visconti took a sharp blade and expertly sliced the tape, keeping his hands clear of the shiny magnetic coating. He turned the aluminium reel clockwise and cut again. He pulled the surplus piece of tape out of the way and then spliced the two loose ends up. He pressed the rewind button, and there was a high-speed babble of music playing backwards.

He started the tape to check this latest edit. Poppy, jazz music brightened up the studio. A finger-snapping accompaniment, a simple but catchy bass riff, a sax player shadowing the chorus line.

'Daaaancin' in the moonlight . . . on this looouhhhng hot summer night . . .'

Phil was smiling, finally happy. Visconti was relieved. Once again, the producer cursed himself for letting Thin Lizzy know about his recording technique with David Bowie. He'd told them how he liked to catch the spontaneous flow of an artist, so he'd record everything – the early experiments, the ad-libs, even the parts that sounded like mistakes. Sometimes these loose ideas actually told you more about the singer's subconscious thoughts than any tightly crafted material.

Therefore, with Bowie, the producer had allowed him to free-associate around a theme that he'd already been working at. Then the pair of them would go over the tape, snipping out lines and words that definitely didn't work. They could edit new phrases into a song, turning chaos into a tidy artefact. By the time Visconti had finished, the track would sound clean and stunning – as if everyone had known what their intentions had been from the start.

But Phil took this process to extremes. He'd spark up a spliff and start singing. Often he was disjointed and incoherent, and

Tony would do his best to make sense of it. When he'd eventually given a shape to the song, Phil would change his mind and decide he wanted to revise the entire lyric. The producer would groan every time Phil did this to him. It was like taking a punch in the stomach.

'Dancing In The Moonlight' had been worth the trouble though. Occasionally, there was a feeling that Thin Lizzy's style had become land-locked – that they couldn't record anything that the band's rocker audience wouldn't appreciate. Also, Phil had a tendency to try the same idea twice, which explained the similarity between 'Emerald' and 'Massacre', between a new tune, 'Killer Without A Cause', and 'Rocky' off the previous album. But 'Moonlight' blew all of those limitations away.

This was Phil's most obvious tribute to countryman Van Morrison – a swooning variation on the latter's 1970 track 'Moondance'. Both singers liked the feeling of romance under the stars, senses over-brimming, the enchantment of a girl. And critically, they were both fans of Frank Sinatra, hence the jazzy lilt to their performances. While Van set his magical scene in October, Phil chose the heat of summer for his action and made the object of his desire a seductive, experienced woman. It was the same situation he'd tried to evoke on the 'New Day' track, six years earlier, but now he'd mastered it.

The line 'I always get chocolate stains on my pants', describes what actually happened when Phil went to see a screening of Martin Scorsese's *Mean Streets* and had an accident with a box of Maltesers. Only Phil could make something as mundane as this sound sexy and strange. On a more significant note, the fledgeling U2 would rehearse 'Dancing In The Moonlight' shortly after its release, making this song a meeting point for three generations of Celtic soul swingers.

Phil struck up a relationship with Van – they'd been introduced by tour manager Frank Murray at a *Midnight Special* TV show in Los Angeles. Van was jamming with blues guitarist Elvin Bishop, and for some reason he asked to speak to Frank, who asked Lynott to come along with him. Phil nearly collapsed at the thought, but they spoke for half an hour, and on future trips to America he would meet Morrison for coffee at the Howard Johnson motel near his home in Sausalito, just over the bridge from San Francisco. Van would even play him acetates of his new recordings, like the *Into The Music* album, which was glorious.

Frank used this crucial introduction in his ribbing games with the singer. He knew he could always better any of Phil's claims now.

'Hey, Phil, who got you into Frank Zappa and "Freak Out"? I did, didn't I?'

'Yeah, Frank, but who turned you on to John Mayall And The Blues Breakers? That was me – right?'

'Never mind that. Who introduced you to Van Morrison? You can't beat that, can you?'

Another player who needed to find his best in the studio was Scott Gorham. He was probably the least egotistical guitarist to play in Thin Lizzy, but now that Robbo was away, he was overdubbing the harmonies himself, layering the noise, working at two jobs. At first he felt he couldn't do it, but Phil pumped up his confidence. By the time they'd got halfway through, Scott realised that he could do anything he wanted to do.

They were working abroad at the Toronto Sounds Interchange studio – hoping to avoid paying so much of the UK tax bill that was now an unwelcome part of the band's success. Phil was flush enough to buy himself a place in London – part of Embassy House, at the corner of West End Lane and Cleve Road in West Hampstead. But if they weren't careful, much of their revenue would be gone. By making the record in a foreign country, they could circumvent a few of the demands.

June 1977 was a fitting time to make an album called *Bad Reputation* in Canada. Phil had embraced the title when a journalist asked him about the band's notoriety. But the authorities in this part of the world were less taken by rock and roll excess. The Mounted Police had arrested the Rolling Stones' guitarist Keith Richards at a Toronto hotel in February after finding him with twenty-two grams of heroin and a smaller amount of cocaine. The legal wranglings would continue for a year and a half, as the music community wondered if he'd go down. Keith eventually got off with a suspended sentence, but the deterrent was still a powerful one.

Thin Lizzy spent their free time walking around the bohemian area of Yorkville, noticing that the punk spirit which had enlivened England the previous summer was now an international force. Phil liked this idea – for years he'd been telling the press that a fresh rock and roll generation needed its say. So he'd socialise with this new breed in local clubs like the Crash 'n' Burn and Larry's Hideaway. The band would get drunk and play on these stages for free, bringing many of their new friends back to the hotel for parties. Downey used to say that the Toronto hangovers were among the worst in the world. Occasionally, Phil would get heavy with any dissenters, and he actually cracked the jaw of a guy who'd bad-mouthed the Irish.

Phil returned to patriotic themes on the record. On 'Soldier Of Fortune', he was playing a mercenary, back from the conflict. He put in oblique references to the pipes of 'Danny Boy' and the Irish National Anthem, 'The Soldier's Song', as Visconti welled up the melodrama, and Downey, partitioned off in the studio behind Perspex screens, played a martial beat on his snare drum.

'Opium Trail' was inspired by a television drama about Oriental triads and the passage of heroin to the west. This subject matter became a worrying obsession with Phil – critics were already alarmed at his romantic take on the story. The advance of the punk style was evidenced on the superbad riffola of the title track and on 'Killer Without A Cause'. So too was the use of stencilled lettering on the cover. Another curious detail about the front sleeve was that no mention was made of the return of Brian Robertson.

Phil was adamant that the fiery Scotsman wouldn't play with the band again. His behaviour in 1976 was unforgivable, the singer insisted. But Scott wanted to get the Famous Four together again. He was already thinking about the upcoming tours and how they'd need another player to reflect the sound of the new record. He kept hammering at his plan.

'C'mon, Phil, don't break the magic circle.'

'No way!'

'Let's give him another shot right off the bat. His attitude's better now.'

'I'm not fucking having it!'

But Scott put up a good case, and they called up Robbo, asking him to add some guitar to the record. He was more humbled now – after leaving Lizzy with his busted hand, he'd convalesced, upset that any time he played guitar after the accident, the stitches would pull open, setting his recovery back. Luckily, his tendons weren't as badly damaged as the doctor had originally thought, and soon he was forming his own band, Wild Horses, with Jimmy Bain, the former bass player from Rainbow. Robbo had financed that project himself, and it had cost plenty, with little now to show for it. So he agreed to Scott's plan, with the proviso that the two Chrises signed up Jimmy Bain for a management contract.

At Toronto airport, Robbo came to appreciate the civic hospitality. He was just about to pass through Customs – he could actually see his old roadie pal Charlie McLennan waiting for him on the other side – when the cops pulled him over. They searched everything, holding him there for hours. They even wanted to examine his orifices to see if he'd hidden any drugs about his person. Robbo was angry; it was like he was a marked man. *How do they know I'm a mate of Keith Richards?* he kept thinking.

Most of the tracks were finished, but he put his piercing tones over several songs, notably on 'That Woman's Gonna Break Your Heart'. But for political reasons, Robbo's name was left off the cover. He was acknowledged on the gatefold sleeve with a less prominent photo of the reformed four-piece, taken on the steps of a brownstone in New York's Greenwich Village. On 20 July – three days before the release of the double-A-side single 'Bad Reputation'/'Dancing In The Moonlight' – the band issued a press release to say that Robertson was back in the gang, although Phil stressed that he was only a 'guest'.

There was a new sense of importance about the band now. Phil would check out of hotels if the beds weren't big enough. They had baggage handlers and a far more expensive operation. This was the result of the band's three-month tour of America in the spring of 1977, supporting Queen.

Phil had watched the extravagant style of Freddie Mercury's band, and he liked it. He never wanted to travel on the cheap again. He liked being seen in the limos, or swishing effortlessly through airports and the best hotel lobbies. The two Chrises would sometimes freak at the bills that were coming in, but the singer didn't care. He also enjoyed sharing his new status with friends and family – bringing his mum and her partner, Dennis, on the road for holidays, taking pleasure from their obvious excitement.

They had played well on that tour, to the extent that Queen began to shorten the support act's time on stage, and even played classical music between the sets – some Chopin to temper the fever of the fans, and to wipe away the memory of Phil's powerful act. One day, the Lizzy people had been hanging out backstage when they saw Queen drummer Roger Taylor crumpling a paper in disgust. He'd just read an American review that praised Lynott and his roaring music, much preferring it to anything Queen played.

Gary Moore had replaced the injured Robbo for that tour, putting in a bravura spell from January to March, before returning to Colosseum II. People used to joke about his dramatic entrances and exits from the Lizzy camp, saving the band's short-term prospects, but often leaving them in disarray. Rather ambivalently, they called him 'Super Sub', appreciating that he'd probably be called back off the bench before long.

Scott used to say that Thin Lizzy was 'the fightinest band'; just to survive with these people, you had to be handy with your mitts. Whenever they hired any road crew, the critical questions were: 'Can you change strings?', 'How much do you normally get paid?' and 'Can you fight?' Almost everywhere they went, there was the possibility of violence. Phil was intolerant of any jokes about blacks or Irish, so that was an obvious flashpoint. Also, the band's interaction with the women of any town ensured that there were always disgruntled locals who wanted to take a swing at them. The volatile effect of drugs and alcohol made life even more perilous.

So although Robbo had told people he was a reformed man, the summer tour beginning in August was unlikely to pass quietly. But no one had anticipated the damage that would happen in Finland. It was the night before the Turku Festival by the south-west shoreline, and the band were hanging around the club at the side of the hotel. The local lumberjacks were incensed that they were talking to the girls from town, and so started pulling people's chairs away when the band went to the toilet, revving up for a fight.

They were picking on the sound engineer, Pete Eustace, who was a hippie vegetarian who wouldn't harm anyone. Finally the Lizzy truck driver, John Rivet, intervened and punched a trouble-maker. Frank Murray, tour manager, tried to stop a massive fight, but John whacked the guy again. A Finnish hardliner tried to smash a chair over Robbo's back as the ruck spread from the disco, through the hall, past the elevator and into the lobby. A crew member, Bill Cayley, took a shocking kick in the crotch – the worst anyone had ever seen. He died some years later of testicular cancer, and his old friends would wonder if his fate was possibly due to that terrible night.

Robbo took about five punches to the face. He finally resolved to beat off these monsters by hurling a table at them. But he didn't realise that the base was made of marble, so he was caught in the helpless position of struggling with this dead weight, both his arms out of action. They battered him plenty. Then the police came, and they took John Rivet away, dragging him over the gravel of the car park, leaving his face raw, and his back lacerated. When Lizzy got him back the next morning, he was so beaten up that he couldn't drive the truck.

Phil and Scott had missed all of this. They were having a smoke in a bedroom upstairs when Robbo arrived, bleeding and protesting, his shirt hanging off his back. They were so stoned that it took a while to understand the Scotsman.

'We got our asses kicked,' Robbo finally explained. 'Here, give us a smoke o' that.'

He was soon numb to the pain and indignity. 'Actually, it was just a wee skirmish. And you should have seen the punch I got on that guy.'

He smoked some more, and the evening's adventures took on a considerably brighter look. 'Yeah, we showed them all right.'

Phil and Scott looked at each other and smiled.

Robbo's body was sore to his bones for the next few dates. The band was starting the shows with 'Soldier Of Fortune', and he was responsible for the opening keyboard chords before resuming his guitar playing. But his hands had been stomped on, and he could barely move. Even though the fight hadn't been his fault, Robbo was blamed for much of the trouble.

Still, Lizzy played on through August, to the homecoming show at Dalymount Park in Dublin, followed by a Saturday night gig at the Reading Festival – cheering the multitudes but ready to head back over to America with Graham Parker And The Rumour, still hoping to make a critical impact over there. This was a sore point. Many UK rock acts signed to Mercury Records had made little impression in America, and some parties felt especially bitter. The Graham Parker song 'Mercury Poisoning' was not unrelated to this problem.

The reviews for the *Bad Reputation* album marked a change in the band's perception in the UK. Until this point, they had enjoyed three years of growing praise. 'The Boys Are Back In Town' had topped the readers' and critics' chart in the *New Musical Express* Christmas polls of 1976 – above newcomers like The Sex Pistols and Eddie And The Hot Rods. But by 1977, some aspects of Lizzy's work were being questioned.

The rock papers were becoming spiky and brattish, just like the new music. Punks had scorned the idea of the love song – romance had no place in their brutal agenda. Patriotism was also rubbished with the Pistols' 'God Save The Queen'. So too were machismo and sexism – many female acts such as Siouxsie Sioux and Patti Smith were trashing the stereotype of the submissive female. Very quickly, the term 'chick' – a favourite Lynott word – was outdated in hip conversation. This drift was evident in the reviews for *Bad Reputation*. Songs like 'Dear Lord', with its sobbing religiosity and the multi-tracked vocals of Visconti's wife, Mary Hopkin, were laughed out of court.

Lizzy still had a mass of loyal fans who didn't care for musical trends, so there was no immediate threat to their popularity, and thus *Bad Reputation* reached number four in the UK charts in October 1977. And besides, Phil was becoming friends with people like The Boomtown Rats – it was actually the Lizzy management who had set up Geldof with his record company. Eventually, Phil would play with members of The Damned and record with some of The Sex Pistols. None of these people disputed his streetwise credentials. And even though The Clash seemed more political and right-on than Lizzy, they'd reflect a similar energy and would borrow the same gangland imagery in many of their best songs.

But the new irreverence bothered Lynott, and he was involved in a famous brawl at the Reading Festival with a *Melody Maker* journalist who'd slagged him off. He became less playful in his interviews, and toned down the references to his womanising. His best response was to play well, and at this stage the band was still peaking. Adding some of the extra new songs to the set gave them a peerless range of tunes – and a lot

of them actually sounded better now than on the old records.

With this in mind, Lizzy began to record the live shows, working on the principle that few bands could better them in performance. In 1975, the British guitarist Peter Frampton had released a double album, *Frampton Comes Alive!*, recorded at Winterland in San Francisco. The record sold phenomenally well throughout the following year, quickly passing the 8-million mark. Whenever Lizzy heard the tracks on the radio, they'd sneer. 'It doesn't warrant that,' Scott reckoned. 'We could top it, easy.'

Sure enough, the flat monitor mixes they heard of their own shows were remarkable. You could hear Phil working the crowd, throwing in his ad-libs and much-practised lines. Songs like 'Rosalie' and 'Cowboy Song' had come so far down the road now that they were like different compositions. Tony Visconti was listening through the tapes – from Toronto's Seneca College Fieldhouse or Philadelphia's Tower Theater, and especially from the Hammersmith shows at the end of 1976 – and he was elated. You could really do something unique with this, he reckoned. A classic double album.

That was the reason they'd become involved with Tony in the first place. Chris O'Donnell had read an interview with him in a magazine, when he'd talked about bands not bringing out their commercial potential. He'd actually cited Thin Lizzy as an example. Now here he was telling them that they had an album on their hands that could live for ever. All he needed to do was to give the record some cohesion, enhance the excitement that was so obviously in there anyway, and to tidy up a few of the gaffes that were unavoidable in a live context.

This approach needed some extra work back at the studio, fixing bum notes and amending the backing vocals. Scott and Robbo were so adrenalised during these gigs that they'd be running up to the mike stands and screaming uncontrollably, then running back to play guitar. The Hammersmith gigs were the most exciting of all, and they formed the bulk of the emergent album, though again it was prudent tax-wise to say that the band had recorded a good percentage of it overseas.

For the 'Dancing In The Moonlight' track, Visconti would take a lead break from one show and drop it into a performance from another night. He snipped out a chunk of Scott's solo on 'Still In

Love With You' because there was a mistake – a 'clam' – in the passage. But he was also happy to leave ragged parts in the likes of 'Cowboy Song' just for the sake of the ambience.

The album was mixed in the spring of 1978, and the management began assembling photos by the band's photographer friend Chalkie Davies. They decided to fill the centre of the gatefold sleeve with a montage of shots – reflecting the colour and vim of their shows. But there was one of Phil's photos there, too. It was a still-life of a tray resting on the mixing desk of The Maison Rouge mobile studio. On the tray were some white powder, a razor blade, a straw and a rolled-up banknote. Everyone thought it was stupid to advertise the band's drug use thus. But Phil insisted. It was his little way of showing off.

Lynott's fondness for the white lines didn't always manifest itself in such a glamorous way. During the forty-date American tour that started in September 1977, Phil had begun to binge on uppers and powders, staying awake until five in the morning, then taking pills to help him sleep. When he got his wake-up call a few hours later, he was tetchy and unpleasant and raged at the crew and band members, using any excuse to vent his foul mood. They'd give him a pill to calm down and the cycle would start again.

The support act for this tour was Graham Parker And The Rumour, who actually out-played them on some shows, most painfully at The New York Palladium. Suddenly, the support band lost some of their privileges – sufficient time to sound-check, and full use of the headliners' equipment. It was a replay of the situation between Thin Lizzy and Queen earlier in the year, only Phil was on the defensive now, and it was a little sad to watch him getting imperious like Freddie Mercury. Anybody who questioned the singer's behaviour would be slammed down. 'Don't shit on my parade,' he'd say.

Frank Murray was unhappy with this. He'd known the singer since the days of The Black Eagles, and they'd had many fine times together. Phil had even been best man at his wedding, and later his wife, Ferga, had designed a lot of the Celtic motifs on the band's customised shirts. But now Frank could either choose to endure the tantrums and messy behaviour – to become a yes man, effectively – or confront his old friend about his dissolute ways. The latter option would mean leaving the organisation. Frank spoke his mind and then got out.

Even so, Phil could still be generous with his help and experience. After returning from America, Lizzy toured the UK with the Dublin punk band Radiators From Space. Lizzy had picked this band themselves, because they'd had some bad luck at home. They'd been banned from Dublin gigs after a nineteen-year-old student, Patrick Coulty, had been fatally stabbed at a Radiators' show in Dublin University's Belfield Campus, on 25 June 1977. They couldn't get any more work in Ireland, so they moved to London, where they were signed to Ted Carroll's Chiswick label.

The Radiators weren't sure if they should accept the Lizzy tour – they felt that their real constituency was in scuzzy clubs like The Vortex, The Red Cow and The Roxy. But they accepted anyway, and before long they'd played in front of many thousands of people and had learnt much about playing live – something that was denied to a lot of punk acts.

Yet the group was upset that they were getting bad sound mixes and weren't allowed to sound-check as much as they wanted. Singer Philip Chevron eventually mentioned this to the headliners, and the next afternoon Lynott personally looked after their needs, standing by the mixing desk, doing his best to see them right. This was far more than they'd hoped for.

Near the end of the tour, Chevron met Phil in a backstage toilet, having a pee. The two bands hadn't socialised so much, since the Radiators could only afford to stay in bed-and-breakfast places after the shows, but the two Dubliners said hello. Both men were a little frazzled – the Radiators hadn't been used to the plentiful stimulants that were on offer, and they'd all gone slightly mad. But Lynott was kind and positive, and he offered his junior some sound advice.

This was a special moment for Chevron. He'd actually been in the audience when Thin Lizzy had played 'Whisky In The Jar' on the Irish pop programme *Like Now* back in 1972. Now here he was, party to a one-on-one coaching session with the man. And Lynott started telling him great things – profound observations about music and how to live your life. At least, that's how it felt to Chevron at the time. His thoughts registered deep in Chevron's psyche, affecting his attitudes towards the world from that moment on. Which was just as well, because when he woke up in a daze the next morning, his conscious mind was a total blank. Lynott's wisdom had somehow bypassed the new-boy's memory faculty. Chevron couldn't actually remember a single word of the conversation. Damn!

13

Robbo was so angry with the situation around him that he pulled a white clog off his foot, turned the carved sole outwards, and swung out. He connected with the head of Sid Vicious, and the almighty *thock* of wood striking bone filled the tiny cabin. Then he sat down on one of the long couches. Sid fell on top of him, his head in Robertson's lap, weeping uncontrollably.

Nancy Spungen was disgusted at the pitiful scene, and she started calling her boyfriend a wimp. Wasn't this the Sex Pistol who'd chain-whipped journalists and glassed his enemies – who'd hacked himself up and took bad drugs and was an icon for disaffected youth? Why was he letting himself down now?

'C'mon, Sid, you gotta *do* something!'

But Sid was all in, and he just cried some more. Robbo was now comforting him, telling him it was all right, stroking his injured, spiky head, thinking, *You're a big softie. You're living the dream and it's not working out.*

Robbo had been off for some Mexican food with his girlfriend, Lita Ford – the Runaways guitarist who was living and recording on a Chelsea houseboat. They'd met up with Jimmy Bain and Kenny Jones, the old Small Faces drummer, and their partners. They'd come back to the boat in a great mood, but when they saw Sid and Nancy already making themselves at home there, the atmosphere turned nasty.

Kenny Jones was irate because a few weeks before, Sid had bottled his guitarist friend Jimmy McCullogh in the face. He wanted revenge and said he was gonna kill the punk – but Robbo persuaded him to go home instead. But as the evening continued, even he got extremely annoyed. Sid was behaving like an asshole, slagging off Thin Lizzy and Phil. He started staggering around the cabin, striking threatening poses, encouraged by

Nancy. Meanwhile, Lita was holding on to Brian's leg, telling him not to react to these dumb insults. But he couldn't restrain himself. The clog came off and the bass player had the arrogance beaten out of him.

Unlike some of his colleagues, Robbo was never fazed by punk. When Johnny Rotten had turned up at one of Lizzy's after-show parties in 1977, many of the older guests felt edgy. The singer Roger Chapman turned to Robbo and urged him to do something. 'Go over and nut him,' he suggested, 'show him what punk really is.' So the guitarist obliged, walking over with his bottle of whiskey and Derek the Dog under his arm, and he pushed Rotten. 'I'll show you punk – you little cunt.' But once the bravado had passed, the two firebrands actually found they had much in common and became good mates.

Inevitably, it was Phil who formed a special understanding with Sid. Few people could talk to the guy. Scott tried his best, but it was as if he was in a different place entirely – he seemed like an idiot. However, Lynott's speciality was oddball characters and outsiders. He used to welcome Sid and Nancy when they called round – mostly very late at night, when all of the other guests, such as Bob Geldof and snooker player Alex Higgins, had gone home. Since the break-up of The Sex Pistols in January 1978, punk's premier couple had become isolated, a situation worsened by their addiction to heroin.

Phil had moved from Embassy House because of complaints from the neighbours. Now he was at Anson Road in Cricklewood, and it was a famous party venue. Sid and Nancy were happy there, at their best watching Elvis movies. Sometimes they were the only people left awake, but they'd try and tidy up the room before they headed home. The only reminder of their visit was the occasional spot of blood on the bathroom walls where they'd been injecting themselves.

Phil found his entry into the punk circle through the office of his publicist, Tony Brainsby. As well as Thin Lizzy, the PR company looked after the profiles of big acts such as Queen and Wings. Brainsby had stuck with Phil's band from the end of 1972 – working on the success of 'Whisky In The Jar' and helping them over the lean years until *Jailbreak* happened. Sticking with the group had been an act of faith. There was certainly little money in the job – Tony used to refer to the band's account as 'the national debt'.

Sometimes Tony conspired to hype Phil into the papers, to compensate for a lack of chart success. In 1974, the singer had pretended to have a hearing problem, and thus found himself talking to journalists about the harmful effects of high decibels in rock and roll. But as the band became established, Phil was a publicist's dream – talking to the music press about his street-fighting, amorous ways, and then buzzing the tabloids in 1978 by judging the Miss World contest. He could charm anybody, sending them all home with the kind of story they wanted.

One of Tony's assistants was Kim Taylor, otherwise known as Magenta de Vine, an Aylesbury punk who knew many of the important shakers in the capital. She eventually took over Sid Vicious's flat in Maida Vale, jokingly promising to frame the blood on the walls. Magenta had turned up for her job interview with Brainsby wearing a leotard, and then told him she had to hurry because she had a transvestite friend waiting for her in the car outside the office in Winchester Street. Of course, she got the gig, and soon the likes of Nancy Spungeon and the Pistols drummer Paul Cook were calling over, and everyone's lives were changing radically.

Magenta was joined in the office by Caroline Crowther: tall, blonde and well educated. Tony claimed that he didn't know her background until after he'd hired her as an assistant – that she was the daughter of comedian and TV personality Leslie Crowther, and had a conviction for a petty drugs offence. When Phil first noticed her at a music biz party, he was intrigued. In turn, she was smitten by his combination of manliness and little-boy-lost appeal. The way he fluttered his eyelids and gave off shy signals in the midst of his posse of regular mates was almost like a *coquette*. Phil started turning up at the office a lot – Tony was amused that he was suddenly keen to do all the press duties that he was offered.

Back in 1975, Thin Lizzy had recorded a song on the flip-side of the 'Rosalie' single called 'Half Caste'. It was a low-key reggae song, with a lyric about the confusing experience of growing up with a mixed background. The boy could travel down to Brixton, but he'd never be fully accepted by the black community there. Equally, if he tried to woo a fair-skinned girl from Richmond, the doors were also closed to him. It was a sad admission. Yet a few years after he'd written this song, he was dating a girl from the Richmond-Twickenham set, and he was progressing happily. In April 1978, Caroline discovered she was having Phil's baby.

Phil, like his mother before him, thought about marriage when parenthood touched him. But he said he would only consider taking the oaths if it was for ever – not just because his girl was pregnant. His romantic nature, and the seed of Catholicism in him, wouldn't allow Phil to think about divorce. So they held off such plans, although Phil was pleased to be introduced to her parents as the steady man in Caroline's life.

On certain areas, the father-in-law and boyfriend agreed to differ. Leslie was a patriot who sometimes listened to recordings of wartime speeches by Winston Churchill. Phil would presently put 'Smash H Block' on the *Chinatown* record sleeve – a reference to the IRA 'Dirty Protest' at Long Kesh Prison in Ulster, where prisoners smeared the walls of the cells with their own excrement in a bid to regain political status. Life had become mighty complicated since these two entertainers first shared that *Crackerjack* TV stage together in 1973.

Phil walked out of the Marble Arch studios into the reception area where his old Dublin friend BP Fallon was finishing off a phone call. He looked apprehensive.

'God, Johnny's a bit out of it, isn't he?'

BP wasn't surprised to hear this. He'd only been managing Johnny Thunders for a short time, but already he knew the form. The guitarist had taken the morphiated stagger of Keith Richards and made a life and a legend out of it. His records with The New York Dolls between 1973 and 1974 were pieces of seminal, fall-about raunch – hugely influential on the Sex Pistols. His next band, The Heartbreakers, ran a publicity campaign with the slogan 'Catch 'Em While They're Still Alive'. Their most famous number was 'Chinese Rocks', a song describing the degradation of being lashed to a heroin habit. The Heartbreakers, along with their one-time satellite Nancy Spungeon, took the blame for bringing hard drugs into the UK punk scene.

Thunders had played with Paul Cook and Steve Jones from the now-defunct Sex Pistols in the spring of 1978, a revue that called itself The Living Dead. These people were assembled again in the summer to record Johnny's album *So Alone*. When Fallon asked Phil about playing in the sessions, he was unsure, but Caroline talked him into it. He brought down a very impressive lump of hash, which was rapidly consumed. Then they got to work.

Sometimes Johnny would liven up and play astonishing music – gruesomely pinned, but still able to relay feelings from the depths of his soul. Other moments were problematic. Steve Jones had a song left over from the Pistols days called 'Black Leather' which he gave to Thunders, who mumbled something about heavy metal, then immediately fell asleep, standing there with his guitar still strapped on.

Phil consented to play a few standards. There was the surf instrumental 'Pipeline', and the rhythm and blues tune 'Daddy Rollin' Stone'. Phil was wary of jamming with musicians he didn't know, since his style of bass playing was so odd. He'd actually strum the instrument, sweeping with his arm, like he was playing chords. Somehow this worked on stage with the rhythm of his singing, but he couldn't manage the timing with just any old drummer. That's why himself and Brian Downey made such a good team – and were less spectacular operating on their own.

But he was having a good time with Paul Cook and they made a fine rhythm section. Phil had to sing on 'Daddy Rollin' Stone' next, and he was enthralled at the idea of sharing the vocals with Steve Marriott. Here was the former singer of The Small Faces, whose music he'd performed in the Dublin halls way back in the days of The Black Eagles. Marriott was the little guy who'd legitimised the idea of blue-eyed soul, and in response to this Phil gave his best.

Johnny Thunders sang as well, and they made an impressive trio – bragging about their low-down, girl-stealing ways, finding a cheery bond in this fave tune. The short-term result of this session was that Phil was now keen to work with the Pistols boys again, at ease with their style and personalities. What nobody foresaw was that Thunders, Lynott and Marriott would all die prematurely in sad circumstances, and that the song they recorded together would have a morbid import as time passed.

The main issue for Thin Lizzy that summer was the release of *Live And Dangerous*. Chris O'Donnell had copped the title from a conversation with Bernie Rhodes, manager of The Clash. The latter wasn't keen on a proposal to have his boys playing with Phil's band, and rather dramatically he started talking about how gigs had to be 'dangerous'. Chris thought that concept was just perfect for his own purposes.

On the album's release on 2 June, Phil told a journalist, 'all the hits are there . . . and it's the end of an era'. It was the last time that Robbo would feature as a full-time member. The band's music would get heavier after this, and the fan-base would fragment. Thin Lizzy's peak was revealed in these grooves.

It was pointless debating how many overdubs were on there. This was simply a great artefact. From the big chord that opened 'Jailbreak', past 'Rosalie' and segueing with 'Cowgirls' Song', through to the rampant crowd-pleasers at the close, it was all textbook rock and roll. Everything was presented at its greatest; the guitar clash of a song like 'Emerald', Phil's rich alliance with the fans, the joy of riffing and ad-libbing according to the thrill of the moment. Even an inspired soundcheck of 'Southbound' was put to use.

Reviewing the record for *NME*, Nick Kent compared *Live And Dangerous* to the great concert recording of the Stones, Jerry Lee Lewis and even Bob Dylan's imperial 1966 *Albert Hall* bootleg. Lizzy, he reckoned, were equal to the finest of them. He called the LP 'a near perfect statement of intent by what is now the best hard rock band in the world . . . Lizzy have always played like warriors and this is an album made by heroes.'

The vindication of Visconti's method was witnessed during the tour that accompanied the album. Masses of new fans now knew Phil's live routines and his manner, and they wanted to participate beyond the limits of the record. So those summer 1978 shows were even more extraordinary as a result. Lizzy was justified for improving on reality because everyone's expectations became even more fervent, and the band was able to surpass that need. 'Still In Love With You' became a heart-breaking moment, with Robertson's guitar raking over the crowd's emotions. This was his grand finale. Nobody could have contrived the likes of this.

There was another ritual now when Lizzy played London. It had begun in 1976, when Phil asked Frank Murray to put some special people on the guest list. The singer would spot them in the audience before a show and point them out to his tour manager; they were the daughters of Cecil Parris. His half-sisters. Ever so quietly, Phil had kept a link between himself and his dad's family. He seemed to be happy to see them there.

Some people at the record company had been uneasy about the viability of a live double album, selling at full price, but *Live And Dangerous* struck number two in the charts – held off the top by the *Grease* soundtrack. It sold over 600,000 copies in the UK, sustained by a long and committed marketing campaign. It was both a commercial and a critical success. In America, they were now signed to Warners, who seemed to be making a purposeful job of selling the band. The management also renegotiated their UK contract – picking this most successful moment to extract more money and assurances on the band's behalf.

They played two nights at Wembley at the end of June 1978 – partly to impress the American promoters who'd come over to see them, but also because the smaller venues just couldn't contain them now. To please everyone in the capital, they'd have to play The Hammersmith Odeon for a week. Their support band was Horslips from Dublin – who shared Lizzy's zeal for Celtic myth and grand music. Their drummer was Eamon Carr, who'd befriended Phil during the poetry days of Tara Telephone in 1969. When they met again, they looked at each other and laughed. Lizzy's managers were grinning too. How had all of this happened? Wasn't someone going to come over in a minute and tell them it was all a mistake, that they should really be this famous, playing the biggest gig in town? Other backstage visitors at Wembley that night included Paul McGuinness, a young manager, and Adam Clayton, bass player with the formative U2. They were all thrilled to be this close to Ireland's greatest band.

Robbo left after the summer tour. He and Phil had reached an impasse, worsened by their combative spirits, by Robbo's habit of drinking two bottles of Johnny Walker's Black Label each day, and by the many chemicals that were being consumed. Gary Moore was contacted, and this time he was offered a permanent job in the band, which gave him a licence to get more involved in the creative workings. But there was a further problem: Brian Downey didn't want to play any more, and pulled out just before an American trip.

Brian was drinking a hell of a lot, and smoking too much dope.

THE BALLAD OF THE THIN MAN

There were problems at home, and he was totally fatigued. He literally couldn't get up in the morning, never mind play. And he felt that the band was working overly hard – a crazy amount of stress. The last thing he wanted to experience was another tour with Gary. He'd shared rooms with him before, and he'd be getting Moore's side of the latest argument through the night, then he'd go outside and Phil would be bending his ear about the guitarist's new problems. It was intolerable.

Later, when he read about the illness ME, Brian instantly sympathised with the people who'd been stricken by this. He'd been somewhere similar himself. His style of therapy was going fishing – so he headed off to the beaches of Cork and started casting out, just like he'd done since he was a kid. On a good day, he was the only person on the shoreline. Sometimes he'd take a little boat out and lose himself in contemplation, maybe hooking a sea bass, wondering if there was any point in returning to London.

He'd been replaced by Mark Nauseef, formerly with The Ian Gillan Band. That meant there were only two members of the *Live And Dangerous* band on stage, so Moore's flash moves were even more warranted. They acquitted themselves well, and by the time they'd reached Australia there were the makings of an exceptional show. On 29 October they played on the steps of The Sydney Opera House – a free show, and a great balmy evening before an estimated 300,000 people. It was an astonishing spectacle.

Phil looked ace in his lamé jacket, leather pants and shiny pumps. These fans had never seen the band before – and never would again – so he knew he had the perfect chance to throw all his best shapes and capitalise on that generosity of spirit. He actually seemed to get better as the size of an audience multiplied – hence the frustration of the band not getting any bigger in America, where Lynott would naturally have been the greatest star.

Phil's healthy appearance ran contrary to the lifestyle he was leading. When he'd visited New York in September, he'd gone to see Sid Vicious perform a post-Pistols gig at Max's Kansas City. The punk had six months left to live, and was playing to subsidise his heroin addiction. Phil and Sid chopped out some lines of cocaine in the filthy toilets, before the Irishman got back to the hired limo and resumed his tour of the city's ripped backside. The Clash were in town, so he met up with them too. He finished the evening at singer Willie DeVille's place in Greenwich Village. He'd scored some Dilaudid, a muscle relaxant, a favourite of Elvis in his last few years. Phil wasn't just imagining the lives of the low-rent drifters – he was socialising with them now.

Brian Downey was running out of money in Ireland, so he rang the London office. He spoke to Chris O'Donnell, expecting to get lectured about his sudden flight. But Chris asked him to come back when the band returned. Brian was surprised; there were no hard feelings, not even from Phil. He wasn't sacked after all. When he met the band again, they were surprised at his haircut and how much weight he'd lost, but were genuinely glad that he was back.

After a few messy dates at The Hammersmith Odeon, Thin Lizzy finished 1978 as The Greedy Bastards – a shameless combination of players from Phil's band, the Rats and the Pistols, playing The Stardust Ballroom in Dublin on 20 December. Steve Jones's guitar was faulty, so he borrowed one belonging to the guy in the support act. This was The Edge from U2, and the kid nervously watched the headliners, hoping that nothing would happen to his precious instrument.

The most dazed soul on the stage that night was Phil. The previous evening, Caroline had given birth to a girl, Sarah Philomena, at Holles Street hospital in Merrion Square, Dublin. He was determined that his child would be brought up a Catholic in the old country, and Caroline was even taking religious instruction to accommodate this rosy desire. The romance and practicality of Phil's life were about to be tested like never before.

The song 'Róisín Dubh' (Black Rose) summed up everything that was great about Phil – his passion, his ripping imagination, his unending ambitions. At the same time, it branded him as a reckless dreamer, prone to sentimental outpourings and wild, elusive ideas. He was trying to condense the entire Celtic spirit – the mythic figures, the history, the great writers, the musicians and hell-raisers – into a seven-minute epic. In the same song, he was also writing the ballad of the band, documenting Thin

Lizzy's incredible history and the personalities who'd passed through. It was big and wide, roaring and emotional. Nothing was going to dilute the grandeur he felt about such themes.

Now that Phil was again working with Gary Moore, he felt that it was right to make his biggest statement. The band had been working up the song in soundchecks over the summer of 1978, but it had never come out well. Moore could fix it if anybody could. After all, when he'd played with the band in 1974, he'd already fooled around with traditional tunes. So he resurrected 'The Mason's Apron' – a dance tune that had been preserved in Irish manuscripts since 1785 – and they built the instrumental passage around this.

They used 'Danny Boy' – the Ulster air that Eric Bell had recorded on the *Funky Junction* LP back in 1972 – thus acknowledging the two Belfast guitarists who'd played with the band. And they raised up 'Will Ye Go, Lassy, Go', which was emblematic of the Scottish influence in the group. And as a final reference to Thin Lizzy's gene-pool, they played something from Scott Gorham's homeland: 'Shenandoah' was the theme music from the James Stewart film about the American Civil War. They even tried some more US folk references, but every time they got to it, it just sounded corny.

Over the top of this musical weave, Lynott name-checked the greats of Irish history: George Best, Van Morrison, Brendan Behan, James Joyce, Oscar Wilde and WB Yeats. He used a down-home expression, 'Ah sure, I was born and raised there', and punned around two famous names. Phil's version was 'Ah Shaw, I was Sean O'Riada' – referring to the playwright and to Ireland's foremost composer. And, of course, Phil paid tribute to Cúchulainn, the original Irish cowboy and the archetype for his fast-blazing spirit.

The character Róisín Dubh was another rich figure from Irish literature. In the sixteenth century when political protest was outlawed, Gaelic poets would write 'vision' poems about a wailing, ghostly woman. She was the black rose, symbolising Ireland, calling out for help from Catholic friends in Spain and Rome – desperate for their armies to come to her rescue. This source was brilliantly developed by James Clarence Mangan into a nineteenth-century poem, 'Dark Rosaleen', which was in turn adopted by Brendan Behan and Luke Kelly from The Dubliners.

As early as 1975, Phil had ended a song called 'Leaving Town' with an invocation to this sad lady.

Lynott's friend Jim Fitzpatrick had stimulated him into writing about this area. He provided the artwork for the album and helped with the sleeve notes. Phil loved the idea of secrets and coded messages. The original poem was a call-to-arms against the English, and that was an image Phil had already referred to in 'Emerald' – the pikes glinting in the moonlight, a further chance for insurrection. But mainly, Phil wanted to celebrate Ireland's durability and glory – a soul power that hadn't been suppressed or lost in the face of many tragedies.

Phil's puns were terrible and the scholarship he based the song on was very loosely executed. The music was bombastic and the patriotism he evoked was a knee-jerk representation of Ireland rising out of slavery. But there was still something majestic about the track. He was trying to catch the breeze, to give voice to the essence of his spirit. He wanted to live up to his nation's finest. At worst, the song was a heroic failure. It was fitting that later on his gravestone in St Fintan's cemetery, Co. Dublin, would be engraved with the grieving legend of Róisín Dubh, his one true love.

In early 1979, Thin Lizzy flitted between the Good Earth Studios in England and the EMI Studios in Paris, assembling their music from a number of sources. *Black Rose* was an album of extremes – a reflection of Phil's ever-fragmenting life. On the one hand, he was relating the joys of parenthood with 'Sarah' – tender jazz-soul, like an old Isley Brothers tune. The next thing you'd hear was the allusion to hard drugs on 'Got To Give It Up'. Phil wasn't just observing heroin use by now – he was indulging.

When the Parisian dealers called around to the Pathé Marconi studio, they offered the band free snorts of heroin. Phil took some, and so did Scott. Soon they were buying the stuff, before sloping off to the clubs. Gary Moore was a straight-edger now – he hardly touched alcohol, never mind drugs, so he was once again out of sync with the singer. He worked hard in the studio – lashing over the tunes with his rapid, glissando style, finally able to make a real impact on Lizzy. Scott was facing new competition now, obliged to react to this peppy agenda.

Tony Visconti wasn't pleased with Phil's loose approach – the vocal ad-libs were more delirious than ever, his decision-making process all gone to hell. When they'd made *Bad Reputation* together, the band had smirked at Tony's white slacks and his Gucci loafers. He seemed so together – even practising his karate moves on Lizzy's drunken crew. And the band thought it was funny that his Welsh wife, sweet little Mary Hopkin – who'd represented Britain in the Eurovision Song Contest in 1970 – was literally shaking if she was left on her own in a room with them. But the humour was harder to find now. People were nodding off at the mixing desk. Even Tony was taking nips of brandy and a few sedatives to make the chore easier.

Somehow, the band's pop sensibility was able to survive. With 'Waiting For An Alibi', they had another hit single, reaching number nine in the UK charts in March. The idea of ruin was a big theme now. The song allowed Phil to replay his fascination with misfits, failures and ageing Romeos. 'Do Anything You Want To' was all libertarian slogans and rumbling kettle drums, closing with Phil's passable Elvis impersonation, and it reached number fourteen in the June charts.

Some reviews for the album were harsh, suspecting that the lyrical ambitions of Phil were lessening, that he didn't care so dearly about his art. And the sleazy territory of 'S & M' and 'Got To Give It Up' wasn't either funny or illuminating. He wanted to be down with the lads, but was also choosing to serenade his baby girl. The vagabond and the good son were fighting it out in Phil's mind as the *Black Rose* album hit number two in the charts in May 1979.

At the same time, a track from Gary's solo LP *Back On The Streets* reached the top ten. It was a slow blues, a homage to the playing of American guitarist Roy Buchanan, whom Phil liked a lot, so he was glad to sing on the number. Gary had created some of the musical motifs while he'd been touring Belgium with Colosseum II, sad and strangely foreign. Phil liked these ideas, and he even agreed to play a stand-up bass on the track, marking the notes on the neck with chalk since there weren't any frets. They played some accordion together on the track, with Phil pushing one end while Gary worked the keys – a hilarious experiment.

Chris O'Donnell laughed when he heard some of Phil's lyrics – the way he sang about 'old Beaujolais wine', when the whole point of that particular tipple was that it was supposed to be fresh and new. But the song's opening line was something different: 'I remember Paris back in '49' didn't seem so dramatic until you discovered that his dad was called Parris, and, of course, Phil had been born in 1949. Once more he was singing in code; he was thinking about his mother and father's courtship and their subsequent split.

Phil's favourite film was *Casablanca* – the story of two lovers who meet in the French capital before the war, and whose lives are then torn apart by global events. Later, when Rick, the main character, is living in North Africa and feeling blue, you see a flashback to his old Parisian days, when he was in love with the beautiful Ilse, and they cruised along the Champs-Elysées and drank in the bars, always happy, until the Germans marched in. Several years later, the couple meet up again, but it is too late to make anything of it. The guy, played by Humphrey Bogart, can only offer the memory of their good times as a comfort. 'We'll always have Paris,' he insists.

That was the ambience of Phil's singing on 'Parisienne Walkways' – of something irrevocably lost. He'd been building on this theme of star-crossed lovers for the past eight years, and now he'd expressed it as well as he could. There would be a postscript to the story in the form of an unreleased song called 'Blue Parris', recorded in November 1982. It was a miserable, self-pitying song, with Phil singing about demons and rejection and clearly realising that the vagabond impulse had been wholly transferred through the generations, father to son.

Gary Moore should have been pleased with the good state of his solo career and his profile with Lizzy. But Phil and Scott were becoming more secretive, now that there was a new habit to conceal. Scott had actually dabbled with heroin as a teenager in California, and now that Phil was discovering these things for himself, it was like the floodgates opening again. And, for a while, the drugs helped to alleviate the problem that the band weren't getting any bigger. They weren't selling any fewer records, but the sales weren't rising either. They found themselves playing the same old venues on each tour. They'd reached a plateau. A little snort here and there would lessen the tedium of this situation. It was like taking a holiday.

Phil was even harder to get through to now. Peter Eustace, the sound man, had already encountered this side of him when they'd been talking about different religious philosophies. He'd been gassing on about Zen and stuff when Phil completely closed down: 'Look, man, don't get inside my head!' He was even more obstinate now. He was also suffering from terrible stomach cramps before gigs, and his performance levels were falling off.

Any hopes of a big push in America were ruined by a messy event in Los Angeles. It was a Warners Records party at The Roxy on Sunset Boulevard, and there was a roped-off VIP area, where signings to the label could socialise in peace. But Phil was caught outside in the standing area, and people were hassling him. He tried to get past the ropes, but a girl from Warners told him there was no room – there had just been a visit from the safety officer, who told them the place was overcrowded. Phil was enraged that he couldn't get in and so he swore and barged past. The girl was badly upset – and news of this altercation spread through the company, costing Thin Lizzy plenty of goodwill. The Americans believed that Phil had shouted 'Suck my dick, baby' at one of their own. Even though the band felt that Phil wouldn't have said this kind of thing exactly, the damage was irreversible.

Gary and the band fell out on 4 July 1979, after an Independence Day festival at Oakland, just outside San Francisco. The next day, he said he was going to quickly visit his girlfriend in Los Angeles, but he'd rejoin them in Reno, Nevada, two days later. He never turned up, and Scott had to carry the show on his own.

The band had a meeting with Moore when they returned. He told them he'd gone off the music, that he didn't feel it was creative any more. But the understanding was that he'd finish the tour. Phil returned the favour by working on Gary's solo recordings in the few days leading up to the LA show. But the guitarist didn't return the favour – he went into hiding at the California home of Glen Hughes, the former bass player of Deep Purple. On 16 July, Lizzy's management officially announced that Moore had been sacked for unreliability. The guitarist didn't go quietly though, and he told the UK press about Thin Lizzy's turbulent ways, as a season of mutual bitching commenced.

They called in Midge Ure to cover the tour. He was a friend of Phil's – they'd co-written a song on the *Black Rose* album, 'Get

Out Of Here'. Midge had become famous in the mid-1970s with the teenybop band Slick, before he teamed up with former Sex Pistols bassist Glen Matlock to front The Rich Kids. His most recent gig was with Ultravox – a synth band, influenced by the likes of Kraftwerk and The Yello Magic Orchestra.

Phil was coming up to thirty. The decade was nearly over, and Thin Lizzy would presently be ten years old. He was intensely aware of the fact that in some quarters they were regarded as an ageing band. So if he could accommodate Midge into the act, this might give them some extra relevance. Midge was heavily involved in the new scene in London that came to be known as the New Romantics. They played Bowie records, film sound-tracks and German electronic music at weekly club nights like Blitz and Helden – making like they were in Berlin during the days of the Weimar Republic, beautiful and decadent.

Phil, as ever, wanted in on this scene. He befriended Steve Strange and Rusty Egan at their Club For Heroes evenings at the Barracuda in Baker Street. He wore cavalry shirts and trench coats and started writing his songs on synths and drum machines. He met other curious souls at Club For Heroes, such as Pete Townsend. On one famous occasion, Phil escorted The Who's guitarist to the toilets and slipped him some of his drugs. Townsend subsequently collapsed on the floor, curling up into a foetal position – his heart was beating erratically and he thought he was going to die – as a young Paul Weller watched in drunken amazement.

Much of this new music was put aside for his upcoming solo album, but Phil wanted to try something with the band as well. For the immediate future, though, it was a case of getting Midge to play the basics, to cover for Gary Moore's absence. On the Concord flight over, the Scotsman listened to *Live And Dangerous*, frantically trying to learn the set. After a quick run-through with Scott at the hotel in New Orleans, he was on the stage at the Louisiana Municipal Auditorium, posing and charging around, bringing life to the beast, amused that Phil was just as keen for him to get the stage moves and the crowd-pleasing poses together.

Ure took immense care over his looks, shaving his sideburns into points, wearing vivid shirts and pegged trousers – a Caledonian futurist. Sometimes Phil would step outside for a photo session and realise that he was outclassed by the newcomer, and he'd blow his stack. The other upshot of this recruitment was that Ultravox would get a management deal from the two Chrises, and would occasionally outsell Lizzy in the charts during the next decade.

The American tour was salvaged, but the Reading Festival appearance at the end of August was called off, causing some rancour in the UK. In September, they toured Japan with Midge – who was now playing synths much of the time – and guitarist Dave Flett, who'd formerly worked with Manfred Mann, as a temporary filler. In their spare time during soundchecks, Midge would constantly play the same keyboard lines, and Phil tried to make a song out of them. He was thinking about the Japanese talent for micro electronics and the damage this might have on Western economies. It was a new kind of Yellow threat. His chorus line was taken from a chant he'd picked up on the football terraces: 'Attack, attack, attack . . . is what we lack.'

Lizzy came back to London for a winter personality change, as they met up with Paul Cook and Steve Jones – their combined forces now known as The Greedies. Their single release, 'A Merry Jingle', jollied up the office parties and the charts, spreading peace and goodwill to all men, just as Phil found himself fixing to get married.

14

Mrs Jean Crowther, mother of the bride, turned to Scott and asked him if he'd written a good speech for the reception. The American was politely terrified. *Oh shit*, he thought, *not a speech*. The weddings back home had never been this complicated – a best man just smiled a bit and maybe took care of the rings. But here in England there were so many formalities and customs; the best man really had to work for the honour of the title.

Even the stag night had been difficult. He'd booked the club in Hammersmith, invited a ton of people and hired four strippers. Phil seemed to be enjoying the evening, but Scott had to deal with all the hassles. At one stage, he had a stripper rebellion on his hands. They'd previously agreed a price over the phone, £50 for the job, but now he found himself shouting at a naked girl who was demanding £70 instead. It was an annoying situation, made worse by the fact that the other guys at the party found this highly amusing. Stan Bowles, the footballer, was looking over and cracking up.

The wedding was on 14 February 1980 – Valentine's Day – at St Elizabeth of Portugal Church in Richmond. It was a traditional Catholic service, even though many guests were unorthodox. Thin Lizzy's road crew helped out as ushers, wearing penguin suits but strutting down the aisles in their cowboy boots. Bob Geldof turned up in a bomber jacket and plaid trousers, accompanied by Paula Yates. Robbo was there with his wife, Dee Harrington. His colleague from Wild Horses, Jimmy Bain, came with his spouse, Lady Sophie, daughter of the Marquis of Bute.

Phil was nervous before the service. He'd realised what he was getting into – the vagabond was about to swear his undying fidelity – and he was awed by the church and the ceremony of it all. Scott had recently had his hair cut – losing almost a foot off his famous locks – so he was more in tune with the serious tone of the ceremony. However, Paula Yates was taking advantage of the high celebrity count to get pictures for her upcoming book, *Rock Stars In Their Underpants*. She wanted to do Scott immediately – he just had to drop his trousers and she'd snap away, but the guitarist wasn't in the mood for all this.

The mood lightened at the party afterwards at The Kensington Hilton. Leslie Crowther was a natural in front of the 200 guests, joking through his speech, making the family members and the rockers feel equally at ease. He even made a racy remark about the day Phil asked him for his daughter's hand in marriage. The legendary answer to the question was, 'Well, you've had everything else, you might as well have her hand.'

Billy Idol, The Boomtown Rats, Eric Bell, Midge Ure, Mary Hopkin, Lemmy from Motorhead, Mark Knopfler, Steve Strange and the other friends thought this was a real laugh. Phil gave a fine speech too – romantic and light. But Scott wasn't even going to try and compete. He read out the telegrams, toasted the couple and wished them the best for their honeymoon in Rio. Caroline was beaming – she was expecting her second child and she looked well.

Shortly after their return, the couple bought a bungalow in Howth, along the north shore of Dublin, backing on to the bay. Glenn Corr was where Caroline was to spend the next few years. A second daughter, Cathleen Elizabeth, was born on 29 July, also at Holles Street hospital. Whenever Phil wasn't touring or working at their London home – The Walled Cottage, 184 Kew Road in Richmond – he'd stay with them in Ireland and enjoy the family life.

When the weather was good, they'd have football matches on the beach with friend and neighbour Jim Fitzpatrick, plus old pals from the 1960s: Brush Shiels, Frank Murray, Terry Woods, Noel Bridgeman, Robbie Brennan and Terry O'Neill. All of the kids, wives and girlfriends would be chatting, laughing and organising the refreshments. It was just how Phil had dreamed his homecomings would be. Caroline was planning to take a degree in drama at Trinity College Dublin, so there were good possibilities ahead of them both.

Philomena came over too, leaving The Clifton Grange Hotel in Manchester after fourteen years. Her son had bought her a place in Howth too for her fiftieth birthday, called White Horses. Together, they purchased The Asgard Hotel nearby, although this was unfortunately destroyed in a fire a short while later. But at least there was an extended family of sorts back in Ireland now. Phil would come over with presents that he'd bought for them on tour – little dresses for the girls that looked fine and always fitted them. He even sang them lullabies at night, putting them to sleep with words he was making up on the spot. That made him smile; while once he'd wanted to be as revolutionary as Elvis Presley, now he was a corny old strummer like Burl Ives.

In interviews, the singer claimed to have reformed his ways. But it was as if he wanted to partition his life – to have the wife and kids in one place, and the Wild One lifestyle elsewhere. He'd pose with his striped shirt and his hair pulled down over his left eye – just like the comic character Dennis The Menace. He even called his dog Gnasher, so he could be more like the famous trouble-maker. In concert, he celebrated the tearabout personality with ever-obvious glee. Backstage, he was still the boy who couldn't say no.

He released the album *Solo In Soho* on 18 April 1980. Scott, Brian and the new Thin Lizzy guitarist, Snowy White, played on some tracks, but the record was presented as the start of a solo option for Lynott. This pursuit of parallel careers was something that Rod Stewart and Brian Ferry had tried outside of their bands, The Faces and Roxy Music. And like these artists, Phil's own work beyond Thin Lizzy was mostly soft and stylised. The single 'Dear Miss Lonely Hearts', released on 14 March, reflected this. The LP was divided between love-struck ballads and experimental ideas – suggesting that Lizzy would concentrate on the traditional rockers in future.

The album also included 'Yellow Pearl', the song Phil had worked up with Midge Ure during the Japanese tour of 1979. It was wilfully novel, with a drum machine, a vocoder and synths, and was chosen as a theme tune for *Top Of The Pops* in 1981, where it was used for the next five years.

Meanwhile, another track, 'Ode To A Black Man', was a bluesy celebration of the musical and political leaders who'd furthered the black cause. Phil name-checked Bob Marley, Martin Luther King, Stevie Wonder, Robert Johnson, Mohammed Ali,

Malcolm X, Haile Selassie and Jimi Hendrix. Phil admitted that he'd been 'living on the wrong side', denying his father's roots, but now he wanted to embrace that culture too. The inclusion of Bob Marley in this list was of special significance; in 1978 they'd met at the *Top Of The Pops* studio. The reggae star handed him a badge of Haile Selassie, the late Emperor of Ethiopia. In return, Phil gave him a Lizzy badge, bearing his own likeness. Bob said thanks, and put it on his shirt. Amazing . . .

'King's Call' was a tribute to the enduring power of Elvis Presley. Phil was singing lines from 'Are You Lonesome Tonight' and remembering how painfully and drunkenly he'd dealt with the news of his hero's death in 1977. August 16 had been a rare break in Lizzy's summer tour that year, and Downey had been relaxing in London when the news came on the television. Immediately, Brian thought of his Crumlin friend, and how badly he'd take the news. Thirty seconds later, the phone went, and there was Phil on the other end, cut up and crying.

The uneven quality of *Solo In Soho* was due to the fact that it was recorded on the move. Parts had been put together at Good Earth, Tony Visconti's new London studios in Dean Street, Soho. Snowy White would later feel angry that he'd unwittingly worked as a session man, thinking he was actually recording for Thin Lizzy. Other tracks were patched together from a visit in 1979 to Compass Point, Nassau. This trip had been set up as a working holiday for musician friends and their partners. But little was achieved, and the stay had degenerated into aggressive scenes when Caroline flushed a stash of Phil's drugs down the toilet. The ad-hoc nature of these recordings was further revealed when two songs from this era, 'Ode To A Black Man' and 'Didn't I', used a few of the same lyrics.

Snowy White was the first regular English guitarist in Thin Lizzy. He'd grown up on the Isle of Wight, which felt like Alcatraz to him during his teenage days. He'd already discovered the *John Mayall And The Bluesbreakers* LP, and then followed the trail of Eric Clapton's guitar influences back to the guys who'd grown up in the Mississippi Delta. After knocking his style into shape during a year's stay in Stockholm, he returned to Britain, touring with Cockney Rebel and Al Stewart. Just like Gary Moore, he befriended and worked with the former Fleetwood Mac guitarist Peter Green, thus boosting his reputation as a dedicated scholar of the blues.

He was touring with Pink Floyd at Madison Square Gardens on Independence Day, 1977. That was the night that Phil had been stoned and had been convinced that the inflatable pig in the sky was pissing on his head. They met up after the show, but it was no big deal at the time. By Christmas 1979 Snowy was in Cliff Richard's band, rehearsing at Shepperton Studios. He met Scott there, who told him that Lizzy were also working in the complex, and were looking for a new guitarist. He jammed with them and was offered the job, though he wasn't sure if he'd enjoy it. Phil assured him that they'd find room for his style.

Snowy was clean-cut, didn't take drugs, and sometimes appeared on stage in a rugby shirt – contrasting with Phil's stony stare and the leather sleeveless jackets from La Rocka, also favoured by the rest of the band. Still, they took him on tour in April, along with a teenage keyboard player, Darren Wharton. The latter had been spotted by a friend of the band's in Manchester. He used to play the nightclubs such as Tiffanys, backing comedians and crooners. Bill Tarmey, soon to be famous as Jack Duckworth in *Coronation Street*, was a regular compère for these shows, as Darren tinkled at the grand piano, wishing he was hanging out with Herbie Hancock and Chick Corea instead.

Darren was introduced to Thin Lizzy at Good Earth Studios in the early spring of 1980. They were finishing the *Chinatown* record – named after the area of London they were recording in. He played keyboard on the title track and told Phil he was a Manchester United supporter. That clinched it – he was asked to pick up a few of the tracks in time for the next rehearsals. He was so excited he learnt the whole set, scoring it all out on manuscripts.

A week later, he was in Norway, watching his first ever Thin Lizzy gig from a riser at the back. They started with 'Jailbreak'. Scott and Phil ran out and Wharton was playing his synth and thinking, *Wow, what a band*. He was like a punter, enjoying the spectacle. He'd never experienced crowds like this. At the jazz concerts he'd seen before, people sat there clapping politely. But these Scandinavian rocker fans, they were the wildest.

Everyone was so excited by this new regime that they didn't realise how laid-back Snowy was. He'd stand by his speaker cabinets, making sure that the sound was coming out the way he wanted. When Phil eventually noticed his introverted ways, he'd rib the new guy, trying to involve him. But that just made Snowy more obstinate, less inclined to be throwing shapes. He became even more static during the gigs. He was a good bloke, but he just didn't want to conform to Phil's idea of stagecraft.

The singer had weathered the rise of punk, and held his own with the Futurist/New Romantic clique. Now there was another subculture to consider – a force from the rock heartland of England, something the journalists at *Sounds* magazine were calling 'The New Wave Of British Heavy Metal'. This music was a reaction to punk – bands such as Iron Maiden, Samson, Diamond Head and Saxon were dedicated to proving that hard rock could still have the same energy levels as the likes of the Sex Pistols.

This genre was basically press-led – most of the bands had no connection with each other, and many were playing barely revised Deep Purple and Black Sabbath licks. But media attention swelled the audience, and gave metal a deal of legitimacy and vigour again. As the tide waters rose, so vaguely related bands like Judas Priest, Mötorhead and Def Leppard enjoyed a lot more attention – the latter freely confessing to their admiration for Phil Lynott and his powerful, tuneful songs. This new community of bands and fans broke off from the mainstream, not caring what happened outside. There were enough of them out there to put their acts into the charts. They liked Phil, and he bonded with them too. *Kerrang!* magazine was launched off the back of this new music, and this journal would support Thin Lizzy thereafter. The singer's interviews in those glossy pages revealed him at his most relaxed and humorous.

Beyond this reassuring clique, the world was less tolerant. The Lizzy single 'Killer On The Loose' was released in September 1980, reaching number ten in the charts. The dominant bassline and the straight, pummelling rhythm were suggestive of Mötorhead. The subject matter – a serial killer hunting down women in a red-light district – was too close to the recent, brutal history of Peter Sutcliffe, the Yorkshire Ripper, for many people. Suddenly Phil was getting attacked for his macho tendencies, and the boy's-own imagery in the music.

Since Phil had saved many of the romantic songs for his own album, most of *Chinatown* was more upbeat and strident. 'Sugar

Blues' was an admission of the singer's fondness for cocaine – just as the inside sleeve shot for *Solo In Soho* showed him tapping his nose in a roguish way. The high spirits and ad-libs of 'Having A Good Time' were endearing reflections of Phil's merry style, but the references throughout the album to Triad gangs, Oriental secrets and street trade were also indicative of some bad habits settling in.

On 14 June Thin Lizzy played a show at the Gaumont in Southampton. Afterwards, they went to The Post House in town, asking if they could step in for a few drinks at a local girl's twenty-first birthday party. The usual rivalries between jealous homeboys and the band broke out and Phil was hit on the face by a glass. His white shirt was covered in blood, and he seemed horribly injured. But when doctors cleaned up the wound in hospital, they found he'd escaped with a minor cut.

But the media made out that he was badly hurt, and Thin Lizzy didn't bother denying those stories. It was publicity, wasn't it? A few days later, they were in New York when the Radio 1 reporter Richard Skinner called up the hotel. Chris O'Donnell took the call, and assured the listeners in Britain that Phil would of course be battling back from his injuries, but he was receiving expert treatment in America to ensure his full recover. Skinner began asking more specific questions. He asked the manager what was the name of the specialist who was treating the singer. Chris was flummoxed for a few seconds. There was no specialist. As he looked across the room for inspiration, he caught the eyes of Phil's personal assistant, Gus Curtis. *That would do.*

'The name of the specialist is . . . Dr Augustin Curtis.'

Phil's solo records weren't selling so well. 'King's Call', released in June, stalled at thirty-five in the singles chart. And while the *Chinatown* album peaked at number seven on 18 October 1980, the sales quickly fell off. Phil was trying to win the approval of the metal fans, the dance futurists, the romantic souls and the older audience who still grooved to Dire Straits and Phil Collins. The terrible danger with this gambit was that he'd end up pleasing no one.

Thus in the spring of 1981, Phil was simultaneously working on a new Lizzy album and some solo ideas. His drug consumption was such that he'd arrive late in the evening at

Lombard Studios in Dublin or Good Earth or the Odyssey complex in London – raring to go – just as the other musicians were tiring. The songs for the second solo album were mainly gloomy – like the proposed title track of the record, 'Fatalistic Attitude'. He was now talking in interviews about feelings of despair. A working title for the next Lizzy LP was *Living Out Somebody Else's Dream*. The singer was also getting weary of his party image, how he was expected to provide vicarious thrills for all his listeners. He was finishing the lyrics for this song on 8 December 1980, the day that John Lennon was gunned down by a fan in New York.

'Are you a poet?' he wrote. 'A lover? A father? Or a rock and roll star? . . . Well, I'm messed up, I'm mucked up, Oh I should shut up . . .'

In May 1981, the 'Killers Live' EP reached nineteen in the charts. Phil began reaching for the panic button. At his insistence, the next Thin Lizzy single was 'Trouble Boys', a rockabilly tune which everyone else disliked. It was actually written by Billy Bremner, the former drummer with Rockpile. The record reached number fifty-three in August, and then headed down. It was their worst-received single in six years.

The band headlines at Milton Keynes Bowl on 8 August, above The Ian Hunter Band, Judy Tzuke, Paul Jones and The Q Tips. It was an uninspiring bill, the weather was rotten and ticket sales were dismal. Phil turned up early, got wasted and played a terrible show. Eight days later, they returned to Ireland, to play in the grounds of Slane Castle. This time they could expect a more enthusiastic crowd, but as with Dalymount Park in 1977, Thin Lizzy would have to defend their title against the latest contenders from home.

U2 and their manager, Paul McGuinness, were intensely aware of Phil's achievements. They used to play 'Dancing In The Moonlight' in the early days. Larry Mullen would entertain friends with his Philo impersonations. Paul used to pick over *Live And Dangerous* as a model for a live show: the rise and fall of energy, the dynamics, the running order of songs and the sheer musicality of the band. That was something U2 had to aim for.

Adam Clayton was on friendly terms with Lynott. Their first introduction in 1978 had been a little embarrassing, as the new boy had rung Phil at The Clarence Hotel where he was staying at the time, unwisely making his call at ten-thirty in the morning. The star was just going to bed, but he said 'Howyeh, man?', and dispensed some brief advice to his fellow bass player. In the following years, it was obvious that Phil was following their career path. 'Youse are next,' he'd tell Paul McGuinness. 'We'll have to move over.' The two bands shared an accountant, Ossie Kilkenny. The Lizzy crew even let McGuinness watch them at work in the late 1970s. He was fascinated by the details and the mechanics of such a huge team – and there was no better example of international success for an Irish band than Phil and the boys.

Respect was one thing, but U2 also realised the importance of distinguishing themselves at Slane. Their second album, *October*, was finished and set for release in the autumn. They wanted to unfurl their backdrop on the stage – just as The Boomtown Rats had done at Dalymount Park – but they messed it up and lost much of the initial impact. By the time it was ready, the crowd had calmed down, and effectively U2 were just warming them up again for Phil. The contenders had also tried to hire a helicopter for the day, but couldn't manage it. Of course, Phil had done exactly that, and had flown over the crowd, waving at the multitudes. Darren Wharton was riding shotgun with his boss, and he was practically expiring with excitement.

U2 suffered roadie problems on the day also – a new guitar tech hadn't understood the band's on-stage tuning arrangements, leaving Bono with some tricky vocal manoeuvres. There was no chance of them blowing the headliners off, even if they'd played their very best, but they had one last gesture to make before the stage was made ready for Thin Lizzy. In the days when Paul McGuinness worked in the film industry, he'd met a guy at Ardmore Studios called Gerry Johnson, a special effects man. Paul hired him for the day, and stashed him on the far bank of the river, in the bushes with his special artillery. At the end of U2's set, he let off a series of fireworks. The Lizzy people were furious – this was an impudent and presumptuous stroke. But Phil just laughed. 'Fair play to them,' he said.

Slane was the last time that Thin Lizzy were the undisputed leaders in Ireland. They carried the day by force of the singer's great rapport with the crowd, and the number of old, blazing songs that everyone adored. But the musicianship was sloppy on

158

the day, and Phil was losing that all-welcoming, delightful aspect of his act. Soon, U2 began having hits in Britain – and, even more significantly, becoming big in America. They'd learnt a lot from the old firm, and now they were adapting those achievements for a new decade.

On 20 August 1981, Phil was fined £200 at Kingston Crown Court in Surrey, for possession of cocaine. He had denied the charges, saying the two packets of cocaine in his jacket had been left there by a friend who'd borrowed it. The cannabis plant in the conservatory was a kind of 'practical joke'. The raid had taken place in November of the previous year by Special Patrol Group officers posing as Gas Board workers. Phil's comment on leaving the court was that the fine was 'a most unpleasant birthday surprise'.

Scott Gorham's body was like a stick of fire. He was taking tranquillisers, trying to get rid of the pain, but it was just making him delirious instead. He was having tantrums, throwing shit around the dressing-rooms, looking for arguments. The pain of heroin withdrawal while touring Europe – sometimes enduring eight-hour road trips between venues – was driving him mad.

It was March 1982, somewhere between Spain and Portugal, and Scott was ranting more than usual. Phil told him that he should just go on to London, that the band would finish the gigs without him. So he flew back, and immediately got into a huge argument at his doctor's office. This guy was supplying the guitarist with the drugs that were meant to get him off the smack, but it only got him more addicted to the medication. The doctor was screaming back at the guitarist. It was a terrible situation. Scott went to a re-hab clinic in Hampstead and stayed there for a while until he got over the worst of it. But inevitably he went back to drugs. There was too much temptation around the band to resist. The only way to definitively stop, the guitarist decided, was to get out of the band.

'Hollywood (Down On Your Luck)' was a grimly suitable single to mark this period – a song about private suffering and public indifference. The record stopped dead at number fifty-three on 6 March. Meantime, Phil was putting a solo gig together, backed by a new outfit, The Soul Band. This included Robbie Brennan, who'd played for a while with Phil in Skid Row in 1968, plus American bass player Jerome Rimson and guitarist Gus Isodore. The last two members were black guys – and Phil wanted to continue the roots renewal that he'd prompted with 'Ode To A Black Man'. The band toured Ireland in the summer, with Phil strumming a double-necked instrument – allowing him to play either bass or six-string guitar. But the experiment wasn't given the time to develop fully, and presently Phil was working again with Lizzy.

While Ireland had once seemed like a retreat, now it was a dangerous town for someone with Phil's lifestyle. Heroin was easily available across town, distributed by prominent figures in the drug families who knew Phil well. Suddenly, the parties at Glenn Corr in Howth weren't so happy. People would nod off in corners or just sit there in silence. Phil and Caroline were arguing a lot as well, as the junkies and dealers moved in and the older friends were often frozen out.

Chris O'Donnell was one of the latter. After eight years of working with Phil, he felt a terrible coldness developing between them. One day there had been yet another trauma with the singer, and he thought, *What's the point?* He'd spent so much of his time developing Phil's life, and he hadn't developed his own. It seemed like he'd always been sending telegrams to congratulate friends on their weddings while he was unavoidably on tour. He counted himself as a sports fan, but he'd missed complete seasons. His waking nightmare was living with the query, 'Didn't you used to manage Thin Lizzy?' He was simply worn out.

Likewise with Snowy White. He left the band after playing the Castlebar Rock Festival in August 1981. He'd lost interest halfway through the recording of what was to become the *Renegade* album, and he'd become fed up waiting around studios – his waking and sleeping hours often at the opposite end of the day to Phil's nocturnal regime.

Renegade was a half-hearted record – Thin Lizzy by the yard. It contained some routine rockers and a token cowboy drama. There was a quirky jazz tribute to Fats Waller that rhymed 'Sigmund Freud' with 'very annoyed'. The singer mused about the prophecies of Nostradamus on 'Angel Of Death'. Phil only sparked on the title track, which pictured a good son who'd become lost and confused, and again on 'It's Getting Dangerous', which became a further account of the wild times of Johnny The Fox, except that now he was cornered, running out of tricks, his heart turned to stone, his soul dying off. The harmonising guitars sounded like a call from another age. Phil was pulling his voice out of the moribund depths, singing like a boy again as opposed to a weary fighter. 'Watch out for the danger,' he called, as the sad record faded away.

Around this time, the management began circulating stories about Phil's imminent film career – that he was to play the lead in a biopic about Jimi Hendrix. News quickly spread, and soon there were telexes coming in from branches of the record company all over the world. 'Do we have the rights for the soundtrack album?' the Australians wanted to know, as the hysteria increased. But there never was a biopic – at least not with Phil involved in it. The Irishman couldn't act – his only role thus far had been a comedy sketch on *The Lenny Henry Show* and he'd fluffed the punchline about twenty times.

The Philip Lynott Album was also released in the autumn of 1982. At its worst, it was obsessed with faddish, ephemeral sounds, and sounded either doomy or cute. Phil's tendency to try the same idea twice was revealed on 'Cathleen', dedicated to his second daughter, a poor song compared to 'Sarah'. But one track really excelled. 'Old Town', co-written with Jimmy Bain from Wild Horses, was his version of 'Penny Lane' – a remembrance of the streets and buildings and their interplay with his emotions.

There was even a lovely trumpet flourish at the end, just like on The Beatles' song. Phil's singing was odd, though. It sounded thin, with a sinusy quality to it. Maybe he'd developed a cold during the recording session. Or more likely, he'd snorted so much cocaine over a considerable period of time that he'd damaged his septum – the cartilage inside his nose was severely degraded. This boy was audibly cracking up.

15

Phil was standing in the kitchen at his house in Kew, wearing his dressing-gown, looking fierce. Around him stood Darren Wharton, Gus Curtis, his personal assistant, plus the new guitarist, John Sykes. They were feeling groggy after the previous night's party, but their boss wasn't in the mood for sympathy. He was holding a huge square of cheese in his hand – a block that he'd bought a few days ago for his own gastronomical pleasure. But there was a great bite out of the corner of it, like something from a *Tom And Jerry* cartoon.

'All right, who's been eating my fucking cheese?'

They giggled like kids. This was too silly to take seriously.

'It's not fucking funny! And if nobody owns up, then I'm gonna find out another way. Here, John, take a bite out of this.'

Sykes bit into another corner of the cheese. Phil compared the two dental impressions. Nope, the guilty man had a twisted tooth, and John's mark was a clean one. It was now Darren's turn, but it became clear that his incisors were differently spaced. That just left Gus, who looked rather guilty as he munched on the remaining corner. And sure enough, it was a perfect match.

Phil was livid, and he stomped out of the kitchen complaining of treachery, as the guests sniggered some more. His anger seemed totally out of proportion to the crime. People had enjoyed masses of the singer's home comforts in the past – his food, his booze, even his drugs. In the days when he'd lived in Cricklewood, Phil would leave the Camden Palace or Club For Heroes early and get himself driven home the long way. Thus, he could stop at a twenty-four-hour shop on West End Lane and buy alcohol and provisions for the likes of Mick Jones from The Clash or Steve Strange – whoever was coming over later. Now, here he was getting irate over a lump of Cheddar.

But that was the deal in the spring of 1983. Emotional extremes. Stormy arguments. The occasional thrill of having new faces in the camp. The miserable prospect of old friends becoming ill and detached. The strange feeling that people were laughing at Phil, rather than along with him. And behind all of these details, there was the pervasive sadness of Thin Lizzy's last tour, as they finally split after thirteen years.

Quitting wasn't Phil's idea – he was the last to agree to such a move. But the tickets for the tour in January weren't selling, and the general consensus was that the band was outdated. Scott was unwell and tired of the endless hustle. The band was heavily in debt, and needed some media interest to start reversing this trend. By announcing that the band was playing its last gigs, they would instantly create a feeling of fondness and nostalgia for the band. And anyway, if they wanted to re-form in the future, that was perfectly acceptable – hadn't Frank Sinatra been making his comebacks for decades?

The band's publicist, Tony Brainsby, put the message out, and sure enough the ticket sales went up and the press eulogised them again. Every country in Europe and beyond wanted to have Lizzy back one more time, so dates were constantly added, and the band looked to be in business until the autumn. Meantime, they were using John Sykes as Snowy's replacement. He was fast and fresh, and had some form with the metal band Tygers Of Pan Tang. Phil had worked on his solo single, 'Please Don't Leave Me', which was produced by a mutual friend, Chris Tsangarides.

The latter also worked on Lizzy's last studio album, *Thunder And Lightning*. The mood was aggressive and Sykes's guitar had the voguish crackle that pleased the head-banging constituency. 'Cold Sweat' was pulled out of an early jam at Pete Townsend's Eel Pie studio – Sykes giving the band a heavily blocked sound that they'd previously ignored in favour of harmonies and riffs. But if the sound of the new music was invigorating, Phil was writing many of his lyrics to order – the same old themes, the corny rhymes, a lack of real poetry. Only rarely, like on the morbid confessional of 'The Sun Goes Down', did he reflect much personal involvement.

On 28 January, two days after the tour started, Phil appeared on the television show *The Tube*. The mood of the programme was irreverent and informal, but Phil completely misjudged the tone. When interviewed, he was paranoid and boorish, humiliating the young girl who'd walked into the dressing-room to interview him. He also alienated the *Top Of The Pops* crew by swearing and misbehaving. They knocked 'Cold Sweat' off the show, and it climbed only one place in the following week, to reach number twenty-seven on 12 February.

The last of Lizzy's four nights at the Hammersmith Odeon was 12 March. The idea was to showcase the band's history, with some of the old guitarists stepping up to play their signature lines. They could put this on a live album which would fulfil their contractual obligation to the record company. Thus another loose end could be tied up.

Eric Bell came early to the soundcheck. In the ten years since splitting with Phil, he'd worked with the likes of Bo Diddley, Noel Redding and Brush Shiels. His profile wasn't huge, but neither was he such a nervous wreck as he'd been back in 1973. He'd kept in touch with his old band, and occasionally their management flew him out to European dates to play 'Whisky In The Jar' and 'The Rocker' for old times' sake. Together with Downey and Lynott, he'd recorded 'Song for Jimi' in 1981, remembering Hendrix and the music that originally inspired them.

Eric looked up at the Odeon stage, and there was Gary Moore, who'd also arrived early. The two Belfast men hugged each other and realised here was the chance to have fun. So they had a massive blues jam, and they were smiling at each other, just like in the old days at The Maritime club in the 1960s. Then the others arrived, and the Lizzy business commenced. There were six guitars on stage, including Phil's bass. *It's like the Spanish Armada*, Eric thought, looking at all the guitar necks raised in the air. *Like a sea of galleons* . . .

It was also deafening. Every player had a bank of four Marshall cabinets, and when they got a chance to take a lead break, most of them immediately went to the top of the fret – to try and get the definitive piercing note. Eric stopped playing, and no one even noticed. Something changed deep inside him that day. He left rock music behind, steering back to the home of the blues.

Thin Lizzy's farewell to Ireland was sloppy and drunken. At the

Royal Dublin Society (RDS) Simmons Court Pavilion on 9 April, Phil wore the same jerkin that he'd posed with on the cover of his second solo record. But now he was bursting out of it. The sleeves were pulled up to his elbows and his forearms ballooned from the cuffs. He'd lost the strut and the smile. It was like watching a bad Phil Lynott impersonator.

When they reached Japan in May, Phil and Scott couldn't get any heroin, and were suffering from awful stomach cramps. 'Still In Love With You' was such an emotionally charged song now – a mutual declaration of thanks between the long-standing fans and the band. But during that part of the set at Tokyo's Kasienken Hall, the pair of them felt so bad that they didn't want to be there. Phil was delirious and putting himself down on stage; he looked over to Scott and his face was wet with crying.

The guitarist couldn't hold his gaze – it was so utterly desperate that he had to turn away. *I can't take any more of this*, he thought. *If I can see Phil looking this bad, then I've gotta get out*. That clinched it for Scott – giving him the resolve to get away from drugs, leaving him with a three-second scene of total horror that was videotaped in his mind for years after.

In his spare time of July and August, Phil played a series of gigs with Downey and Sykes at Swedish folk parks – billed as The Three Musketeers, and supplemented by Mark Stanway, the keyboard player from Magnum, and an Irish guitarist, Doish Nagle. They returned for Lizzy's last great gesture in the UK, Sunday night at the Reading Festival on 28 August. This was an ideal chance to give the band a ritualised send-off. Sykes was now happily integrated in the gang. The crowd was totally partisan: enthusiastic long-hairs who loved the excessive posturings of this band, the people who'd liked *Thunder And Lightning* most, and who weren't bothered by the yardsticks of cool, credibility and fashion.

Phil gave them the favourites and allowed Sykes to dazzle on the new tunes. He revived an old ballad, 'A Night In The Life Of A Blues Singer', which morosely painted up the life of an artist in decline, still compelled to slog it out until the end. But there were two songs which defined Thin Lizzy on this shivery night. 'Cowboy Song' had the intimacy of a campfire sing-along; the crowd knew the words and the rites – providing the whooping coyote calls on cue, singing the last line for the band, knowing too well that they were directly headed for 'The Boys Are Back In Town' and an ultimate dust-up at Dino's.

Phil had lost some of the top range of his voice, and he often coasted around the lower, guttural notes. But as the band finished with 'Still In Love With You' he was exceptionally great, soaring high and making each little accent in the tune work for him. Whenever he came to the chorus line, 'Is this the end?' the crowd would cry, 'Nooooooh!' and Phil would have to pledge his undying affection to them all over again. It was terribly sad. He was demonstrably adored by so many thousands of people, even at this point.

The absolute end was 4 September at Zeppelin Field in Nuremberg. This was 'Monsters Of Rock', a package tour of Europe, featuring Thin Lizzy, Whitesnake, Mötorhead and Meat Loaf. Robbo was out there, playing with Mötorhead. His hair was cropped short and dyed red now – after a psychotic introduction to the band in New York, he'd become convinced that they'd only hired him for his rock and roll looks. So he went berserk in his hotel room, chopping off his locks and messing with hair colour. He even bought a pair of silver hot pants to test their tolerance to the limit.

But Lemmy the singer let him get on with it. He used to laugh as Robbo blazed away on stage, oblivious to the fact that the lighting rig – shaped like a Lancaster Bomber – was being lowered on to his head, causing the roadies to push him out of harm's way. Lemmy was a sociable chap, and when Scott wandered past the dressing-rooms at Nuremberg, he called him over and offered some refreshment: 'Here, have some of this.'

Lemmy licked his wart-encrusted finger and dipped it into a huge bag of amphetamine sulphate. He proffered the glistening present to Gorham, who instantly felt nauseous. Meat Loaf walked in, introducing everyone to his girlfriend called Wonder. Robbo was in hysterics. He was thinking of Wonder Loaf – the sliced bread that he bought back home from the supermarket. But the comedy was lost on the big American, who got sulky and mooched off.

This package tour of bands had played the night before at Kaiserslautern, also in Germany. Somehow Scott and Brian Downey had got lost on the autobahn, and Phil was wandering around before showtime in a panic. Robbo said he would fill in, and Philthy, the Mötorhead drummer, was a huge Lizzy fan. So they quickly rehearsed, and were ready to take the stage when the missing boys walked in. Philthy was gutted.

Nuremberg was another emotional night. By the time they got to 'Still In Love With You', the 35,000 crowd, the crew and all the members of the other bands lining the wings were in pieces. But Phil and Scott had already done all their grieving, and they'd gotten used to the fact that the band was done for. They just felt ill and wanted to get this one over with. They surveyed the emotional scenes around them and they were thinking, *Is this ever gonna end?*

They split at Heathrow airport the next day. Nobody made a big deal of it. Darren Wharton was one of the most optimistic people there. He assumed that the veterans just needed a rest. Even Robbo had understood as much from his conversations with Phil at the hotel bar in Germany. 'Sure, if we ever run out of money,' the singer had told him, 'we can always start Lizzy again.'

16

Phil's band was finished and his marriage was fragmenting. He didn't read books any more and practically all his friends were involved in the music business. Unlike Brian Downey, he couldn't just cut out and go fishing. Phil didn't even like the countryside – once he was out of the car, he wanted to get straight back to the dirt and the danger of the city. His public personality had been built on the concept that he was a winner – effortless on stage, big in the charts, ahead of the pack, lucky in love. He was the guy who'd always been in control, but as 1984 began, Phil was plainly losing it. All he could do was to shuttle around London and Dublin and fret over his future prospects. What did he *mean*? What could he *do*?

Well, he could start another band. So in the early spring, he began rehearsing and writing, eventually setting up the gear at Howth Community Hall, near Glenn Corr. John Sykes had been offered a job with Whitesnake, and his absence was a blow to Phil. But the singer resumed his connection with keyboard player Mark Stanway, who in turn suggested guitarist Laurence Archer, formerly of White Horses.

Brian Downey played drums for a while, but he didn't feel that the music compared well to Lizzy, and he was unhappy with Phil's erratic working hours. He was replaced by Robbie Brennan, who'd worked with Phil in 1982 in The Soul Band. He had also been the drummer of Auto Da Fé – the folk-influenced act which Phil had produced over the previous two years. Doish Nagle, who'd toured with The Three Musketeers, played rhythm guitar.

They warmed up with some Irish dates in April, complementing their new songs with Lizzy standards. Phil had been messing with the name Slam for the new act, but an early newspaper feature on the act used the headline Grand Slam, which he liked even more. In May, they moved to London and began working at E'Zee Hire Studios in the north of the city. They practised for ten hours a day, six days a week – an exhausting pace designed to make the new act into a workable option. Phil had insisted on having a full concert PA system in the room, obliging everyone to blast away like they were actually performing before an audience. Robbie, who'd been used to a more genteel style of late, was sweating a terrible amount, thrashing off a lot of weight in the process. By the end of this three-week period, he was fitter than he'd been in years.

Given that both the public and the music industry were indifferent about his new project, Phil worked his band harshly, sometimes terrorising individual members. The musicians turned this into a kind of joke. 'Whose turn is it today?' they'd giggle, as the grim process began at two o'clock every afternoon. One of the recurrent victims of his anger was Laurence, who didn't have all of the skills needed to play on the older songs. Every time they started on 'Parisienne Walkways', it was an embarrassment, because the new guitarist simply couldn't hold those long, sustaining notes the way that Gary Moore could. This led to terrible barrackings afterwards.

Phil was listening to a lot of Gil Scott Heron and the new rap acts; Grandmaster Flash and Melle Mel's 'White Lines (Don't Don't Do It)' was a favourite. He had a vision of Grand Slam putting some of that funky aspect into their act. Robbie had some technical grasp of musical tablature, and he assumed that the singer shared this. One day he was talking about the different number of musical bars in the chorus lines of a new song. How did it break down again, Phil?

'I don't fucking know! The first line is like "Father O'Malley and Father O'Callaghan went to town today." And the second one is like, "Father O'Malley and Father O'Callaghan went to town *again* today." Just sing that rhythm to yerself. Okay?'

A much-improved band played some more Irish dates at the end of the month. Phil was back to playing small gigs, with a basic road crew. He was in a scary mood during these gigs. When they appeared at The Rialto in Derry, the bass player of the support band accidentally knocked off the power supply. Phil chased him up the stairs and was just about to smash a whiskey bottle over his head when the rest of the band pulled him off.

After leaving Omagh in Northern Ireland, they headed south for the border. They were stopped en route by armed members of the Royal Ulster Constabulary, who were edgy about the sight of so many reprobates travelling together. But when Phil explained who they were the cops cheered up, even joining the band in an impromptu photo session, complete with machine-guns and brandy bottles.

On 21 May, they were still on tour when the press broke the news that Phil and Caroline had separated. She was now living at her parents' home near Bath, yet stressing that there was still some hope for the marriage. Even though she had enjoyed some wild times in the past, Caroline had resolved to take her daughters away from the messy scenes that inevitably surrounded her husband. Phil now had the house at Kew to himself and he was often deeply unhappy there.

When he returned from visits to Sarah and Cathleen, he'd lock himself in a room – sometimes for days – crying and inconsolable. Occasionally, a member of Grand Slam would argue the point with him, saying that you couldn't bring up kids in such a crazy environment, but Phil would turn nasty and threaten to sack him. And while Kew was treated like an open house, with friends and various chancers staying there for indefinite periods, there was one unbreakable rule: nobody was to interfere with the kids' room, with the drawings on the walls or the toys stacked up where they'd been left.

His drug intake worsened – soon he was spending £1,000 a week on cocaine, often adding heroin to the bill. Phil normally accounted for his domestic expenses on the stubs of his cheques, but he never recorded his outgoings for drugs. Soon, his chequebooks were full of blank stubs. Robbie and Doish were also participating in this excess, but they always knew they could escape the worst of it and get back to the relative calm of Dublin. But there was no place Phil could retire for peace. Fans and freeloaders called at all hours.

One night, Robbie heard a faint voice calling from upstairs. He went to the master bedroom and discovered the singer, totally naked, having a cocaine seizure. Even though Robbie was a drummer, he would never be able to explain the horrific beat of the guy's heart that night. He made him sip cold water, slowly trying to get Lynott's metabolism back to normal. It was appalling. But the next day Phil acted like nothing had happened, and soon he was hammering his system all over again.

He was sucking on oxygen bottles and Ventolin inhalers on tour now – heroin usage had aggravated his respiratory system, and now he was suffering from severe asthma attacks. Those intense Grand Slam rehearsals at the start were especially valued now, as the band members were invariably wrecked before they got on stage. On the fast numbers like 'Yellow Pearl' and 'Cold Sweat', Phil could raise some of that old vigour. But the ballads were excruciating.

Just like Elvis in his post-Priscilla days, he revealed much of his personal sadness on stage. On 'Sisters Of Mercy' Lynott cried out for the love of his mother, describing his weariness and squalor, begging for deliverance. The singer was too proud to ask for help when he was off stage, but the song told everything without flinching. 'I have travelled from Dublin to Saigon,' the lyrics said, as the showman shook his fist at the crowd. Behind the leather glove, there were trackmarks where he'd been shooting up. It looked like a cat had scratched the hell out of him. On his left arm was a horrible open sore, left by a hypodermic needle.

The most graphic and upsetting of the new songs was called 'Harlem'. Phil wrote it with Crumlin in mind, but he didn't think it sounded rock and roll enough, hence the change. Again, he was singing about his fall from grace – evoking a junkie ambience in his backstreets story. And once more, he was calling for the Lord's help, confessing to weakness and depression, capping the chorus line with a cautionary 'don't do it' message. Musically, it was a great song – mournful soul like The Commodores' 'Night Shift' – but the words were so despairing.

In happier days at Howth, Phil used to take his daughters to the Church Of The Assumption on a Sunday. He'd stand at the back, waiting for the end of the service, then he'd stop off at The Royal Hotel, where musicians used to play for the fun of it. There was a band of local folk musicians called Clann Éadair, some of whom worked as fishermen. Phil used to sit in on these sessions, playing acoustic bass, occasionally joined by his American musician friend Jerome Rimson, now resident in Ireland. Phil decided to work with this band and together they recorded 'A Tribute To Sandy Denny', which was released as a single in September 1984.

This was Phil's folk version of 'King's Call' – a farewell to the former vocalist of Fairport Convention, whose lovely, clear voice had prompted many Irish rockers to evaluate their own traditional heritage in the late 1960s. Phil's elegy was beautiful, almost Elizabethan in its melodic pitch. His keening vocals were also evocative of the first single he ever sang on, Skid Row's 'New Places, Old Faces', back in 1968.

Phil had forgotten nothing. He'd actually pre-empted the renewal of interest in folk music in 1980 when he teamed up with old friend Terry Woods to record the Appalachian standard 'Tennessee Stud'. During some spare minutes in the studio, Woods, Lynott and members of the Galway-based act De Dannan recorded a rousing version of Ewan MacColl's 'Dirty Old Town'. Two years later, he helped Terry's former partner, Gaye Woods, to fashion a contemporary Irish feel on her records with Auto Da Fé.

Despite some rowdy London shows in June 1985, a suitable record deal for Grand Slam wasn't available. By the end of the year, Chris Morrison had put around £100,000 of his own money into the band. They played The Marquee again in December, showcasing a new, sympathetically crafted song called 'Gay Boys', but still there was no major interest. This situation wasn't helped by the fact that the album of Lizzy's farewell tour, *Life/Live*, sounded turgid, and peaked at number twenty-nine in November – despite the historic presence of Robbo, Gary Moore and Eric Bell on the recordings from the Hammersmith shows. The press was only interested when Phil gave his support to The Anti-Heroin Campaign. He told them that he'd been a user, but he had quit now. 'I want to do as much as I can do to de-glamorise the whole thing,' he insisted.

Grand Slam officially split at the beginning of 1985. Phil had twelve months of his life left when he flew to San Francisco to work with his former friend Huey Lewis. The American wanted to recapture the fighter in Lynott's music – to have him singing in a high register, upfront and committed. He had him perform on an old Clover song, 'I'm Still Alive', plus a Laurence Archer number, 'Can't Get Away'. The song 'Harlem' was now called 'If I Had A Wish'. It was more of a love song now, losing some of the unique dread in the transition. But it was still heartbreaking. Assisted by these tapes, Chris Morrison got him a solo deal with Polydor.

He had ten months remaining when he showed up at a Pogues gig on Saint Patrick's Day. Everyone was glad to see him, especially the band's manager, Frank Murray, and they went back to Kew for a party. Phil loved the idea of The Pogues – like Thin Lizzy, they'd taken the spirit of Irish music, especially of those roaring old Dubliners' records, and they'd given it a contemporary zip. He was in fantastic form that night, until his drugs connection arrived and his personality changed. He suddenly wanted to keep out of the way of Frank and the others – they'd know that he was pinned.

In May, he was at number five in the UK charts, playing with Gary Moore on the pop-metal single 'Out In The Fields'. They wore scarlet hussar jackets and sang about the stupidity of sectarian conflict in Ireland. While he was overweight and breathless, there was still something majestic about the singer. Gary used to lecture him about his drug habits. Phil thanked him for his concern, but still carried on.

One of the many promotional calls for the single found them at Sky TV, where Phil's old girlfriend, Gail, now worked. She was involved in music programming, and she took him to lunch during breaks in the filming. His clothes and his hair were a mess, and she told him so. But he denied everything – he painted her a completely false picture of his life.

Whenever he met with former friends, that was the deal now – deception, shame, maybe aggression. If people criticised him, he could be hostile. Alternatively, he could allow all this emotional mess to pour out, which was also unsettling, because the next time he might completely deny what he'd said. Tim Booth, his mate since the days of Orphanage and Dr Strangeley Strange, met him in The Dockers pub in Dublin, and Phil's skin was practically purple with toxins. Tim said hello, but Lynott didn't recognise him for about thirty seconds. Then he caught on, and spent a long time apologising afterwards.

There was a terrible loneliness about his wanderings around his home town. One night he turned up at a kids' dance in

Howth's Summit Hill disco. All the little girls were thrilled, but the older boys reckoned that he'd lost about a foot in height and that he looked terrible. They felt embarrassed that he'd chosen to walk into a teenage party.

On 13 July, he watched Live Aid take off at Wembley Stadium. Bob Geldof had become globally influential in setting up this show to benefit the thousands of Ethiopians suffering from famine. Midge Ure, the one-time Lizzy guitarist, had also been a critical influence, co-writing the 1984 Band Aid anthem 'Do They Know It's Christmas/Feed The World'. U2's career would flourish after a dramatic performance on the day. But Phil – who as a kid was made to go around his Crumlin school collecting for the 'black babies' – was overlooked. All he could do was to bring a bass guitar into the RTE studios in Dublin and donate it for the auction.

Five months left to live, and he holidayed in Marbella. The owner of the Cuba disco there was an Irishman, Maurice Bolan. Phil agreed to put on a show as a favour, on Tuesday, 6 August 1985. He called out Robbie and Doish of Grand Slam, plus a guitarist from the Dublin band The Lookalikes, Sean O'Connor. The first time the musicians met him at the club, he was in the cubicles, doing his druggy business. His last headlining show was a fiasco.

There were several drug busts around this time – he was easy to catch now. On 19 September, he was let off a charge of possessing cannabis by a Dublin court. His own lawyer called him 'a drugs victim and a tragedy'. Justice Gillian Hussey said, 'I wish he would give up drugs; he is only destroying himself.' Phil celebrated the outcome by guesting on the Gary Moore gigs in September, at The Manchester Apollo and The Hammersmith Odeon.

His first single since leaving Thin Lizzy was an old Grand Slam number, 'Nineteen'. It was inspired by a night in a Texas bar when a roughneck had walked up to the counter and said, 'I'm bad, gimme a beer.' He was a biker, and he'd worn the colours of his gang, the Nineteenth Chapter. Phil clicked with the concept, remembering that as a kid of nineteen, he was just as irrepressible himself.

Phil didn't want a straight metal track. He was bored of all those limitations. This was the era when Michael Jackson was working with Eddie Van Halen, and ZZ Top were fooling around with sequencers. Therefore he agreed to try out some stuff with dance producer Paul Hardcastle, who coincidentally had a number-one hit with a song about tragic soldiers in Vietnam called 'Nineteen'.

The pair met for work at the Roundhouse studios in Chalk Farm in north London. To get the young rebel feel of the song, they borrowed a motorbike from a nearby shop and began to record the revving sound in the studio. Soon the place was filled with exhaust smoke and the engineer was going mad, but Phil thought this was hilarious. He'd brought lots of beers along and he smoked a bit of spliff, but Hardcastle didn't notice that anything was badly wrong. He was an old Thin Lizzy fan, so he was enjoying this. Near the end, he remembered the funk of the 1976 track 'Johnny The Fox Meets Jimmy The Weed' and he suggested that Phil should update this idea, and try some rapping on his new record. Lynott was totally up for it, and he managed it first time. It sounded great.

Paul had spent a little time at the house in Kew and he'd been telling Phil about his recent marriage. Two days later, there was a knock on his own front door and a present arrived. Lynott had sent over the jukebox from his home that the producer had been admiring. A present from the old fox. He could be considerate in other ways too. When the mixing of the record kept them up late for a couple of nights, he sent flowers to Paul's wife, with a note saying, 'Dear Delores, sorry for keeping him out. Love Phil.'

But kind gestures couldn't disguise his poor physical condition. Phil was drinking a bottle of liver-pummelling brandy a day, and was routinely injecting heroin into the veins of his feet. He'd leave a cheque out in the garden at Kew, under an ornamental gnome; and it was discreetly swapped for a batch of heroin. Unlike the old days, when he naïvely joked about his naughty behaviour, he was simply a user now, forced down to a base, subsistence level.

Yet Phil was like his Crumlin soul brother Brendan Behan – so strong, dodging mortality so many times, that people figured he'd survive anything. That was the illusion. But of course Brendan had eventually died of his excesses. When the writer Normal Mailer saw Behan in New York near the end in 1964, he figured he was 'carrying an incredible fatigue inside him. He was like a giant in chains.' That's how Phil looked in the video for 'Nineteen'. Despite the biker action and the grand Californian backdrop, he was manifestly tired, hunching up, running slow.

Scott Gorham called over in December. He'd been in America recording some new stuff, and he wanted Phil to hear it. They hadn't met for a long time – which was part of the guitarist's therapy for quitting heroin. He'd been instructed to leave behind everyone who was taking drugs, so that he could break those habits. He'd been treated by Dr Meg Patterson, who'd also succeeded with Eric Clapton and Pete Townsend. Scott didn't want to stay at the hospital, so he'd returned to his place in Putney. Meg's son had come over to help him, clearing the house of drugs and any paraphernalia associated with his old ways.

Any time he felt bad, his young guardian would throw on a coat, and they'd walk the streets together. They discovered that golf was a welcome distraction, so Scott and his new friend would take to the course in the freezing cold, wearing masses of sweaters and shirts. The guitarist was going through the agonies of withdrawal, and dealing with it by pitching and putting through the worst of the winter of 1984–5.

But when he called over at Kew at eleven in the morning, he felt marvellous. He was therefore upset to notice that Phil's face and body were puffed up, and that he was wheezing – but the singer also insisted that he was off the heroin, he really was. Just then, the phone rang. Phil was informed that one of his several drug charges had been dropped, so he marked the occasion by filling a tall glass to the top with vodka. He drank it in one gulp and filled the glass again. He asked his friend if he would care for a tipple, but it was far too early in the day for Scott.

Phil was talking about getting Thin Lizzy back together again – it seemed like such a natural thing to do. He even picked up a guitar and tried to strum out a few chords, but it sounded fuzzy and unfocused. Scott didn't have the heart or the mental strength to say anything, but inwardly he thought a reunion wasn't likely in the near future. *You're not in any shape to write anything or to go on the road*, he figured. But he didn't want to disappoint the guy, or to damage the chance of a band reunion later in 1986.

'Let's think about it,' he said.

When Phil promoted 'Nineteen' on television, he was gasping through interviews, the confidence totally gone from his eyes.

Occasionally he'd rally, talking about future production adventures with the soul man Tom Dowd, and also suggesting that a Lizzy reunion was possible some time. In December, he mimed to the single on a Christmas special of the kids' show *Razzamatazz* – presented by his DJ friend, David Jensen. Playing drums on this occasion was Brian Downey, who hadn't seen him for two years and was shocked by the squalor he'd witnessed at Phil's place: junk-food boxes, untidy rooms and creepy individuals abusing the singer's hospitality. What made this scene all the more poignant was the fact that the new songs Lynott had written sounded fabulous.

Tony Brainsby was still arranging the singer's press coverage, setting Phil up with a few rock journalists. After a day of such duties, the two old associates were loosening up for the Christmas break. The singer admitted to Tony that he wasn't well. 'You have to listen to your body,' Phil said. 'It's telling me to quit. That's when you know it's time to stop.'

When he'd gone, Brainsby walked into the main office and said something strange – half to the girls who worked for him, half to himself.

'I've just been talking to a dead man . . .'

Philomena flew over to share Christmas 1985 with her son at Kew. The decorations were up and he'd bought little wind-up presents for his daughters' stockings, and they played with them together. He wasn't his lively old self, but his ma travelled down to Bath to pick up Sarah and Cathleen to bring them back for a celebratory party.

Jimmy Bain, the former bassist with Rainbow and Wild Horses, was still around when she came back. He was a regular feature at Kew, but Philomena didn't like him at all. Phil seemed even more lethargic, but he cheered up when he saw the kids and they had fun for a bit. Then he started vomiting. Bain disappeared.

Brian Robertson arrived with some presents. He was living up the road with Chrissy Wood and her boy Jesse James. He knew there was something amiss, since Bain had rung up earlier, looking for somewhere to stay. He said that things were getting 'heavy' down at Phil's. Brian had refused as he didn't want this character around his adoptive kid. Jesse was six years old, the son of Ron Wood, guitarist with the Stones. He was holding a present that he'd wrapped himself. He loved Phil – they always had a fantastic time together – and he was looking forward to seeing his big friend again.

Robbo pressed the buzzer and Philomena ran out in tears, not knowing what to do. Her son had climbed into a bath with his clothes on, complaining that he felt cold. But then he'd been unable to get out again, and she had to drag him out herself. So Brian went up to the room to see him. The place was a tip. Phil was lying on the bed, and it seemed like he was losing control of his body, which was scary. Still, the singer wanted to talk with his friend, and he tried his best to say a few personal things. Robbo hugged him, and then went downstairs. He told Philomena to call a doctor. Something was severely wrong.

A Harley Street doctor known to the rock fraternity came and administered an injection. Robbo sat down with Philomena and had a few whiskeys. He explained that the problem upstairs was drugs-related. Then he had to explain to Chrissy and Jesse James that they wouldn't be able to hand over the presents just yet. He told the boy that Phil was suffering from the flu. Privately, he didn't think his mate was going to make it. As they drove off, he realised he might soon have to break some terrible news to Jesse.

Big Charlie McLennan came over on Christmas Day. He was joined by Graham Cohen, a friend of the Lynott family since the days of The Clifton Grange Hotel. When Philomena had rung Glenn Corr in Dublin to speak to her partner, Dennis, it was clear that she needed extra help. Graham, who was staying there as a kind of housekeeper, offered to fly to London.

But the private doctor had told them to leave Phil until he got better by himself. They felt so helpless. By the afternoon, there was no improvement, and when Caroline rang from Bath to wish everyone the best for Christmas, Philomena was still terribly worried, and she told her what was happening. She quickly drove up, assessed the situation and recommended a place in Wiltshire named Clouds Clinic.

Caroline took the girls back to Bath, while Big Charlie and Graham drove Phil off to this discreet clinic. But by now, the singer was semi-comatose, and Clouds wasn't able to offer the treatment he needed. So, in the last remaining hours of Christmas Day, they put Phil in an ambulance for the half-hour journey to the intensive care unit of Salisbury General Infirmary.

Over the next eleven days, Phil slipped in and out of consciousness. He'd talk to the nurses – even flirting a little and singing in a very weak voice. He'd suddenly remember moments from his childhood: how they once had a dog in Manchester but the nasty landlord made them get rid of it. Recognising that his condition was grave, he asked to see a priest. Near the end, he realised the dreadful situation that he'd put his mother into. 'Merciful Jesus,' Phil gasped, 'what have I done to you?'

He was put on a dialysis machine and a respirator, as his system weakened. Septicaemia was travelling through his blood-stream and there were multiple abscesses in his organs. His body was effectively closing down. Philomena stayed at the hospital for days on end. Charlie and Graham put on hoods to reduce the risk of further infection and then washed his body and powdered him afterwards. Since the wards were short-staffed over the holiday period, they found many ways to help out.

A few select friends and relations came to visit, ignoring the reporters who were waiting outside, aware that a shocking drama was unfolding. Philomena and the others spent much of their spare time in the visitors' room, making coffee for the families of other seriously ill patients. Sometimes they just sat there, looking at the magnolia walls and the high ceiling, convinced that Phil was going to get better and that he'd truly want to reform his ways when he came out of there. He was only thirty-six years old, they reasoned, and he had an awful lot to achieve yet. Sure, he was a warrior and he'd fight his way off this sick-bed as well. He would, wouldn't he?

On 4 January 1986, Philip died.

17

His face was everywhere. On the fans' T-shirts, on the tickets for this special gig, on the back panels of dozens of biker jackets, on the posters that the hustlers were selling outside. And within Dublin's Point Depot, it was exactly the same. There was Phil on the screens surrounding the stage – film of him hunched up on a barstool, sad and vulnerable singing 'Borderline'. Next time you looked up, he was brash and laughing at his own act as a 1970s playback revealed his proudest times. As the audience became inflamed by the memories and the ceremony of this astonishing night, there was a spontaneous reaction – something that hadn't touched this town for more than a dozen years:

'LIZZZ-ZZEY! LIZZZ-ZZEY!! LIZZZ-ZZEY!!!'

It was just like *Live And Dangerous* all over again. Thousands of voices – the old Dubs, the teenagers, the rockers, the relatives and compadres, the many admirers who'd flown in from Japan, Scandinavia, America and the UK – were all chanting and partaking of this emotional, irrational ballyhoo. Philip was ten years dead, but tonight at least it felt like he was as big as ever, practically tangible, his spirit dominating the shape and the intensity of this event.

His music was in the ascendant once more. Bands like Guns N' Roses, Bon Jovi, U2, Oasis and Def Leppard had paid homage to him in one way or other. In the UK, Primal Scream had been encoring with 'Don't Believe A Word'. Across the Atlantic, Smashing Pumpkins had recorded a version of 'Dancing In The Moonlight', cutting into the sad essence of the song. Phil hadn't even been aware of how many artists he'd influenced when they'd been teenagers; only now was his legacy starting to ripen.

This night in Dublin was the perfect time and place to mark the rehabilitation of his art. It was 4 January 1996, and many of the bad memories had been dimmed. He was no longer the *Sunday World* rocker – those stories had been picked over until there was little left to sensationalise. Anyway, just like with Elvis, the public exposure of his declining years had actually made everyone more aware of his raw humanity – he was the guy who never pretended to be faultless, and now everybody knew plenty of the awful details that were behind his lyrics. Thus his best music transcended the scandalising.

And so the crowd chanted – around 8,000 of them – and the songs pinballed through this fine venue that hadn't even been operational when Phil was alive. People were pointing to the back of the stage and gasping, because there it was – the mirrored Thin Lizzy logo, big and bright, hanging above the speaker stacks and the drum kit, just like it used to. In the quiet years, it had rested in the stairways of Slattery's, one of Phil's old haunts, but now it was gloriously restored.

Even the organisers were a little startled at the reaction to this show – much of the merchandise had actually run out at the start of the night, and they could have sold even more tickets if the venue had been bigger. But this wasn't really a night for cashing in. It was a belated wake and a watershed, an occasion for remembering Phil at his best and for passing that feeling on. Some of the people that night hadn't even been born when 'Jailbreak' had come clanging out of the radio speakers. But now such songs were relentlessly played on the national FM shows, hailed as perennials. Also, there had been an obligation for Irish radio to schedule a percentage of home-grown music in their programming, so that was another reason why Thin Lizzy songs were still so widely known.

Backstage, Sara and Cathleen Lynott were taking all this in. Sarah could only barely remember what her dad's shows were like, and her sister couldn't recall much at all, but now they could directly witness his acclaim. Of course, Philomena was there too, and she was greeting a lot of the old crew members, who'd also reunited for the occasion. Many wore something to remind them of their old boss – a ring, an earring or some little trinket that had been passed on to them, and which had become their palpable link with the man. Now they were hugging and laughing, telling their favourite Lizzy stories, a lot of which they'd been too sad to relate before.

Phil had died at an especially bad time. The mood in Britain was totally anti-drugs in 1986, and the media presented Phil as the worst kind of loser. The coroner's report stated that the cause of his death had been multiple abscesses due to septicaemia brought about by intravenous drug use. This was the era of Thatcherite self-restraint and moral correctness, packaged as 'family values' and AIDS awareness. Heroin addicts were the ultimate folk devils – 'junkie' Boy George was publicly exposed and hounded by the tabloids six months after Phil had gone. So it was hard to celebrate Phil's life back then when so many people were sermonising over his demise.

But people were overlooking some of that now, considering the wider focus to his life. Likewise with the music: on his death, he was often regarded as the heavy-metal yahoo with the studs and the gloves, as if that was all there was to his creative journey. By 1996, there was a growing affection for his early records, and particularly those roaring tunes from the mid-1970s. Street-fighting rock and roll was current again – and you just had to hear Noel Gallagher from Oasis play guitar on his song 'Step Out' to realise he'd been impressed by Lizzy's version of 'Rosalie'. Noel, talking to *NME* in October 1995, was upfront about the sources for his song: 'The inspiration for the two parts of the tune come from Thin Lizzy and Stevie Wonder.'

Meanwhile 'The Boys Are Back In Town' – the song nobody in the camp had especially rated when Lizzy recorded it in 1976 – was being recognised as a classic. Bon Jovi had recorded it for a drugs-awareness album, *Stairway To Heaven, Highway To Hell*, and they'd hardly dared to tamper with the original. It was on the soundtrack to the imminent *Toy Story* film and they played it on the *Gladiators* TV show every time the warriors came out for combat, and the spectators sang along. It had also been a constant feature on American radio after the Gulf War, as DJs used the sentiments of the song to welcome their soldiers home.

A television documentary, *The Rocker*, on Phil's life had just been finished. Directed by the Irish writer and presenter Shay Healy, it collated stories from old friends and band members and was illustrated by many pieces of rare film, including the old 8mm footage that Little Mick had taken of The Black Eagles and Skid Row, plus some video film of Phil at play with his daughters. Most heartening of all were the many testimonies on the programme from established rock stars. They'd all made an effort to express their debt to the guy.

Bono from U2 was unstinting. 'He never could have lost his crown,' he mused, 'and always will be King of Dublin. He was much more of a Dub . . . there's more of what we think of Dublin in him. Maybe I envied him for that.' Van Morrison remembered his good tunes, star value and their talks together in San Francisco – how they were both 'connected'. Huey Lewis summarised the good side of his old buddy's fast-burning style: 'There are some people who don't accomplish half of what Phil did in a whole lifetime.'

Slash from Guns N' Roses was mindful of the singer's final undervalued years. 'It's a sad state of affairs when someone passes away and then you realise how great they were,' he reckoned. Jon Bon Jovi explained that while Thin Lizzy didn't have a huge profile in America, his own band, and several others, had been inspired by Phil's use of that Lone Ranger mythology: 'The essence of an electric rock band singing cowboy songs – we just took it to the next decade.'

A compilation album, *Wild One: The Very Best Of Thin Lizzy*, was primed for release just after the gig, and this would sell 100,000 copies in the UK alone. Chris O'Donnell was walking through the crowds at The Point, handing out copies of the CD to people he knew, looking wistful. 'Quality stuff, this,' he'd say, before smiling and moving on. The next step was the remastering of six of the band's albums from the 1970s, beginning with *Fighting*. Again, these would sell well, and the reviews in the press were mostly all rapturous.

Philomena Lynott's book, *My Boy*, had been published in November 1995. Her account corrected much of the gossip about the singer's birth and death. She didn't flinch when detailing his last days at the hospital, deliberately drawing attention to the dangers of drug abuse. But she also gave a fair amount of dignity to the lives of herself and her son. The book wasn't simply aimed at rock fans – this was a fearsome human-interest story, and shortly after its release it reached the top of the Irish book charts.

For one reason or another, Phil's image was back on the magazine covers. His cavalier smile seemed attractive again; the positive side of his career was more meaningful than the wastage at the end. For a guy who could hardly imagine himself getting old, who always travelled in the front of a car so that he'd die faster if it crashed, here he was, forever young – while all his friends and relations were ageing.

Smiley Bolger was a DJ from Dublin's northside. He'd met Phil during the 1960s and saw The Black Eagles when they played the Club A Go-Go in Abbey Street around 1966. When Thin Lizzy's career was on the rise in 1975, he was a guest reporter for *Starlight* magazine, touring England with them and even humping gear, listening to Phil saying, 'This is it, we're going for it', and sharing that excitement.

He'd meet Phil around Grafton Street when the band became famous, and the singer would always ask about his mother and suggest they have a pint nearby. Lynott would find something in his pocket to give him – a tape of some alternative Lizzy mixes, a badge, a book, some trinket or keepsake. In turn, Smiley would tell him about his latest schemes and happenings. The DJ still had that 1960s spirit about him, the urge to create an event just for the hell of it.

One of these ideas was an alternative Eurovision Song Contest. Since Ireland's Johnny Logan won the proper event in 1980, the following year's contest was held in Dublin. Bolger and his pals ran a spoof of the night at McGonagles bar, with everyone singing daft songs. Phil guested on the old Percy French number 'Mountains Of Mourne', which Smiley later released on his 1981 EP, 'What 'Bout Ye!!'.

The DJ used to make little photocopied books that he'd give to his friends. All of these activities – the music, the happenings, the handbills and booklets – Smiley used to call them 'vibes'. Phil was part of that generation too, and he liked the idea. One time they were sitting in the pub, and he said to his mate, 'Do a vibe for me sometime, Smiley.'

He held his first vibe for Phil at The Northumberland Arms in London in 1987, and thereafter marked the anniversary of his death in Dublin clubs and bars. He involved Eric Bell, Brian Downey, Brian Robertson and many of the musicians who'd come into contact with the man. They had music, videos, poetry and slides. They also worked up a recorded tribute of Phil's poetry and music, *Ode To A Black Man*, which Smiley distributed privately on cassette. And even though 4 January was a bad time to do anything – people were skint and tired after the Christmas parties and the weather was often miserable – he attracted the likes of Sinead O'Connor, Adam Clayton and Elvis Costello, plus many regular fans.

Philomena turned up at the third anniversary vibe. She'd been in a poor way before this – scarcely able to walk into Phil's room at Glenn Corr, crying all the time, sleeping on the settee, sometimes drinking vodka. Because she'd never allowed herself to see her son's coffin, she allowed herself to believe that he was simply away on tour. She was mad with grief. A friend from Manchester, Percy Gibbons, came over and helped her recover. But Smiley's vibe was important in the healing process as well.

After that night at the Sides club, Philomena went home and had a party – listening to her son's music and watching the videos again. By the following year, she could hardly get out of The New Inn gig, because so many people wanted to say hello and get her autograph. She was meeting all these people who loved Phil, and that was a comfort. But not everyone was so pleased. Some parties felt that these nights were amateurish and small-time. Brush Shiels even accused Smiley of making a profit and putting on 'poxy' bands. So the DJ showed his accounts to the press, revealing that he'd taken a minimal fee to cover expenses.

Independently of Bolger, other people were making sure that Lizzy's music would be remembered. On 17 May 1986, the RDS Showground in Dublin hosted Self Aid, a concert inspired by Geldof's Live Aid, aiming to fund job initiatives in Ireland. Most of Ireland's swelling number of world-famous acts were there, which made Phil's death even more sad. The headliners were U2, but they were followed by a surprise act: Scott Gorham, Gary Moore and Brian Downey – there to sing Philip home in front of 30,000 people.

Bob Geldof guested on 'Cowboy Song' with his usual cracked tones. This was an especially moving show for him because he was breaking up his band The Boomtown Rats after the gig. Gary Moore sang 'Don't Believe A Word', and at the very end, something special happened. The band struck up 'Whiskey In The Jar' and the stage was filled by all of the musicians who'd played earlier in the day, including U2. This collective – backed up by what seemed like the entire crowd – raised a tremendous cheer for their absent friend.

STUART BAILIE

Also in 1986, during the USA For Africa recording session which produced 'We Are The World', Phil's old friend Huey Lewis was approached by Bob Dylan, who expressed a personal feeling of loss at the Irishman's death. Huey made his own personal statement at the British Phonographic Industry Awards in February 1986. When presented with the Best International Award, he walked up on stage and accepted the honour in Philo's name – recognising the man who'd taught him so much about stagecraft a decade before.

A lot of bands who passed through London would manage to get hold of Scott Gorham's number. They'd express their sympathy, and often asked him to guest with them on stage. But Scott turned them all down, choosing to come to terms with Phil's departure in a private way. Eventually, he formed another band, 21 Guns, and he was in his usual guitar shop one day, getting his Les Paul fixed, when Pete Townsend walked in. They started chatting, and Pete offered the American some time in his Eel Pie studio. Then they talked about personal things. Townsend explained that he hadn't had the chance to mention it before, but he was really broken up when Phil died. He'd experienced tragedy in his own band when The Who's drummer, Keith Moon, died in 1978 of an overdose of a drug that was supposed to curb his alcoholism. 'It's funny,' he said, 'but I miss Phil more than I miss Keith.' Scott realised that Pete didn't have to say such a thing, so it was probably heartfelt.

In 1991, the record company released a single called 'Dedication'. This was based on a Grand Slam demo, but Scott and Brian Downey played over the basics, and it was presented as a Thin Lizzy track, complete with a video spliced up from old footage. It reached number thirty-five in the charts, and a compilation album, also titled *Dedication*, made number eight in February.

Phil's birthday was celebrated in 1993 with a gig at Malmö, Sweden, attended by Philomena, Eric Bell and Brian Downey. The following August, there was another celebration, 'Are You Ready?', at Wolverhampton, with Downey, Robertson, Bell and Darren Wharton. This show was augmented by Ain't Lizzy, who, along with Limehouse Lizzy and Norway's Bad Habitz, were popular, Phil-inspired calls on the tribute band circuit.

John Sykes was involved in the most ambitious project of 1994, when he toured Japan in November with Gorham, Downey, Wharton and his bassist friend Marco Mendoza. Scott was mindful of the fact that the tenth anniversary of Phil's death was looming, so he wanted to see what could be done. He was satisfied by the Japanese experience, and vowed that whatever happened on January 1996 would be professional and exciting. Several other tributes had failed because there was no one as versatile or charismatic as Phil on the microphone. There had been an unsuccessful tour in the past with Bobby Tench singing, but Sykes was the best thus far, especially on the *Thunder And Lightning* era songs.

Smiley had done his bit in Ireland. Gorham and Sykes were showing enthusiasm in their own project. The genius move was getting Lizzy's management and several other diplomats to unite the different factions for the tenth anniversary – nostalgically titled 'King's Call' – and to come up with something that reflected Phil's style and diversity. To everybody's credit, that's what happened.

Brian Robertson couldn't perform at The Point because he'd been in Sweden before Christmas and a fan accidentally broke his thumb. Gary Moore was missing – possibly in Dublin, although no one was completely certain. It was just like old times, really.

As with the previous years for the vibe, some of the younger Irish bands played off, representing the ongoing influence of Lizzy. So The Frames, Lir and Whipping Boy all participated. All of these chose to play Philip's early songs, hailing the earnest young songwriter who graced those Decca albums. The latter group had actually recorded a version of 'Shades Of A Blue Orphanage' as the flip-side to their fine 'When We Were Young' single, establishing the bloodlines ever further. Lir had gained a mythical stature in Dublin – people said they could play the entire *Thin Lizzy* album note for note.

Steve Collins, the hard man from nearby Cabra – the WBO Super-Middleweight Boxing Champion Of The World – came out and recited 'Warriors'. Steve was a music fan; in the build-up to his two successful fights with Chris Eubank, he'd pumped himself up with music from U2, House Of Pain and a specially commissioned tune from The Chieftains called 'Celtic Warrior'. He'd fought his way up through the shitty side of the sport, and he allied with the struggles and triumphs of the country's musicians. Phil Lynott was his man, all right.

That was one of the many regrets people felt – that Phil had not lived to see the success of so many Irish sportsmen over the last ten years. He would have adored the victories of the national football team, especially their World Cup performances under Jack Charlton. In many ways, Paul McGrath had been Lynott's equivalent on the pitch: tough and relentless, a black Irishman who did his job brilliantly and then partied when the work was over. How great it would have been to see them together at their best.

Brush Shiels appeared at The Point singing 'Old Pal' – a ballad addressed to his one-time amigo. He'd released this as a single in 1986, and some people had been surprised at the sentimentality of the words. But in spite of his abrasive front, Brush had cried when he'd heard that Phil was dead. So he saluted his memory again at the vibe and then travelled home to listen to the rest of the show on the radio. It was one thing to say your farewells, but for Brush not to headline a gig was still hard to take . . .

Eamon Carr relived the old beatnik days of 1969 by typing up a poem live on stage while a folk band, Toss The Feathers, charged through 'Sítamoia' ahead of him. He was highly emotional at the end of it. This feeling was even more accented when Philomena walked on stage and tried to speak to the crowd, but she broke down after a moment, overwhelmed. Even Henry Rollins, the straight-edged, hardcore American singer who'd made Phil the subject of many of his spoken-word tours, was left speechless on stage – the video screens magnifying the tears in his eyes.

Although Eric Bell had vowed never to play 'Whisky In The Jar' after leaving the band, it had become his trademark ever since. And so he strapped on the same 1969 Fender Stratocaster that he'd used back then, and he buzzed and raved over the notes, drawing the song out until it seemed like he was telling the crowd the story of his life. He cut out with 'The Rocker', lifting the atmosphere, readying the crowd for the big send-off.

The Lizzy band comprised Gorham, Downey, Sykes, Wharton and Marco Mendoza. They played 'Jailbreak' and all the pyrotechnics fizzled and the audience yammered with joy. Sykes carried the tunes through cool moments like 'Emerald' and

'Don't Believe A Word'. On 'Bad Reputation', Andy and Michael from Ulster noise-makers Therapy? stepped up, loving the occasion and the still-wonderful rumble of Brian Downey's drums. Rollins returned for 'Are You Ready' and he was in command of his energies once more.

All this was brilliantly rehearsed and presented to the best of everyone's abilities. Scott was smiling a lot – delighted to be bringing the music back home once more. He'd been taken aback at the rehearsals the day before when people kept looking to him for approval. He was the boss in the band now, and many artists who were stars in their own right were now deferring to him. There was Joe Elliott and Rick Savage from Def Leppard, for instance, who helped out with 'Cowboy Song' and 'The Boys Are Back In Town' – tunes that had set the standard for their own band in their formative days of 1978. Meanwhile, there was Midge Ure over at the right of the stage, making no fuss, just pleased to be involved, as 'Róisín Dubh' summoned up the fuss and the grandeur while reeling off that legendary roll call of heroes in the winter night.

So many strands of music were represented throughout the show – folk, blues, rock, Celtic soul and psychedelia. Jerome Rimson and Gus Isodore had saluted him on stage as a black man in an industry that didn't always give him a fair break. Richey Buckley, Van Morrison's old sax player, had played a be-bop version of 'Dancing In The Moonlight', highlighting the jazz in his act. And, of course, Smiley Bolger was there, reflecting an era and a class of Dubliner who would always value the down-home personality of Bold Philo.

There was no figure out there with such a rich spread of experience and personality. No one person could fill those boots. Nobody ever would.

Most of the fans left the venue in a happy mood, following the trail of the River Liffey back into the centre of town. Some would visit Phil's grave the next day, travelling out to Sutton, north of the city, overlooking Dublin Bay. They'd look at his flat gravestone, designed by Jim Fitzpatrick, embellished with Celtic knotwork, an Irish cross and bearing a dedication to Róisín Dubh, the famous black rose. Many would leave flowers and personal tributes at the windswept site.

A few concert-goers headed for Grafton Street, for the after-show party at Lillies Bordello, the liveliest venue in town. They'd gas some more with former friends and exchange phone numbers, amazed at the number of proud fathers who'd included either Phil or Parris in their sons' names. Philomena sat downstairs, surrounded by drawings, framed pictures and gifts that the fans had brought for her. She couldn't even talk by the end, she was so overwhelmed. A few months later, she'd meet up with another fan of her son, Bruce Springsteen, who was keen to pay his respects.

Some of the old crew were telling ghost stories, relating how they could feel Phil's presence at home or in hotel rooms. They'd talk to him a while, and that was reassuring. As a result, they weren't afraid of death any more; they believed that he'd be waiting to throw a great party for them on the other side. Another topic of conversation was the lookalike who turned up at The Point – a black guy who'd perfected the whole *Solo In Soho* look. He wore a dark coat and a skinny tie, a pencil moustache and the hair pulled down over his left eye. Somehow, he'd blagged his way into the backstage bar, and he stood there in the corner, smiling at everyone. He was maybe six inches shorter than the original, but it was still good and fitting to see him drinking there with the rest of the stars.

Inevitably, it ended at three o'clock in the morning, with people staggering down Grafton Street under the rain and the stars, remembering the last sentence of the sleeve notes that Phil had written for the *Jailbreak* album.

'The music sailed out into the night,' he'd envisaged, 'then upward towards the skies, travelling on that thin border between reality and imagination.'

The exact significance of those words might have been lost over the years, but the essential drift was as potent as ever. The old romancer was gone, but he'd touched the fibres of his town with rock dreams and adventure and grand possibilities. Hearts were full, the bad times forgotten. We were all perpetually in love with him.

Bibliography

Books

Behan, Brendan: *Confessions Of An Irish Rebel* (Lancer, 1967)

Behan, Brian: *Mother Of All The Behans* (Arena, 1985)

Behan, Dominic: *My Brother Brendan* (Leslie Frewin, 1965)

Best, George (with Ross Benson): *The Good, The Bad And The Bubbly* (Lagan, 1990)

Coughlan, John (editor): *The Swingin' Sixties* (Carrick Communications, 1990)

Dunphy, Eamon: *Unforgettable Fire: The Story Of U2* (Penguin, 1988)

Geldof, Bob: *Is That It?* (Penguin, 1986)

Geraghty, Des: *Luke Kelly, A Memoir* (Basement Press, 1994)

Kinsella, Thomas (translator): *The Tain* (Oxford, 1990)

Lynott, Philomena (with Jackie Hayden): *My Boy* (Hot Press, 1995)

O'Connor, Ulick: *Brendan Behan* (Black Swan, 1985)

O'Neill, Capt. Francis: *Irish Folk Music* (Norwood Editions, 1973)

O'Toole, Fintan: *A Mass For Jesse James* (Raven Arts, 1990)

Power, Vincent: *Send 'Em Home Sweatin'* (Kildanore Press, 1990)

Prendergast, Mark J: *Irish Rock: Roots, Personalities, Directions* (The O'Brien Press, 1987)

Pryce, Larry: *Thin Lizzy* (Star, 1977)

Putterford, Mark: *Philip Lynott, The Rocker* (Castle Communications, 1994)

Turner, Steve: *Van Morrison: Too Late To Stop Now* (Bloomsbury, 1993)

Articles

Barton, Geoff: Not So Lean Times For Lizzy (*Sounds*, 16 August 1975)

Chevron, Philip: Return Of The Lonesome Cowboy (*Hot Press*, 30 May 1981)

Chevron, Philip: Philip Lynott Obituary (*Hot Press*, 30 January 1986)

Dellar, Fred: Tape Special – Phil Lynott (*New Musical Express*, 6 October 1973)

Doherty, Harry: The Thin Man (*Melody Maker*, 24 April 1976)

Doherty, Harry: Lizzy's Cocky Rebel (*Melody Maker*, 6 November 1976)

Doherty, Harry: Ireland's Own (*Melody Maker*, 8 January 1977)

Doherty, Harry: Cutting It Thin (*Melody Maker*, 16 July 1977)

Doherty, Harry: Wedding News Story (*Melody Maker*, 23 February 1980)

Etherington, Jan: The Lizzy In A Tizzy About His Dad! (*Titbits*, 22 January 1976)

Graham, Bill: The Loss (*Hot Press*, 30 January 1986)

Graham, Bill: You Can Always Hear The King's Call (*Hot Press*, 21 February 1991)

Graham, Bill: Answering The King's Call (*Hot Press*, 27 July 1994)

Hayes, Dermott: The Boy Who Thought He Was Bullet-Proof (*Mojo*, December 1993)

Jones, Allan: Elite Hotel (*Melody Maker*, 14 August 1976)

Kent, Nick: Live, Dangerous And As Hot As It Gets (*New Musical Express*, 31 March 1979)

Kent, Nick: The Boys Are Back On Vinyl (*New Musical Express*, 27 May 1978)

Mackey, Liam: Ballad Of A Thin Man (*Hot Press*, 5 March 1982)

Mann, Richard: Dangerous Liaisons (*Guitar*, Vol 6, No 3, 1996)

Parsons, Tony: Somewhere In Philadelphia (*New Musical Express*, 7 October 1978)

Salewicz, Chris: I Take It Serious Wharrado, Know Wharramean? (*New Musical Express*, 18 October 1975)

Salewicz, Chris: Liz Schiz About The Biz (*New Musical Express*, 10 July 1976)

Salewicz, Chris: How The Laid-Back Californian Met The Drunken Scot And The Heavy Black Irishman (*New Musical Express*, 18 December 1976)

Salewicz, Chris: A Peep Into The Soul Of Phil Lynott (*New Musical Express*, 10 September 1977)

Salewicz, Chris: Gary Goes With A Grouse (*New Musical Express*, 28 July 1979)

Shiels, Brush: The Man (*Hot Press*, 30 January 1986)

Silverton, Peter: Disgusting Of Tunbridge Wells (*Observer*, 23 June 1996)

Slater, Dan: We'll Never Divorce (*Woman's Own*, 30 July 1983)

Snow, Mat: No Sweat (*Q*, April 1992)

Stokes, Niall: Saga Of An Ageing Orphan (*Hot Press*, 2 September 1977)

Sutherland, Steve: The Boys Are Backing Down (*Melody Maker*, 26 February 1983)

Welch, Chris: Thin Lizzy Band Breakdown (*Melody Maker*, 1 November 1975)

Thanks also to the back pages of *Kerrang!*, *New Spotlight*, *Disc*, *City Week*, The Thin Lizzy World Wide Web Site and the Roisín Dubh Web Site. The musical archives of Paul Mauger have been invaluable.

I am also indebted to *Black Rose – The Thin Lizzy Magazine*. This is contactable via Adam Winstanley, 1 Parson Court, Maynooth, County Kildare, Ireland.